A JOB TRAINER'S MANUAL

ABOUT THE AUTHOR

Kathy Morris is currently the coordinator of the Transition To Work Project in Cincinnati, Ohio. In 1977, while living in southern California, she developed a **new** method of placing low functioning rehabilitation clients into jobs. She would train the clients on the job, an idea that caused many professionals to be skeptical. That is now the **new** method of working with lower functioning clients. Kathy brings not only her personal experiences to this book, but also her education. She holds a M.S. in Rehabilitation Counseling from California State University, Los Angeles, and a B.A. in Early Childhood Education from Hillsdale College, Hillsdale, Michigan.

A JOB TRAINER'S MANUAL

Supported Employment
for Low Functioning Rehabilitation Clients
and Disabled Secondary Students

By

KATHLEEN C. MORRIS, M.S., C.R.C., L.P.C.

CHARLES C THOMAS • PUBLISHER
Springfield • Illinois • U.S.A.

Published and Distributed Throughout the World by
CHARLES C THOMAS • PUBLISHER
2600 South First Street
Springfield, Illinois 62794-9265

© *1989 by* CHARLES C THOMAS • PUBLISHER
ISBN 0-398-05536-X
Library of Congress Catalog Card Number: 88-25115

Printed in the United States of America
Q-R-3

Library of Congress Cataloging in Publication Data

Morris, Kathleen C.
    A job trainer's manual: supported employment
for low functioning rehabilitation clients and disabled secondary students/by Kathleen C. Morris.
        p.   cm.
    Bibliography: p.
    Includes index.
    ISBN 0-398-05536-X
    1. Vocational rehabilitation—United States—
Handbooks, manuals, etc. 2. Handicapped—Employment—United States—Handbooks, manuals,
etc. I. Title.
Hd7256.U6M67 1989
362'.0425—dc19   88-25115
                                              CIP

This book is dedicated to the memory of Beverly Rinear. Bev was an excellent job trainer, friend, mother, and was liked by all who knew her. Her clients will always remember the help she gave them both on the job and in their personal lives.

SCOPE, PLAN, AND PURPOSE

THE *Job Trainer Manual* was written as a **how-to** book for job trainers working with low functioning rehabilitation clients and/or special education clients. It covers **practical information** the job trainer needs to know when training clients in jobs. The methods described in this manual are used by the Transition to Work Project in Cincinnati, Ohio. The modifications and experiences cited are from personal experiences since 1977 while training clients in jobs in Cincinnati and southern California. The author discusses many different aspects of the trainer's job, including the relationship with employers and co-workers, as well as professionals and parents who are involved with the client.

This book differs from similar books for job trainers, in that the training methods are presented according to the client's **individual learning style.** Learning problems are defined and the **Client Analysis** focuses on identifying how the client learns best. The assessment is included in the book. Should the trainer have a need for an assessment in a specific area not included, the format may be followed in developing new assessment tools.

The process involved in doing a thorough **Job Analysis** is discussed, and examples of analyses are included. The **Job Match** meeting is critical to the placement of the client in a job. During this meeting, the Client Analysis and the Job Analysis are compared to determine if there is a good Job Match. Included in this manual are notes from Job Match meetings where a job was accepted and one where the job was rejected.

Training on the job is centered around how the client learns. Numerous modifications and personal examples are presented to give the job trainer ideas on working with the client. Modifications are given for traditional jobs in which clients have worked: janitorial/housekeeping, dishwashing, bussing, laundry, clerical, and assembly/packaging.

Working with the employer is crucial to keeping the job. There are many different types of employers and many different methods of working with them. Ideas are presented and personal experiences are cited to help the trainer.

Knowing when to begin **phasing out** of the work place is sometimes difficult. In this manual, guidelines are given for the trainer. **Follow-up** is also discussed as well as what happens if the client fails in the job.

Travel training is covered in this manual, as many times it is the trainer's responsibility to teach the client how to travel to work independently. The steps involved in travel training are outlined for easy reference.

This manual is intended for the paraprofessional job trainer with little or no training prior to being hired as a trainer. The book is written in an easy-to-read manner with many practical ideas for the trainer.

K.C.M.

PREFACE AND ACKNOWLEDGMENTS

IT IS DIFFICULT to decide who to acknowledge first, because so many people contributed to the knowledge I have gained over the past thirteen years. I must say that without the support and backing of Rev. Arthur B. Ihnen of Saddleback Community Enterprises, Mission Viejo, California, I certainly would not be where I am today. He was willing to back me and my new ideas about placing clients with mental retardation in jobs. Thus, in 1977, when we were awarded a grant from the California Department of Rehabilitation, we were at the forefront of a new technique of placing and training the rehabilitation client in competitive employment. I want to thank him for standing up against all the probing questions from others about the cost and man-hours involved. He believed in the program and my ideas about placement. That program is still going today, eleven years later, and is now called Supported Employment. I am proud to have been associated with Art and Saddleback Community Enterprises.

While Art allowed me to place and train clients in competitive jobs, the program would not have been successful without the first employer to hire one of our clients. Dick Burns was that person who hired my first client to clean his brand new restaurant. Barbara Brown helped convince him to hire one of our clients. She worked at the workshop at the time and later married Dick. Without his support and the support of the manager, Frank, I might have given up.

There are many other people that I have learned from over the years, both professionals and clients. Although I am not at liberty to name clients due to confidentiality, they are the ones who taught me how to be a job trainer. Many of their stories are in this book.

Chris Hill Davis and Anna Knoles were not only top-notch professionals for whom I worked at the Rehabilitation Institute of Orange County (RIO) but great friends as well. From them I learned about clients who had disabilities other than mental retardation, such as the closed head injured, diabetic, learning disabled, and more. While at RIO I was also given the opportunity of task-analyzing every job task that the janitorial training program introduced to the clients enrolled. I helped establish a pre- and post-test to determine what skills the clients needed to work on and what skills they had learned. The information I learned in those few months has helped me work with clients in janitorial jobs over the years.

My evaluation skills were developed while attending California State University at Los Angeles. I was lucky to have Doctor Robert Hadley for as many testing classes as possible. He taught us to never be content with superficial information, and to look at all the possibilities. Should he ever read this book, he will find portions of his lectures and seminars throughout.

After moving back home to Cincinnati, my experiences continued to grow. I continued to learn about different disability groups while a Work Adjustment Counselor at STAR Center. Jan Welsh was a good teacher/counselor in helping me adjust to the job.

Lois Goodman Stiglitz probably opened my eyes more than any one person in the recent years. She made everything make sense by teaching me about learning styles. I had always figured out how my clients learned through trial and error, but she brought sense and order to it. Lois, I hope I didn't disappoint you with the *cookbook* in this book, but, believe me, it is necessary for trainers to understand how to observe their clients' actions. Working with Lois at Learning Capacities with Jewish Vocational Service were some of my most enjoyable years, professionally.

I must thank the members of the Management Team of the Transition to Work Project in Cincinnati for their support not only in my daily duties as Transitional Coordinator but also for the encouragement they have given me to write this book. The Cincinnati project was originally the idea of Don Buchheit, Special Education Supervisor with the Hamilton County Office of Education and Sandy Kerlin of the University Affiliated Cincinnati Center for Developmental Disorders. They continue to lend their expertise to the Management Team. Doctor Jean Marie Britt of the Great Oaks Joint Vocational School District has worked with me in hiring job trainers. Together we have learned quite a bit. Evaristo Giglio and Mike Igney, the Area Supervisor and Assistant Area Supervisor of the Ohio Bureau of Vocational Rehabilitation, have been great support. Mike is my supervisor and has spent many hours listening to me and assisting me in solving problems. His calm, quiet manner has helped to reduce my stress level more times than I care to remember. Darlene Cunningham from the Rehabilitation Services Commission in Columbus also sits on our Management Team and was the person who first mentioned the need for a manual of this type. After talking to her about it, she encouraged me to take on the project.

Two friends, Keith Kleespies and Jackie Smith, were gracious enough to spend their precious time assisting me by reading my first draft. Keith is a graphic artist and knew nothing of the subject before reading the book. Jackie is the Work Study Coordinator that works closely with the Transition to Work Project in Cincinnati. Their comments were invaluable in assisting me to clarify points I wanted to make. Jackie made sure I explained the educational support correctly, and Keith made sure that a new job trainer could understand it. I appreciate their time and candor.

Not only did Keith read the book, but he also drew the figures that are used for the client analysis. He taught me that art is serious work, which I knew already. What I didn't know was that an artist doesn't just **draw a few figures.** Like a job trainer, he doesn't want to do the job halfway. He was willing to take time out from his busy schedule to draw the figures for me. I certainly thank him for all his assistance.

Mary Lou Motl has been extremely helpful to me throughout the entire process of writing and locating a publisher. She is owner of Custom Editorial Productions, an editing and typesetting company working with textbook publishers. She has given me advice and encouragement from the beginning.

On the home front, I must thank my family, my husband and daughter for putting up with me for the past year while I have been writing. Bill has been so supportive and willing to do things like watch Kimberly, go shopping and little things around the house so I could work on the computer. It won't be long before Bill can have the computer back and play games anytime he wants. He'll also have to share the TV with me again and let me watch some shows I want to see. It'll be just like old times!

Our daughter is eight years old now and has started writing a book and is asking questions about turning things in to the publisher. She sometimes follows those questions with, "What is a publisher?" She has quite a lot to learn.

I also want to thank my parents for housing my duplicate copies of the book. When this undertaking became bigger and bigger, I became more paranoid about my work being destroyed. Thanks mom and dad!

Kathy Morris
3952 Harvestridge Drive
Cincinnati, Ohio 45211

CONTENTS

A JOB TRAINER'S MANUAL

Chapter 1

WHAT IS THIS ALL ABOUT?

"SEE THAT brand new shiny stainless steel? I want you to keep it looking that way. Your job is to keep this whole restaurant looking as clean and new as it does now."

Those were perhaps the most frightening words I've ever heard. They were uttered by the first employer who ever hired one of my clients from a work activity center. My client was a high functioning mentally retarded young man who had had several jobs before I began working with him. He had lost the jobs for various reasons: lack of speed, poor quality, and interpersonal problems.

I was inexperienced in this job. I had never cleaned anything except my apartment. I had no idea how one cleaned a restaurant. It seemed like a big order to keep it looking like new!

I was never sure if my client was more scared about the job than I, although I don't see how he could have been. After all, all **he** had to do was clean and do what I told him. It was up to **me** to decide what to do and in what order to do it. That would have been fine, except I had NO PREVIOUS EXPERIENCE in industrial cleaning. This experience was my introduction into my new job (in 1977), now called job training.

The purpose of this book is to share my experiences with people who are new to the job of teaching jobs to others so they don't have to **reinvent the wheel,** as my former supervisor would say. By sharing the things I have learned, perhaps the reader will not make the same mistakes I did. This manual will help the trainer understand the concept of job training before beginning the job, a luxury I didn't have. I have worked with approximately 100 clients since that first restaurant in a variety of work places, performing a variety of jobs. In the last 10 years I have trained about 20 people how to teach clients to work. It would have been easier had I possessed a manual to assist in the training of job trainers. Thus, this book was conceived. Hopefully, the experiences and tips in this manual will help the reader be more competent and at ease while training her clients on the job site.

3

ASSUMPTIONS

The Reader

Before deciding if this book fits your needs, it is important to discuss several assumptions I made about you, the reader. First, it is assumed that most readers are new to the field of rehabilitation and have never worked as a job trainer with a person who is disabled. Secondly, it is assumed that the trainer does not know what a **learning style** is, how to task-analyze a job, the **do's and don'ts** in working with employers, or recording materials.

Although this book was written for new job trainers, it may also be helpful to persons who know one or more aspects of the job training process but are **lacking experience** in some areas. For example, a person who has experience as a work evaluator may know how to determine learning styles and perform task analyses but not have an understanding of how to work with employers, perform the daily duties of a trainer, or phase out from a job.

Over the past few years, several **administrators** have asked me about what one looks for in a job trainer. Perhaps this book may help administrators to determine the type of individual to hire by understanding the **actual job duties** to be performed.

Hopefully, this book will be a **commonsense guide** to all who use it. The reader will probably not find anything that is brilliant and new, just usable information that one learns from experience. My goal is to help the trainer learn as much as possible about being a job trainer before actually beginning to work on the job. To me, job training is one of the most challenging and rewarding jobs there is! Good luck, and by all means, have fun!

What This Book Doesn't Do

This book does not address the philosophical question as to whether job training is an appropriate method to utilize in working with your clients. This book is for the job trainer who has been hired to carry out specific duties of teaching clients jobs. It is considered a handbook or manual to assist the trainer in the daily aspects of her job.

Likewise, this book does not address the time or cost involved in training clients on jobs. That topic should have been resolved before the job trainer was hired and the program was started.

This book does not address the **placement process** or how to locate jobs for clients. Much information has been written about that topic. Information on job placement can be located in most rehabilitation facilities or university libraries.

DEFINITIONS

In order to make sure we are using the same language and jargon, let us look at several definitions that are used in this book. It is possible that your program will use a different word or phrase to describe a function or job title listed in this book. Don't give up because the names aren't the same, look at the description to be sure this does or doesn't fit your needs.

Job Trainer

In this manual a job trainer is anyone whose responsibility it is to teach a client a job. A job trainer can work within a rehabilitation setting (i.e. work activity center, sheltered workshop, or work adjustment program). A job trainer can also work for a rehabilitation program but outside the physical facility of a workshop, for example, teaching the client a janitorial job in a factory. A job trainer may also be employed by a school system for the purpose of teaching the client (student) jobs either within the school or classroom or on a job site in the community, either paid or volunteer.

Job titles may vary. Some trainers may be called coaches, on-site trainers, or employment training specialists, to name a few. No matter what the title, some aspects of the jobs will be alike. It is those common aspects that will be discussed in this manual.

The material discussed in this manual applies whether the trainer is involved in a long-term training or a short-term training period. The same principles apply, for example, when working with an employer for one week or six months or longer. The goals remain the same: to assist your client to work independently on his job.

For the purpose of this manual, job trainers will be referred to in the female gender, as the majority of the trainers I have known are women.

Client

The word **client** will be used throughout this manual to indicate the person receiving the job training services. The word client is a rehabilitation term that is used throughout the country. The client in this manual is a person with a disability who is most likely receiving services from a state vocational rehabilitation agency, a private non-profit agency or a school system.

It is assumed that without the assistance of a job trainer, the client would have great difficulty in either learning or keeping a job. Of course, many variables must be considered: the severity of the disability, the physical environment, the co-workers, the supervisors, a change in the supervision, transportation, and more. You, the trainer, should know before you start working with the client the areas in which you will need to focus your training. (This will be discussed in Chapter 4.)

Clients are as diverse as the normal population. You will find some very easy to work with, some stubborn, some lovable (watch these, they can **get away with murder!**), and some extremely frustrating. On those frustrating days, remember that without the client you wouldn't have a job either!

My experience with clients has mostly been with persons who are 18 years old or older. Therefore, the information in this book was written with adults in mind. My clients have been from just about every disability group, with the majority being mentally retarded, learning disabled, and emotionally handicapped. The principles in this book can apply to any client with whom the trainer works.

The client will be referred to in the male gender. Thus, by using both genders when discussing a trainer and her client, it may eliminate confusion as to whom is being discussed.

Employers

For the purpose of this book, employers are those persons who have hired the client. The employer may be the owner of a business, the immediate supervisor, or perhaps the person in charge of production at a rehabilitation facility. The employer has direct responsibility to assure that your client is performing the job tasks correctly and with the necessary amount of speed and productivity. The job trainer may work with several levels of supervisors within a given work place. Working with employers is extremely important, and for that reason, I have devoted Chapter 8 to this topic.

Co-Workers

The term **co-workers** refers to the client's peers on the job. These are the people with whom the client works who do not have supervisory authority over the client. Sometimes, the co-workers can either make or break a job for a client. Relationships with co-workers are discussed further in Chapter 8.

Job Developers

A job developer is someone who locates jobs for your clients. This may or may not be one aspect of your job. Job developers may have a variety of titles: employment specialist, job placement counselor, or work study coordinator, to name a few. A job developer may be hired by any number of agencies, usually through rehabilitation agencies or schools. The duties are primarily the same: to locate appropriate jobs in the community. As a trainer, you will most likely be working with the job developer to communicate your client's progress.

Teaching and Training

Throughout this manual, I will use the terms **teaching** and **training** interchangeably. Some people may disagree with the terminology, arguing that **teachers teach** and rehabilitation professionals **do rehabilitation.** Having been both a teacher and a rehabilitation professional, let me assure you that there is a considerable amount of teaching involved in job training!

Consider for a moment the act of **clocking in** which for some clients may be extremely difficult. It is the trainer's responsibility to teach the client how to perform this task correctly. This may involve teaching the client to identify the words

Monday, Tuesday, etc.. It may require teaching the client to use a code number for his name and **punch in** on a computer or cash register.

Teaching is the primary responsibility of the job trainer who is training a client to perform the duties required on a job. It is with the teaching of jobs that the trainer will find one of the greatest challenges and the most rewarding aspects of her job.

Work Evaluation, Work Adjustment

Work Evaluation and **Work Adjustment** are rehabilitation terms that the trainer may hear from time to time. The definitions given for these terms are my own. They are functional and general and will give the trainer a broad understanding of the terms. Should the reader want to learn about Work Evaluation and Work Adjustment in more depth, there is a wealth of information written and can be located by inquiring at a rehabilitation agency or library (preferably a university library).

Basically, the purpose of a traditional Work Evaluation program is for the client to learn about himself in vocational terms (i.e. to learn his strengths, areas of interests and aptitudes). Work Evaluation programs are usually found in a rehabilitation facility where the client goes for a specified amount of time. While in Work Evaluation, the client would most likely be given a series of paper/pencil tests (e.g. interest inventories, aptitude tests) as well as work samples. Work samples are tests that simulate work (e.g. electronics assembly, lab technician, stock clerk, clerical/receptionist). The purpose of the Work Evaluation is to have the client try out different jobs to determine his interest and aptitude for the occupation. He can do this without having to spend precious time and money in a training program, only to find out when the training is complete that he dislikes the occupation he has been trained to do. The Work Evaluation program allows the client to experience the job before deciding if he would like to pursue training courses in that occupation.

At the end of a Work Evaluation, the evaluator gives a report enumerating the client's strengths and limitations, interpretations of test scores, and information on the client's work habits and attitudes.

Work Adjustment is the next step in traditional rehabilitation. When a client finishes a Work Evaluation, the recommendation may be a period of Work Adjustment to help the person improve his work habits and attitudes. For example, the client may have arrived late each day or perhaps he was unable to accept criticism in an acceptable manner. A Work Adjustment program would focus on improving the work habits and attitudes identified during the Work Evaluation program. **As a job trainer, you will be doing Work Adjustment at the work site.** It just isn't always called that.

Sheltered Employment

Sheltered Employment is just that. It is a job within a setting that is sheltered or protected from some of the pressures of a competitive job. In traditional rehabilitation, there are sheltered workshops that hire clients who have been able to maintain a productivity rating of 50 percent but are not able to maintain the standards necessary for competitive work. These clients usually have been through Work Evaluation and Work Adjustment and may have not improved their work behaviors or habits enough to maintain a competitive job. In a sheltered workshop, clients are generally paid on a piece-rate basis (i.e. they are paid for what they produce) through special arrangements with the Department of Labor. Without sheltered workshops, the disabled people who are employed there would not be working at all.

The new focus of rehabilitation is to place clients directly into competitive employment. By moving directly into competitive employment, clients avoid going into sheltered workshops. The philosophy is that by giving the client the training and support on the job through the assistance of a job trainer, he is able to become gainfully employed. Thus, clients who may have been placed in Sheltered Employment a few years ago are now being placed into competitive jobs.

Supported Work

The program for which the trainer works may be titled **supported work.** This term is new to the rehabilitation community at the time of this writing. The Supported Work Model was developed by Paul Weyman of Virginia Commonwealth University. He has written several books and journal articles about the model. My own general definition of supported employment is the placement of a person into a competitive job in which he **may not have been ready to work** in the traditional sense. By that I mean that the client may be displaying some behaviors or attitudes that are not considered appropriate for competitive work. Intensive training is given on the job by a job trainer for an extended period of time. After the phaseout period when the trainer slowly withdraws from the work site (see Chapter 9), the client's progress is followed for an indefinite period of time. Services are given when/if problems arise at some point in the future.

Rehabilitation Terminology

If you are working with rehabilitation clients, you may want to know some of the jargon that the counselors use. The purpose of the state rehabilitation agency is to rehabilitate persons with disabilities and help them obtain competitive jobs. When a client has obtained a job, that is called a **placement.** After a client has been working without assistance from that agency, they can be **closed successful** or enter **status 26.** This, of course, is the goal for which each counselor and client strive.

There is an established system through which the client proceeds in order to reach his end goal of competitive employment. First, the client completes an application to enter the intake process. He must be declared **eligible for service,** which means that his disability poses a substantial handicap to employment. Not all persons are eligible, and if that is the case, the client is generally referred elsewhere. Once eligible, a plan or **Individualized Written Rehabilitation Plan** (IWRP) is developed in order to outline the expectations for both the client and the counselor. The client may enter a **training status** if he is involved in a Work Adjustment or training program. In the case of the client who receives job training services, this plan will state the need that the client has for those services. Once he enters a job, he moves to **placement status,** where he will be until his case is closed.

There are times that the client does not succeed on the job. Depending on the reason, the counselor may choose to either continue working with him until he is successful, or close his case **unsuccessful.** If the case is closed unsuccessful, the client will no longer receive services from the state agency. There are times that a client may need to be **interrupted** from a program. This usually happens if the client is hospitalized or for some reason is unable to continue with his IWRP.

The rehabilitation professionals are usually willing to answer questions you may have about the system. They may be able to provide you with a flowchart of the different statuses in the rehabilitation system for your reference.

WHAT STEPS ARE USED IN A JOB TRAINING PROGRAM?

The method of job training described in this manual is being utilized currently by the Transition to Work Project in Cincinnati, Ohio, which is the program that I coordinate. It is not necessary to follow all the steps outlined in this manual; however, if you do, your client should have an excellent opportunity to maintain his job.

Step 1: Intake

Every program has its own method of intake. I would caution you to make sure that the entrance criteria is relevant to the program goals. For example, our entrance criteria are basic. The client must be enrolled in the school system, he must want to work, the parents must be willing to cooperate, and the client must have a need for a trainer. You may wish to reexamine your criteria after reading this manual.

Step 2: Client Analysis

The job trainer performs a client analysis or assessment to determine how to best work with him (i.e. determine learning styles). The assessment involves several procedures: reading and interpreting referral information, observing the client in his present environment (e.g. classroom or rehabilitation facility), and performing the assessment itself (see Chapter 4).

Step 3: Job Analysis

Once the job developer locates an employer willing to hire your client, the trainer will visit the work site and perform a detailed task analysis on the job. This will be discussed in Chapter 5.

Step 4: Job Match

Once the client analysis and the job analysis have been completed, then a job match meeting is held. Since the Transition to Work Project involves high school students, the parents are invited as well as the client, counselor, teacher, trainer, job developer, and any other person involved with the client's vocational program. At this meeting, the two analyses are compared to determine if the client has the capability of adequately completing all the required job tasks. If not, the job is turned down. If the consensus is that the client can perform the tasks after a training period with a job trainer and at some point work independently, then the client is taken for an interview. See Chapter 6 for further information.

Step 5: Training

The job trainer accompanies the client to the job site and trains the client until he can do the job independently. This is not as easy as it sounds, as it is the most lengthy step and is the hardest to implement. Chapter 7 discusses this aspect of the program in depth.

Step 6: Phaseout

Once the client can consistently perform most of the job tasks over a period of time, the trainer slowly withdraws from the work place. This is begun only after a meeting is held with the employer, job developer, and trainer. Phaseout may start with the trainer coming in fifteen minutes after the client has started working, or the trainer may leave for a period of time in the middle of the shift. This depends on the portions of the job the client can do independently. Final phaseout occurs after another meeting in which the employer agrees that the client can work independently. Chapter 9 gives guidance on how to phase out with a client.

Step 7: Follow-Up

Once the trainer has phased out, then follow-up occurs. The length of time for follow-up depends on the perimeters of your program. Chapter 10 discusses follow-up.

Travel Training

Travel training is an important aspect of working with the client. It is teaching of how to travel to his job independently, whether that is walking, riding public transportation (e.g. bus or taxi), or car pool. Pedestrian skills, such as teaching the client to cross streets, are important aspects of travel training. Since this is not training on the job per se, I have included this in the Appendix.

The methods to accomplish the steps outlined above will be discussed throughout this manual. Being a job trainer can be a lot of fun and very rewarding. However, it is a complex job that quite often requires quick thinking, a bit of acting, and a lot of **creativity!** Have fun and good luck!

Chapter 2

WHO IS INVOLVED
IN A PROGRAM LIKE THIS?

EACH PROGRAM that employs job trainers is unique. The funding sources differ, thus the structure is different. For example, I have worked for programs that were funded by a non-profit organization, jointly by a non-profit organization and an adult education system, and a state rehabilitation agency in conjunction with other agencies, including a school system. Because of the variety of funding mechanisms, each program works with people in different roles.

Because the Transition to Work program is a joint project between four major agencies (i.e. Ohio Rehabilitation Services Commission, Hamilton County Office of Education, Great Oaks Joint Vocational School District, and University Affiliated Cincinnati Center for Developmental Disorders) we work with a wide variety of persons, many of whom are professionals. The following list may sound overwhelming, but once you learn a little about the role a person plays and get to know the person, you will be able to relax a little.

CLIENT

Obviously, the most important person to everyone is the client. I spoke briefly of the client in the first chapter. Hopefully, the client wants to work and has a work ethic (see Chapter 7). If this is the case, your job will be much easier, as all you have to do is teach the client the job tasks. It rarely is that easy! Get to know your client before you start working with him on the job. You both will be more relaxed when the job begins.

REHABILITATION COUNSELOR

The rehabilitation counselor is an extremely important part of any program in which the state agency is involved. They quite often control the funding for the client and, ultimately, you. The counselor works for a state agency and generally refers clients to rehabilitation programs or schools for training. The rehabilitation counselor can be a great resource for the trainer. The counselor usually has information about the client from all aspects of his life and, therefore, has a complete understanding of the client. If you have questions about medical or psychological reports, the counselor can be of assistance in interpreting them for you. I have known many rehabilitation counselors during my career in rehabilitation and I can't think of one who would not be helpful to you.

It is important to understand that a counselor working for a state agency must operate under state and federal guidelines. There are laws that determine the amount, type, and length of services a client may receive from the agency. It is sometimes frustrating to work with the system, but, unfortunately, there isn't a lot you can do to change it.

Sometimes, counselors interpret the laws differently. You may find that one counselor may accept one form of information, but another won't. There are inconsistencies any time you deal with people. For example, you and your friend may be reading this book but interpret a particular section differently. It is not that either of you are interpreting it differently on purpose, it is just that each of you have your own experiences to use as reference and may look at things from a different perspective.

PARENTS

If your program includes school-aged clients or clients that live with their parents, you will most likely communicate with them. Parents can be influential over their son/daughter and their job performance. This can be either positive or negative. Supportive parents are wonderful to work with, as they will reinforce behaviors at home. For example, if your client walks to work and arrives five minutes late, you can ask the parents to be sure that he has left the house in time to get to work. Of course, this is the client's responsibility and you must make sure he understands this, but the parents can make sure that the alarm is set correctly.

On the other hand, some parents will sabotage the client's job. This is a strong statement, but unfortunately it is true. I have seen this happen many times. Usually when this does happen, the parent isn't too sure that he wants his **baby** working in the cold, cruel world. The parent who sabotages will find something about the job that he doesn't like. It may be the transportation, the co-workers, supervisor, job trainer, or the job itself. Some parents have high status needs for their children and want them working as a computer programmer rather than a dishwasher or laundry worker. They fail to accept the realities of their child's disability. For example, I have worked with parents who insisted that their child should work in the clerical field, even though the client could not read.

Parents who sabotage always win, unless the client is not living in the house with the parent. You can fight it and attempt to make the parent understand, but they will win and the client will ultimately stay at home and not work. It would be much easier on the client and the trainer if the parent were truthful about his/her feelings before the placement starts. Ultimately, the client receives double messages from the parent ("I want you to work, I don't want you to work."). Then you have an additional problem to resolve: the client's self-esteem and confusion. If the client is living in a group home, there is hope because you will gain the support of the group home personnel.

Some parents want to be involved with every step of the training, some feel that the client needs to go through this process on his own, and some parents don't care. For parents of school-aged clients, the first job is a difficult first step for them as well as their son/daughter. They need to be assured that you are not going to take their child and put him in a job and leave him without support. Many times, we train the parents almost as much as we do their child. This usually takes the form of reassurance. For example, when parents are concerned about their child taking buses, we often take them to watch their child transfer. The delight and amazement on their faces is as exciting as watching the client's happiness when he finally has learned a difficult task.

On the other hand, the parent who does not want to be directly involved but is interested in the client's progress is attempting to assist the client in maturing and becoming a responsible adult. This parent will support you and be ready to assist, if necessary. This must be extremely difficult for a caring parent to do as he/she stands back and watches. There are some parents who do not care and will not become involved. Obviously, you will not be able to count on the parent for support.

Parents can be a wealth of information. After all, they have watched the client grow up, and they know the client's likes and dislikes, what the client responds to in a positive manner, and more. Don't ever discount the parents. They can make or break the client's job.

GROUP HOME PERSONNEL

Many clients live in group homes. There are several types of group homes, each with its own purpose. Some homes teach independent living skills, including budgeting, shopping, safety procedures, community mobility, and more. This type of group home is for the client who can reasonably achieve some form of independence, either maintaining an apartment alone or living in a supervised apartment. For the clients who will not be able to achieve that level of independence, there are group homes that take care of the client's needs. They will be interested in exposing the client to the community, but the client will most likely not be able to live alone in the future.

Depending on the group home and the purpose, the staff will be supportive of the client working. Some group homes mandate that the client be in some kind of day programming, and the client must be off the premises each weekday. Thus, if your client is working evening shifts, that may present a problem to the structure of the group home. Likewise, if your client has weekdays off, that will present a problem, as the home is usually not staffed during the day. The reason the client is to be at the home at night is that the programming and classes are taught at night.

The group home that houses that client who is not learning independent living may not be totally supportive of the client working. I have seen this happen when the client's schedule was different from the others who live in the home and all attend a local workshop. The staff of the group home may have additional paperwork, as the client's salary may need to be reported monthly to the Social Security office. I must say that this is **not typical** of group homes, but this does happen and you should be aware.

When a client lives at a group home, he has certain goals for which to strive. Quite often, those goals will be similar to the ones that you are working on at the job site. I suggest that you stay in close contact with the group home, especially if you are working on behavioral goals, as you can assist each other.

JOB DEVELOPERS

As mentioned in the first chapter, job developers are people who locate jobs for your clients. In some programs, this may be part of the job trainer's responsibility. Job developers may be hired by the school systems and be called work study coordinators, or they may be on the staff of a rehabilitation facility, or a job developer for the state rehabilitation agency. In any case, you will need to work closely with the job developer in order to make your program run smoothly and to help maintain a good relationship with the employer. It is important to understand the basic orientation of the three types of job developers so you can understand their priorities.

The **work study coordinator** is an employee of the school system and thus views the client from an educational standpoint as a student in the school who will be working. Quite often, the work study coordinator has been a classroom teacher who has moved into the position of developing jobs. Depending on the creativity of the work study coordinator, he may be able to imagine excellent modifications for the client to maintain the job and discuss that with the employer when negotiating the job. It is important to be aware that work study coordinators have many duties in addition to job development. They teach job-seeking skills in the classroom (e.g. interviewing techniques); develop curriculum according to the policy of the school district; document for legal purposes; communicate with employers, parents, students, teachers, job trainers; and more during all phases of the job.

The **placement counselor from a rehabilitation facility** is looking at the client from the standpoint of an adult who is ready to work. The placement counselor may teach job-seeking skills to a group of clients, working on things such as interviewing skills and filling out job applications. The placement counselor may have a wide variety of clients on his case load. He may work with recovering alcoholics, people with learning disabilities or mental retardation, and people with physical or medical disabilities. The placement counselor will spend time to get to know your client before looking for a job. He will accompany your client to the job interview and negotiate the job placement with the employer. The placement counselor may not be able to devote as much time to your client as the work study coordinator because of the wide variety of clients with whom he works. The counselor also has numerous duties related to his job within the agency for which he works.

The job placement specialist who works for the state agency usually has a case load of at least one hundred clients. He will meet with your client and discuss the type of job needed. We have discovered that the techniques for locating jobs for our clients in the Transition to Work Project in Cincinnati are quite different for the placement counselors in the state agency. They approach employers with qualified applicants who can walk into a job and be successful. A different approach is used to sell a client who is not job ready and comes with a trainer who may stay up to six months with a client. For that reason, Transition to Work has an agreement with the state placement specialists that when they locate an employer that may be interested in hiring one of our clients, they contact our program and we will develop the contact. This has worked well for everyone concerned.

TEACHERS

If your program involves students, you will want to be in touch with the classroom teacher. Depending on the school, the teacher may have the student in her classroom for up to five or six years. The teacher is a wealth of information. Be sure to set up a communication system with her. She will be knowledgeable about the student's behavior, academic skills, moods, and physical problems. I do want to caution you that the student's behavior may change considerably on the job. Behavior problems may disappear, the client's attitude may change, and his self-esteem may improve! This can be a touchy area, depending on the teacher's investment in the student. The teacher may become somewhat jealous when the student's behavior problem that she has been working on for years is suddenly no longer there. This would be difficult for anyone who has spent hours daily to change something, and suddenly the change occurs because of an outside force. I do not mean to imply that this happens often, but be aware of this when you go into the classroom and mention the fact that the client does not have the problems on the job that the teacher said he had.

On the other hand, the reverse can also be true. The client may suddenly begin to display problem behaviors that were never seen in the classroom. If this is the case, you will need to investigate the possible reasons for the changes. If you and the others on the team (i.e. parents, teachers, work study coordinator) think that the client is reacting to the new situation but will change his behavior once he is settled into the job, then you will need to help him through his adjustment period. If that is not the reason, you may need to consider another job for him. My experience has been that the client is more likely to show positive changes rather than negative.

WORK SUPERVISORS

Because of the importance of the relationship between the supervisor and employee, I have devoted Chapter 8 to this topic. In that chapter, I explain the different relationships one might have with an employer. Please see that chapter for information on the topic.

This may be only a partial list of the people involved in your program. If you are employed by a rehabilitation facility, for example, you will also be working with the staff of the facility. The important thing to remember is that you are all working toward one common goal: assisting your client to become a mature worker and maintain his job.

COMMUNICATION

It is essential that you **communicate** on a regular basis with everyone involved in the program. It is important to know the **chain of command** for your program. Who do you speak to about problems, with your client or the employer? The Transition to Work job trainers have weekly job trainer meetings in which each client's progress is discussed. Besides the trainers, the work study coordinators and state rehabilitation counselors attend. The state counselors are scheduled to attend once a month, and the work study coordinators are invited to each meeting. At the meetings the job trainers report on the client's work week, including any problems or positive accomplishments. This is an excellent time to discuss problems and brainstorm ideas on how to best deal with a situation. Many excellent ideas for modifications have originated during job trainer meetings. For example, at one trainer meeting, we were brainstorming about how a client would carry his janitorial supplies from one floor to another and to the other building in an apartment complex. After hearing some ideas, one trainer suggested a golf bag. All the supplies fit into the bag, he could hoist it over his shoulder and carry his mop bucket. We implemented this modification and the client was able to carry everything in one load.

Communication about all aspects of the client's job is essential for the success of your program. Programs that lack communication have many problems and gain a reputation for not providing a good service. As a result, referrals for clients slow down, and if the communication does not improve, the referrals may stop. Communication is critical to your program and cannot be overemphasized.

Chapter 3

PERCEPTUAL MODALITIES

EVERYONE learns differently. Some learn better by watching the task, others by listening to instructions. Think back to your school days when you were in class lectures. Some people took notes on every detail, others sat back and listened. Most likely there were several people with tape recorders. Some people study better when they write everything by hand. These examples represent different learning styles.

This section will present the three basic modalities of learning, additional information related to how one learns, as well as considerations for job retention. Once you understand the different learning modalities, you can use the information to assist in determining if you have a good job match and how to teach your client job tasks in the most efficient manner. The following information was compiled from several sources: *Educational Assessment of Learning Problems* by Wallace and Larsen (definitions); Learning Capacities, Jewish Vocational Services, Cincinnati, Ohio; and ten years of personal experience working with clients in jobs.

The information presented in this chapter will define what the different modalities of learning are and how to assess the client. Modifications to assist clients in performing difficult job tasks will be discussed in a later chapter. Should you desire more information on learning modalities, there are numerous books written on the subject in the special education section of a university library. Books on this topic may be listed under *learning disabilities*.

VISUAL MODALITY

Before discussing the visual modality, we must discuss the difference between **visual acuity and perception.** (These definitions are general and are composites from the sources mentioned above.) Acuity is the ability to see clearly and in focus. Eyeglasses assist persons with acuity problems to see clearly. Visual perception is the way we perceive what we see, whether we perceive things as they were intended. For example, some people may perceive things sideways, backwards, or upside down.

You may be saying to yourself that this sounds like dyslexia. In the programs in Cincinnati for which I have worked, we did not use that term. We considered dyslexia as the inability to read, a very general term. By following the methods used in this manual you will learn some clues as to **why** the person can't read. This philosophy is the same for dyscalculic, the inability to do mathematics, and dysarthric, the inability to write.

The following are some of the components that make up one's visual modality:

Visual Discrimination

Wallace and Larsen define visual discrimination as the "ability to note differences and similarities among forms, letters, and words." A person with a problem in this area will most likely have difficulty reading, matching numbers or shapes. Jobs that may be difficult for a client with this type of problem include filing and other clerical tasks involving precise reading ability. The client may have difficulty performing dishwashing or housekeeping/janitorial work. In these jobs it may be difficult for the client to see the dirt. Inspecting jobs and others that require fine visual discrimination will also be difficult for the client to perform well.

Visual Spatial Relationships

Wallace and Larsen describe visual spatial perception as the "determination of the positions of objects in space." A person with a spatial problem may bump into walls while walking, write uphill instead of on the line, leave unusual gaps between letters when writing, he may be unable to copy a simple shape or design, or when cleaning, he will be unable to replace objects on a desk as they were. The most significant thing about a person with a visual spatial perceptual problem is that **he will not be able to recognize that he has a problem.** So when you ask him if his drawing looks exactly like yours, he will insist that it does. He is unable to see the placement of objects as they actually are. This is important when the trainer attempts to modify a job task for him. Jobs in which a person with spatial problems may have difficulties include housekeeping/janitorial work, as he may not be able to replace objects on a desk or table exactly as they were or he may run into furniture with the vacuum cleaner; some food service work, if the food or dishes must be placed in a certain pattern or design; laundry work, as folding evenly may present a problem; and clerical work where centering or spacing are of the utmost importance.

Visual Figure-Ground Perception

The "ability to focus upon selected figures and screen out irrelevant stimuli in the background" is how Wallace and Larsen define figure-ground. Some people have difficulty reading pages such as this, because they are unable to pick out and focus on the words or sentence that they want to *readastheyallruntogether*. A person with a figure-ground problem will have difficulty picking out an object if surrounded by other things, such as a paper clip on a cluttered desk or table. Several examples of jobs that require the use of figure-ground perception include dishwashing, where he is required to sort silverware and empty bus pans. This could be dangerous, as he may become injured by a sharp knife that he does not see. Folding laundry may be difficult, as the client will be folding white over white which is difficult to perceive. Janitorial work will also be difficult for the client with a figure-ground problem, as it will be difficult to locate dirty areas, especially specks of dirt on tweed carpets. Clerical workers with this problem will have difficulty locating files in a crowded drawer.

Visual Closure

The ability to identify a whole object when only a portion is presented is called visual closure. Some people are unable to **imagine** what portion is missing from a drawing of a face in which the nose has been omitted. Likewise, if presented with separate letters, C-A-T, they are unable to perceive the letters as a whole word. This problem can cause obvious difficulties on jobs where reading is involved. Likewise, a person who sets tables may have difficulties determining if there is a spoon missing, for example. An assembler may not be able to determine if all the parts of a product are assembled.

Visual Memory (Imagery) and Visual Sequential Memory

Wallace and Larsen define visual memory as the ability to remember items that one sees. Visual sequential memory is the ability to recall the items in a specific order. The ability to learn from demonstration is directly related to one's visual memory. Many jobs rely on a person to remember what he sees. Janitors must remember what items were on a desk or in a room, a laundry worker must remember the steps to fold each item, a dishwasher must remember the procedure to operate the various machines, and a clerical worker must remember the name and correct spelling or system when filing.

Visual-Motor Integration (Eye-Hand Coordination)

The ability to coordinate movements of the hand with the eye is called visual-motor integration. Many tasks we do daily involve this coordination. Dialing the telephone, writing, playing ball, driving, typing, making a sandwich. The list is endless. This combination of perceptual modalities is extremely important vocationally. Jobs which require the use of visual-motor integration include: food service (dishwashing, salad making, cooking, hostessing), janitorial/housekeeping (dusting, vacuuming, scrubbing), laundry (folding or hanging clean laundry), clerical (typing, filing), and assembly.

AUDITORY MODALITY

As in the visual modality, there is a difference between **auditory acuity and perception.** Auditory acuity is the ability to hear clearly. Perception is the way we receive stimuli, whether we perceive things the way they were intended. For example, some people may hear the word **mat** for **nat.** People who have a difficult time hearing clearly are said to be hearing impaired. Hearing aids are modifications used to assist some hearing-impaired people.

The following are some of the components that make up the auditory modality. Once again, modifications to assist the trainer will be listed in Chapter 7.

Auditory Discrimination

Wallace and Larsen describe auditory discrimination as the "ability to distinguish between and among such variables as intensity, pitch, phonemes, and words." A person with auditory discrimination difficulties may not hear the difference between similar sounds such as b/d, m/n, and s/z. Jobs that may be difficult for a client with this problem include any with verbal communication. Examples are receptionist, fast food, order taker, jobs which require lengthy verbal instruction such as janitorial work and housekeeper. Most likely, a person with an auditory discrimination problem will also have difficulty understanding language usage.

Auditory Memory and
Auditory Sequential Memory

Auditory memory is the ability to remember what one hears. Auditory sequential memory is the ability to remember what one hears in the specific order in which it was given. For example, you are using auditory sequential memory when your friend tells you his phone number and you try to remember it without writing it down. A person with an auditory memory problem will have an extremely difficult time retaining any verbal instructions. If given a long string of instructions, he may only remember either the first or last bit of information. Once again, most fast-food restaurants would not be appropriate placements for people with this problem.

Employers must be cautioned as to this problem, because many times the client will nod his head in agreement when someone is talking to him. When asked if he understood, quite often he will answer affirmatively. He is the client that you may instruct to clean the women's restroom after he finishes the hall, only to find him sweeping the front walk. It is clients with this problem that employers will often say, "He's here everyday and is a good worker, but I just don't understand him. I tell him what I want him to do in the morning and he says he understands, but when he starts working, he goes off and does something else." Often, the employer may interpret the client's behavior as intentional and label the client as having a **behavior problem.** If the employer is not aware of the problem, your client may eventually lose the job as the employer becomes so frustrated trying to communicate with him.

Auditory Figure-Ground

Auditory figure-ground is the ability to select, separate, and listen to words, sentences, or specific sounds from background noise. A person with this problem will have difficulty following a conversation or concentrating on a task when there is background noise, such as traffic, people talking, music, typewriters, etc.. Headphones or earplugs are sometimes effective in helping a person deal with this problem. It is difficult for people with auditory figure-ground problems to work in any noisy environment.

Auditory Blending

The ability to hear a group of sounds coming together into syllables or words is called auditory blending. A person who does not have this capability will have extreme difficulty learning to spell, as he will not be able to blend letters or syllables into words. He will be unable to blend the letters d-o-g into the word dog. I once worked with a client who could not identify ending sounds to words, however, beginning and middle sounds were correctly identified. This client was concerned because of his inability to spell. This was the major reason he was unable to master the task. Thus, clerical work would not be the optimum job for a client with this problem.

MOTOR PERCEPTION
(TACTILE-KINESTHETIC)

One can learn through the motor channel by either the sense of touch or by movement. When a person wants to remove his keys from his pocket, he is able to determine by the feel of the object whether it is a key or coin. The sense of touch was utilized in this example. An experienced window washer learns the use of a squeegee by the feel of the hand movement. Thus, when we look at the motor channel, this difference should be kept in mind.

Fine Finger Dexterity

The ability to coordinate the fingers to pick up, handle, or manipulate small objects is called fine finger dexterity. People with problems in this area will have difficulty picking up coins, small screws, pins, etc.. If asked to sew on a button, for example, the person may have difficulty not only holding the button in place initially but also manipulating the needle. Jobs in which the client with fine finger dexterity problems may have difficulty include food preparation, bussing, janitorial work, clerical work (i.e. filing, typing), and assembly work.

Gross Motor Perception

Gross motor perception is the ability to effectively use the larger muscles. This involves activities such as bending, stooping, lifting, carrying, walking, running, etc.. People who have difficulties in this area are quite often clumsy and **uncoordinated.** A person with gross motor difficulties would have difficulties in jobs such as dishwashing, janitorial, laundry, stock work, general laborer, and lawn maintenance.

Bi-Manual Coordination

Bi-manual coordination is the ability to use both hands together to accomplish a task. Peeling an apple, running a buffer, folding a sheet, and typing all involve bi-manual coordination. Many jobs involve the use of bi-manual coordination: food preparation, janitorial, clerical work, stock work, lawn maintenance, and general labor.

Sensitivity

Some people are unable to receive a sensation through their fingers, legs, toes or other parts of their body. A person with this problem would have difficulty picking up and grasping objects, as he is unable to determine if he is gripping the object. Although this is rare, the job trainer may occasionally have a client with this problem. The client should not be placed in a job where there is danger to the affected part of the body (e.g. extreme heat or cold, dangerous machinery or tools).

Motor Sequencing

Motor sequencing is the ability to perform motor tasks in a specific order. For example, a dishwasher scrapes, rinses, places the plate into the dish rack, and **sends it through** all in a specific order. Motor sequencing is the ability to learn and retain this order. A person with excellent motor sequencing ability may be able to perform a task with his hands without watching them. A person who has difficulty in this area may have problems on any job involving specific steps such as dishwashing, laundry, lawn maintenance, and janitorial work.

Directionality

Directionality is the term that explains the way one causes one's hands or eyes to move to turn, move, or follow to achieve a specific purpose. For example, one knows that to read, the eyes move from left to right. Likewise, when wanting to draw water from a tap, one knows that the hot water is on the left and the cold on the right. We also know that most taps turn the same way. These directions have been learned through repetition throughout one's life. There are some clients who have difficulty deciding in which direction to move their eyes and/or hands. A client with a directionality problem will have to think carefully before performing the movement required. A client with this problem may likely try to take a lid off a jar, only to give up in frustration. When asked to try it in front of you, you may discover he has been attempting to turn it the opposite way. Directionality problems can affect clients in many different jobs. Many times, modifications can be made to assist the client on the job. A person with this problem may have trouble deciding which way to send the dishes through the dishwasher. If required to set a table, the busser may reverse the silverware items. A janitor may mop himself into a corner, and a laundry worker may not know which side to fold first. The clerical worker may have trouble filing by dates or deciding which end of the paper to place through the copy machine first. Assembly/packaging jobs require numerous directional decisions.

Crossing Midline

Some people are unable to cross midline, which is a vertical line that divides the body in half. This is not a common problem; however, if you are working with clients with mental retardation, you will work with clients who have difficulties in this area. If your client has a midline problem and is asked to move an object from the right side of the table to the left without moving his body, he will switch the object from his right hand to his left at his midline. When doing paperwork, he will place the paper to one side of his midline or sit sideways in his chair. He does this so his writing hand is always on the side and never needs to cross midline. Most of the clients I have seen who had this problem have learned to compensate very well and the change from one hand to the other is not obvious. Although this is a definite problem, modifications assist in helping the client to work successfully. Jobs in which people with midline problems may have difficulties include janitorial work, food service, laundry, lawn maintenance, general labor, and clerical.

LANGUAGE OR SYMBOLIZATION

Symbolization refers to language. Is the client able to apply meaning to words? The area of language and language development is extremely complex. The material presented below is general in nature.

Receptive Language

Clients who have receptive language problems may have difficulty understanding **verbal or visual** input. For example, if you ask him to find the clock and you give him pictures of a clock, a chair, and a child, he may have difficulty. Likewise, if you were to ask him to perform a series of tasks, he may have difficulty, not because he cannot hear, but because the language is not processed correctly. For example, if you were to ask him to open the door, he may give a puzzled look instead. A person with this difficulty may also have problems understanding written instructions, although he is able to identify words. Again, this is because of the problem processing the language used, not the ability to see clearly.

Another aspect of receptive language is the **time** one takes to process input. A client with a problem in this area may pause for what seems like an extended time period before answering. This is often interpreted as lack of interest or inattentiveness. If this happens with your client, he may be taking this time to process what he has heard. An example of this is the person who catches onto a joke long after everyone else has finished laughing. The client must be allowed the necessary time to process information when given instructions.

Some clients may appear to understand verbal instructions. When asked to repeat them to you, they **parrot** your words but did not comprehend what you said. For example, if you asked the client to sweep the floor, he may respond by saying, "Sweep the floor." After repeating what you said, he may remain standing as if no command had been given.

Jobs that may be difficult for a person with receptive language processing problems include any in which the instructions are given verbally, especially quickly or in passing.

Expressive Language

Receptive language involves processing language that begins with another person or one's surroundings. Expressive language involves the ability to think through and process an idea or thought and the time to choose appropriate words or language to say. In short, receptive language deals with what you receive from others, and expressive is what you generate within yourself to express to others.

Clients with expressive language problems will be unable to explain ideas or name objects, although they may be able to identify the object or act out the idea, using the motor channel. I have heard so many trainers, teachers, and people in the rehabilitation profession ask a client to repeat instructions. If the client has an expressive language problem, he won't be able to do this. The instructor becomes upset with the client because he **wasn't listening.** When working with a client with this problem, ask him to **show** you what he is supposed to do. If he can carry out instructions, he has accomplished what you wanted him to do. Jobs that are difficult for clients with expressive language problems include any that involves the necessity to generate language.

Language Usage or Development Level

When working with any client, it is imperative that the trainer communicate with the client with language the client is able to understand! Using vocabulary the client understands is imperative! Likewise, when presenting concepts or ideas, make sure that the client has the ability to understand them. How many times have I heard employers discuss abstract concepts with clients! One trainer complained that an employer was discussing computer programs with a developmentally disabled client. Another employer discussed the **inner self** with a client. The client may nod as if he understands the conversation when he actually has little or no idea what was said. It is extremely important for the trainer to discover the client's level of understanding and converse with him on his level. This does not mean that one talks down to the client or treats him in a childish manner. **Be sure that the employer understands the client's language level before the client is left alone on the job.**

MISCELLANEOUS CONSIDERATIONS

Although the following items listed are not considered learning modalities, they certainly must be considered when working with a client on a job.

Planning and Organization Skills

The ability to plan and organize one's **work area, time, motor movements, and personal day** are all crucial to job retention. If a client is unable to organize his work area, he most likely will be unable to work efficiently. I once worked with a client in a maintenance job. His work room was in such disarray that he had only a small path in the center in which to walk. The mess was so overwhelming to him that he was unable to clean it up without assistance. Quite often it is possible to teach the client how to organize the work area. This is fine until new parts or tools are introduced, at which time it is necessary to reteach the organization.

Many clients have difficulty planning and organizing their **time.** When given a fifteen-minute break, the client may spend thirteen minutes eating, leaving little time for using the restroom. Thus, when the client goes back to work late from break, he is in trouble. The trainer must **structure the time** for the client. In this case, the client may eat for ten minutes then go to the restroom before the bell rings.

A client with planning and organization problems will have **difficulty deciding the most efficient method of accomplishing a task.** He is likely to work with the materials as they were randomly placed on the work area, without rearranging the items. I have seen clients in assembly jobs actually having to stand and reach over the finished products to pick up the components necessary for the assembly. Another client who was collating printed matter would become confused as to which paper went on the top because he picked up the papers in a different order each time, sometimes using the opposite hand. It was necessary to teach him to work consistently by picking up the paper with the same hand so he could see his ring (the thumb was to be on the bottom). It is possible to teach the organization, if the job is repetitive.

Your client may have difficulty getting to work on time. It may be because of problems planning his **personal time.** Thus, it is necessary to help him plan his day, creating a listing of what he does in the morning and the time allowed. Of course, it is imperative that he set the alarm clock for the proper time. I worked with a client once who started his work at 9:00 A.M. and was chronically late. When asked what time he got up, he answered that he arose between 8:30 and 8:45. Since he had a 25-minute bus ride, it was no wonder he was late! With assistance in planning his personal time, it was possible to help the client improve his punctuality.

Social Perception or
Judgment-Making Abilities

This is sometimes a major problem with clients, as they are unable to pick up subtle social gestures, expressions, and verbal communication. Your client may not understand when a person makes a sarcastic statement or makes certain facial expressions (e.g. rolling his eyes). For example, if the person said, "Nice job," sarcastically, the client would **not** interpret the statement as meaning that he made errors. He would think he did a good job. Sometimes a client will laugh inappropriately at jokes told by co-workers when it is apparent that he does not understand the meaning.

The ability to understand the **cause-and-effect** relationship falls under the topic of judgment. A client may not understand the consequences of his behavior. In the example above, he may not realize that the co-workers know he doesn't understand and are embarrassed to be associated with him. Or, the co-workers may continue to tell jokes and laugh at him without his realizing what is happening.

Some clients may continually ask the same question, have difficulty determining when to end a conversation, or decide when to allow a discussion topic to end. In this instance, the client will continue to discuss the topic or ask questions that will cause others to feel uncomfortable. Should this behavior continue, the client will find himself alone at breaks and lunch. **These behaviors are the most difficult to modify, as no two situations are the same.**

Frustration Tolerance

The client's ability to withstand pressure is crucial to most jobs. The bottom line for job retention is usually quality and quantity. Many times the pressure is placed on the client for added speed. The client's ability to handle pressure of this nature is imperative for job retention. Clients handle pressure in a variety of ways. One client may deliberately slow his work pace or stop altogether, while another may throw objects. Profanity may be used, or the client may walk out and say he doesn't want the job any more. The trainer must know how far the client can be pushed and be ready to step in to assist the client in dealing with the frustrations of the job.

Diet

The client's diet can affect his work performance. If he is not properly nourished, he will not have the necessary energy to accomplish his job tasks. I have worked with many clients whose breakfast consisted of a soda pop. This is an area in which the trainer has little control. Some excuses for an unbalanced breakfast include lack of time, no food in the house, "My mom won't fix me any," and "I can't stand to eat breakfast."

SOME BEHAVIORS THAT NEGATIVELY AFFECT JOB PERFORMANCE

It is my opinion that most clients lose jobs due to inappropriate behaviors on the job. Because of my strong feelings on this subject, this opinion will be voiced throughout this book. You will find below some of the behaviors that will cause your clients to lose their jobs. These problems are functional in nature and directly interfere with job performance.

The vast amount of problems that are diagnosed by psychologists and psychiatrists will not be discussed in this book. The trainer will need to study the referral information on clients with identified psychological problems and discuss the specific problems with someone knowledgeable on the subject.

Work Ethic

Although work ethic is not a behavior per se, the client's job performance is directly related to the presence of a work ethic. Simply speaking, I perceive a work ethic as the desire to work, to earn money, and to perform well on a job resulting in inner satisfaction. I have worked with many clients who are thankful to have a job and strive to do well and have the supervisor, family, and friends pleased with his work. The satisfaction of bringing home a paycheck is identified with being normal. Clients with a good work ethic will be willing to do all the duties required and will strive to maintain the quality and quantity expected on the job.

On the other hand, the client with a poor work ethic will not care if he completes all his work or if his quality is good or not. Many times he will talk about going home as soon as he arrives for his shift. He gives the overall appearance of not caring. When asked if he wants to earn money, he sometimes shrugs his shoulders.

Unfortunately, quite often the client with a poor work ethic is not in need of a paycheck. If he is not working, he gets to play or watch T.V. and do as he likes. His daily needs are taken care of by family. Often, the family is ambivalent to the client working, as he is still viewed as a child who is dependent on them. Sometimes it seems as if the parents are as dependent on the client (e.g. for companionship at home) as the client is on the parent for the necessities of living (e.g. shelter and food). Typically, a parent who fosters dependence does not require the client to perform jobs (chores) at home. Thus, the client is ill-prepared to enter the world of work.

Sometimes the client's work ethic seems to be good when the job begins, but once he becomes settled in the job or bored with the repetition, his attitude may change. Another factor that may affect the client's work performance is his perception of the pressure. If the pressures of the job are perceived as too great, he may start displaying behaviors noted above. **Unless the family is genuinely supportive of the client working and displays a work ethic by expecting him to perform well, the client will most likely have difficulties dealing with the shock of his new job.**

Attention-Seeking Behaviors

Many times the client is used to being the center of attention at home, church, and sometimes at school. When the client begins a new job, he is usually not the focus of attention. However, the attention from the job trainer is enough to satisfy his need. When the trainer starts to phase out and the client is no longer receiving the constant attention, he may begin some behaviors to bring attention to himself.

Some clients are creative in their methods of attracting attention to themselves; thus, there are as many ways of accomplishing this as there are clients. A general way to describe clients who seek attention is **manipulative.** For this reason only a few of the most common behaviors will be discussed.

1. **Interrupting.** Probably one of the most frustrating behaviors a client can display is to interrupt. Some employers have great difficulty with this behavior. When a client interrupts, he is not showing good judgment, which, in fact, may be part of his disability. One employer complained that the client interrupted an important meeting to ask if he could have a drink of water. Obviously, this type of behavior will not go unnoticed.

2. **Asking numerous and/or inappropriate questions.** A common way of seeking attention is to either ask many questions throughout the workday or ask inappropriate questions. An example of an inappropriate question is asking if he should proceed to the next step, after the client had been performing the job correctly for some time. Asking personal questions is also inappropriate. A client once asked me how many children I had, why I waited so long after I was married to have a child, and did I have a problem conceiving. I was glad the client asked those questions of me and not the employer. He was instructed to never ask questions of a personal nature to anyone at work!

Sometimes a client is persistent in asking questions. If he is not satisfied with an answer, he may continue asking it many times. This also is irritating to an employer or co-worker. An example of an irritating question is, "Am I doing a good job today?"

3. Asking for help when it is not necessary. Sometimes a client will pretend he does not understand something or cannot perform a portion of his job and needs assistance. For example, a client may **forget** where the supplies are located or **need assistance** to lift an object. In these examples, when questioned as to where he **thinks** the supplies might be located, he suddenly **remembers**. And when asked if he ever lifted the object before, he answers affirmatively and proceeds to do so at your request.

4. Deliberate poor quality. A client may suddenly start making errors when the job trainer withdraws, realizing that if his quality is not good, the trainer will come back. This is especially noted on jobs in which the client works independently. A behavior program is sometimes necessary to work on this issue (e.g. the trainer only comes to see him when his work is correct).

5. Talking or laughing to himself. When working in an area near co-workers, the client may either talk or laugh to himself in order to receive attention. This behavior tends to be irritating to others as they attempt to concentrate on their job tasks.

Compulsivity

A client who displays a compulsive behavior will focus on completing a task precisely. If he is folding a towel, the ends must meet perfectly or he does it again. This behavior is a mixed blessing, in that the client's quality will be excellent, but his speed will suffer because of it. The employer is looking for a balance between quality and quantity. Two towels folded perfectly in the period of one-half hour is not acceptable.

Distractability

The client who is easily distracted by either noises or visual stimuli will not complete all the work expected. There are some effective modifications that may assist the client for some jobs. However, if the work station is in the middle of a heavy traffic area, the trainer will need to be creative in devising an effective modification.

Perseveration

When a client perseverates, he will continue to perform a task until instructed and sometimes made to stop. For example, if the client was instructed to draw a box on a paper, he will continue to draw boxes until either the paper is withdrawn or the trainer places her hands on top of the client's so he cannot continue. The client may also perseverate verbally by repeating a sentence or asking a question until made to stop. Specific rules must be made for the client who perseverates (e.g. you may only touch this one time or you may only ask a question one time a day).

Unwilling to Accept Supervision

Sometimes a client will be unwilling to accept supervision from the employer or the trainer. Although this was discussed above in the section about work ethics, it is my opinion that sometimes a client is unwilling to accept supervision because he thinks his way is better. This is commonly called being **stubborn.** The client may really want to work and enjoy the praise, but truly think that his way is the best. Common behaviors related to not wanting to accept supervision include **ignoring or walking away** from the supervisor or trainer. Quite often, the client will continue with the task while the instruction is being given.

Sometimes the client may display his opinion by **talking back** to the supervisor. Of course, this behavior is not tolerated often by employers.

Inappropriate Interactions/Advances to Co-Workers

A client may want to become too friendly with his co-workers. He may, for example, ask if he can go to someone's house or come to a party. Or, as a client of mine did, he may ask a young woman to unbutton her blouse so he could "see what was underneath." The client in that example was severely reprimanded but not fired. He was lucky. This behavior is rarely tolerated.

Boredom

A common myth is that mentally retarded clients do not get bored. That is not my experience. I have found many of my clients becoming bored on simple repetitive jobs. When this happens, several behaviors may occur. The mind starts to wander and the client becomes **inattentive** to the task at hand, which affects the work quality. He may take **numerous restroom breaks or start talking on the job.** He may **withdraw into his imagination,** especially if he has psychological problems. He may also become lax in his **attendance and punctuality.** When this happens, the trainer must become involved immediately!

What's Next?

The information presented in this chapter is critical to working effectively with your client. Before you begin working with him, become acquainted with the terms. You may want to discuss this chapter with some of your co-workers to help you become familiar with the information. In the next chapter you will learn how to assess your client to determine his own learning style.

Chapter 4

CLIENT ANALYSIS

THIS IS perhaps the most controversial chapter of the manual. I have been told many times, and I have told others, that a client analysis cannot be written in **cookbook** form. My opinion has changed since I have observed trainers attempt to assess their client's learning styles without direction and training. Due to the lack of experience of the paraprofessional job trainers, they were making some incorrect assumptions about their clients. It is my opinion that guidelines can be given **cautiously,** in order to assist the trainer in analyzing the client.

This chapter is intended to be a **starting point** for you to learn about assessing an individual's skills and weak areas. Assessment is a complex skill. Master's degrees are offered on the subject and evaluators are generally required to have experience before they are permitted to evaluate clients without direct supervision. Therefore, you are not expected to learn everything about assessment from this manual. The basics are here for you to learn. If you find yourself confused, I suggest that you seek out a professional evaluator and present your data to him, or you may write to me in care of this publisher.

WARNING!

Due to the complexity of administering, observing, and interpreting assessments, be advised that by reading this chapter, **you will not be qualified to present yourself as an evaluator!** This point is so important that you will see it repeated throughout.

WHAT TO EXPECT

This chapter consists of samples of exercises you may want to give to your clients. The purpose of the exercises is to give a rough estimate of what the client's learning style is, or to determine how you will teach the client any new job task.

The information in this chapter is based on information from a variety of sources: *Educational Assessment of Learning Problems* by Wallace and Larsen; Learning Capacities, Jewish Vocational Service, Cincinnati, Ohio; Doctor Hadley's testing courses at California State University, Los Angeles; and about 12 years of experience working with a wide variety of clients in facilities and on jobs. This information is commonly used in special education classrooms, especially with the learning disabled. Thus, teachers can be a resource for you. Although the information presented is similar in nature to that used in the Learning Capacities program in Cincinnati, it is basic and does not begin to encompass the scope of information the learning capacities specialist finds during an assessment. If the reader is interested in further information on assessing clients for learning styles, the special education section of a university library, specifically, learning disabilities, will be of help. I found the book *Teacher's Handbook of Diagnostic Screening: Auditory, Visual, Motor, Language, Social-Emotional, Developmental Skills,* by Mann, Suiter, and McClurg, to be interesting and helpful.

WHY IS THIS NECESSARY?

The client assessment is necessary in order to determine how you intend to teach the client on the job. By giving the assessment, you will be able to decide if the client is able to learn to do specific job tasks. You will make observations of the client and his performance on tasks in order to assess all of the learning modalities presented in the last chapter.

This is your chance to start building a rapport with the client, your chance to get to know him and his chance to meet you and begin to feel comfortable with you. I cannot emphasize enough the importance of developing a good relationship with the client **before** he starts his job. He will be nervous on his first day of work, and you will most likely be the only person he knows. **He needs to know his job trainer before the first day of work.**

HOW MUCH TIME DOES THIS TAKE?

The length of time the assessment takes depends on the client. If he is high functioning and understands most of the tasks, it can take as little as two or three hours. If the client is lower functioning or slow, or if it is one of your first assessments, it can take much more time.

Because of the amount of time needed to perform the assessment, I suggest that you plan on two sessions with the client. There are several reasons for this suggestion. Many times, in the first session the client is very anxious. His performance will not be a true picture of his abilities. If you see him a second time, his anxiety is usually reduced. I should mention that it is good to see your client while he is anxious, because he will probably react in a similar fashion on his first day of work.

When scheduling your client, ask if he wears glasses for reading. If he does, ask that he bring them to your session. If he doesn't like to wear them, he may **forget** to bring them and you cannot assess the visual channel accurately. If he is scheduled for a second session, he can be required to bring them.

The client may not have the stamina to attend to the tasks for a three- or four-hour period. It is imperative that you collect data that is as accurate as possible. A tired client will lose concentration and have difficulty working well.

ADVICE FOR THE BEGINNER

Although this is complex information, do not let yourself be intimidated. By following the advice listed, you should do fine:

1. **Read all the information on learning modalities** until you are sure you have absorbed it. Find a good listener and tell him about the way people learn. If you can explain it to someone else, then you most likely understand the concepts.

2. When reading the information about learning modalities, **try to apply it to yourself.** It is helpful if you have an idea of your own learning style. It has been said that a person tends to teach in his own method of learning. This certainly makes sense. However, not everyone has the same learning style as you. I tend to be a visual learner, and tend to use demonstrations, written instructions, maps, diagrams, etc.. When working with a client who is an auditory learner, however, I must concentrate on using my mouth and not my hands.

3. Once you understand the learning modalities, then move on to the **exercises.** Read them until you have memorized them. They will seem simple to read and understand, but when you are face-to-face with your first client, you will want to reach for the book and reread. During the session you will not want to make your client wait while you read. This may affect his confidence in you. My advice is to overlearn.

4. While you are reading the exercises, it is important to **learn the process** involved in administering them. They are all written with the same format. Define what you want to learn, things you need to consider when administering the exercise, the type of instructions you will give, possible modifications you will use, and what you intend to observe.

5. **Observations are crucial!** It takes concentration and practice to be a good observer. I suggest that you use the "Observations" sections of the exercises to practice. It is not necessary to confine your practice to your clients. I am constantly watching people working. For example, when eating out, I almost always observe the food servers, bussers, and other employees. Have you ever had a waitress take an order for a table of four without writing down a word? That's an auditory learner!

6. **Before administering these exercises to your clients, practice on friends or loved ones.** You will begin to get the feel of what you are supposed to do. I STRONGLY ADVISE YOU TO WORK IN PAIRS WITH ANOTHER TRAINER IN ORDER TO GIVE EACH OTHER FEEDBACK. IT IS IMPERATIVE THAT YOU BE HONEST WITH THE OTHER PERSON. THIS IS NOT A TIME FOR SOCIAL GRACES. AFTER ALL, YOU WILL BE DETERMINING HOW TO WORK WITH CLIENTS WHO NEED YOUR ASSISTANCE!

7. Once you are comfortable with administering and interpreting the exercises, you may **make up some exercises of your own to give.** If, for example, you have a client who wants to be a janitor, then you will need to assess him on janitorial skills. Therefore, you will need to observe and try to teach him to dust, sweep, vacuum, and clean a restroom. In the interest of time and space, I did not include these tasks in this manual. However, if you work slowly and write out what you intend to do, in the format provided, you should be alright. If you decide to make up more assessment tools, be sure to keep in mind that they should:

    a. Always be able to give you the information you desire.

    b. Be affordable. Some of the best assessment tools I made were from scraps. One time I needed to have a young woman learn to count the fish in a fast-food restaurant. In her case, it was important to teach with the actual fish or a close facsimile. She was unable to generalize from counting pennies, for example, to counting fish, so I made some **fish** from carpet padding. They were approximately the same color, texture, and size as the real fish she would encounter on the job.

    c. Be practical. It may not be practical to have a client actually triple a recipe for chili because of cost and disposal problems afterwards. However, it is practical to provide measuring utensils and have the client measure water or perhaps flour, while tripling the amounts from recipes.

    d. Make it only as complex as necessary. Sometimes it is easy to get caught up in making something quite elaborate when it is not necessary. For example, one could make an elaborate color chart to use in determining if a client is able to discriminate between colors. While there is nothing wrong with this, the trainer could very easily use items in the examining room for this purpose (e.g. asking what a particular color is in a painting or on some of the assessment tools). The time and effort for the chart could have been better spent on another project.

    e. After making any new assessment tool, **always practice on a co-worker or friend to make sure you didn't forget anything.**

8. When looking for ideas of how to assess your clients, I suggest talking with a teacher. If you are not working with school-aged students and don't know any teachers, you may want to go to a teacher's supply store. You will find reading-readiness

workbooks with visual exercises of all ability levels, multicolored counters which can be used for many things (i.e. color discrimination, counting, spatial perception), reading comprehension books by grade levels, games, and many more things. I have spent many enjoyable hours browsing, buying, and getting ideas. If the supply store prices are expensive, you can go to a toy store to buy the supplies you need.

9. Again, I want to emphasize that you will **not** be considered a work evaluator by following the instructions in this manual. You will know some of the basics about observation and have some ideas to start you off when you assess clients.

Getting Started

Hopefully, you have a **quiet area** in which to administer your assessment. Ideally, the area should have a table, chair and adequate lighting for reading. This, unfortunately, is not always the case. I have assessed clients in women's lounges, storerooms, halls, and even in my car. I hope you are able to find an adequate place to work.

During the administration, I suggest that you have a **pad of paper,** as well as the list of possible assessment exercises, available on which to take notes. This is extremely important, as it is easy to forget details after you finish. If my client asks me what I am writing, my answer is usually, "I am writing down what we are doing. Because we will do so many things together, it is easy for me to forget."

Some clients will be extremely interested in what you have written about them and may wish to look at your notes. If you sense this will happen, I strongly suggest you keep your comments to strict observations. Do not editorialize or write opinions. You may write a specific sentence the client said, for example, "The television set talked to me this moring," instead of writing that this person sounds crazy or says strange things.

You will probably want to devise your own abbreviation system, unless you take shorthand, as you will not want your client to have to wait for long periods while you write. I use an **L or R** for handedness or direction, arrows for up or down, etc..

I have included the form we use with our client analyses to guide you (see Figure 1). This analysis was devised by the job trainers themselves. The trainers are not expected to give each exercise listed, as that would take weeks! Instead, the trainer should select a core of exercises to administer. I would suggest that the ones with instructions and asterisks be included, as they are good basic exercises that can give you excellent data. As you look over the list, you will see that the only limit to what you do in a client assessment is your imagination.

When meeting your client, it will be necessary to **introduce yourself** to him. I usually explain that I will be teaching him his job and I want to get to know him. While we are meeting, I am going to have him do some things for me so he can teach me how he learns, so when he starts his job I will know how to teach him. Obviously, this explanation is far too detailed for some clients. Part of the assessment is adjusting your language level to the client's.

FIGURE 1

TRANSITION TO WORK PROJECT

STUDENT/CLIENT ANALYSIS EVALUATION LIST

Student_____ Reading Level_____ Math Level_____
Job Trainer_____ Open Learning Channels_____
Date(s)_____ Medications_____

-----------------------VISUAL PERCEPTION-------------------------------------

	+/-	Comments
A. Have you ever had your eyes tested? When?		
B. Any problems seeing? Seeing clearly? Peripheral visison?		

	+/-	Comments
1. Visual Discrimination		
1a *Identifying shapes (folder)		
1b *Identifying pictures (folder)		
1c *Identifying words (folder)		
1d *Word & Number Match (folder)		
1e Reading flashcards (flashcards)		
1f Labeling envelopes w/stickers (box of stickers)		
1g *Sorting plastic utensils (setting a table bag)		
1h Putting a puzzle together (puzzle)		
1i Stapling papers together (stapler)		
1j Pulling Weeds, not grass, flowers, etc.		
1k Sweeping - dirt, rice, etc.		
1l Sorting nuts and bolts (box)		
1m Typing		
1n *Word & number find (see 4.b)		
2. Position in Space		
2a Putting alphabet in order (envelope)		
2b *Setting a table (bag)		
2c *Copy objects		
2d Centering the nuts and bolts (round container)		
2e Labeling envelopes (box of stickers)		
2f *Folding a tablecloth, etc. (setting a table bag)		
2g Sweeping		
2h Moving about in a building		
2i Writing name, sentences, etc.		
2j Putting playing cards away (playing cards)		
2k *Copy pictures		

* Instructions Provided

VISUAL PERCEPTION (Continued)

	+/-	Comments
3. Reversals - Is the student left or right handed?		
3a *Word & Number Match (folder 1d)		
3b Giving directions of left and right (see 9b)		
3c Telling time (clocks)		
3d *Word and Number Find (see 4b)		
3e *Copy pictures (see 2.k)		
4. Figure Ground		
4a Identifying items on advertisement (folder 4a)		
4b *Word and Number Find (folder 1d)		
4c Identifying money		
4d Identifying buttons (box of buttons)		
4e Identifying bobbypins (small box)		
4f Putting a puzzle together (puzzle)		
4g *Sorting plastic utensils (see 1g)(setting tbl. bag)		
4h *Folding a Tablecloth, etc. (see 2f)		
4i Abstract Card		
5. Midline		
5a Observing		
5b Drawing a straight line across the board/paper		
5c *Copy Objects (see 2c)		
5d Instructing to move an object from left to right and vice versa (without turning body)		
6. Color Discrimination		
6a Pointing to colors in the room		
6b Identifying colors of clothing (bag of material)		
6c *Copy objects (see 2c)		
6d Putting a puzzle together (puzzle)		
6e Identifying shades with buttons (box of buttons)		

* Instructions Provided

VISUAL PERCEPTION (Continued)

	+/-	Comments
7.0. Visual Sequencing		
7.0.a *Drawing the Next Shape (folder)		
7.0.b Putting Scrambled Sentences Together (folder)		
7.0.c Putting Scrambled Comics Together		
7.0.d Putting a puzzle together		
7.0.e *Identifying the next object (folder)		
7.1. Visual Memory		
7.1.a *Remembering Objects		
7.1.b *Drawing an identical picture (see 2k)		
7.1.c *Setting a Table (see 2b)		
7.2 Visual Sequential Memory		
7.2.a. Putting Written numbers in order (flashcards)		
7.2.b. Putting alphabet in order (envelope)		
7.2.c. *Folding tablecloth, etc. (see 2f)		
7.2.d. Putting playing cards in order		
7.2.e. Putting days of week in order		
7.2.f. Putting months in order		
7.2.g. Spelling		

AUDITORY PERCEPTION

	+/-	Comments
8. Auditory Discrimination		
8a *Repeating words while standing - behind		
- left		
- right (folder)		
8b *Repeating sentences - The girl got a ball, doll, and an airplane (folder 8a)		
8c Identifying noises from tape (tape)		
9. Auditory Memory & Auditory Sequential Memory		
9a *Repeating list of words, numbers		
9b *Follow the Directions		
9c Demonstrating activities asked from a deck of cards- get 3 of hearts, etc., put in envelope, etc.		
9d *Repeating sequence of a story (folder)		

* Instructions Provided

Transition to Work Project - Ohio RSC - September, 1987

.... AUDITORY PERCEPTION (Continued)

	+/-	Comments
10. **Auditory Figure Ground**		
10a Following directions while listening to a tape of -noise (tape)		
10b -music (tape)		

.... MOTOR PERCEPTION

	+/-	Comments
11. **Hand-to-Eye Integration & Fine Finger Dexterity**		
11a *Setting a table (see 2b) (setting a table bag)		
11b *Sorting plastic utensils (see 1g)		
11c Threading a needle (small box)		
11d Sewing a button (small box)		
11e Sewing a hem (small box)		
11f *Copy objects (see 2c)		
11g Paper clipping (paper clips)		
11h *Copy pictures (see 2.k)		
11i *Folding (see 2.f)		
11j Stapling (stapler)		
11k Removing staples (stapler remover)		
11l Tearing perforated items (folder 11l)		
11m Putting playing cards away (playing cards)		
11n Putting a puzzle together (puzzle)		
11o Cutting - a line/difficult pictures (scissors)		
11p Stacking coins (box of money)		
11q Wrapping coins (coins in wrapper)		
11r *Picking up coins, small objects (see 9b)		
11s Pulling weeds		
11t Writing numbers/letters		
11u Writing name in cursive		
12. **Directionality**		
12a *Demonstrating understanding of the list of directional words - put the can on top of the.... (see 9b) (folder 12a)		
12b Assembling nuts and bolts (nuts & bolts)		
12c Cutting a circle (scissors)		
12d Mopping		
12e Sweeping		
12f *Folding Tablecloth (see 2f)		
12g Doing aerobics with a tape of music and demonstration (tape)		

*Instructions Provided

MOTOR PERCEPTION (continued)

	+/-	Comments
13. Bi-Manual Coordination		
13a Observing		
13b Threading a needle (small box)		
13c Picking up a chair		
13d *Sorting plastic utensils(see 1g)(setting tbl.bag)		
13e Typewriting		
13f *Folding tablecloth (see 2f)		
13g Shuffling Cards (playing cards)		
13h *Follow directions (see 9b)		
14. Touch Sensitivity		
14a Identifying same objects from 2 bags (2 bags)		
14b Identifying different items in containers		
14c Demonstrating different water temperatures		
15. Gross Motor Dexterity		
15a Walking a straight line		
15b Picking up heavy objects - chair, etc.		
15c Throwing - beanbag, ball (ball)		
15d Catching (ball)		
15e *Folding tablecloth (see 2f)		
15f Mopping/sweeping		
15g Picking up large trash bag, carrying and throwing in dumpster		
16. Coordinated Body Movements		
16a Jogging		
16b Skipping		
16c Hopping		
16d Jumping rope (jump rope)		
16e Jumping jacks		
16f Lifting heavy box & put on high shelf		
16g Doing aerobics (tape)		

*Instructions Provided

Transiton to Work Project - Ohio RSC - September, 1987

MOTOR PERCEPTION (Continued)

17. Motor Sequencing	+/-	Comments
17a Doing aerobics (tape)		
17b *Folding a tablecloth (see 2f)		
17c Putting nuts & bolts together (nuts & bolts)		

COGNITIVE PERCEPTION

18. Language	+/-	Comments
18a Answering questions - personal data, hobbie, etc.		
18b Proofreading		
18c Reading a list of words (flashcards)		
18d Filling in application (see 18d)		
18e Explaining - sick days, lost time card, etc.		
18f Reading ability		
18g Comprehending (see 18f)		
18h *Following directions (see 9b)		
18i Reading/understanding instructions for - medicine (see 18i)		
18j Reading/understanding instructions for - cleaning (see 18j)		
18k *Following directions - auditory (see 9b)		
18l Following directions - visual		
18m Following directions - simple worksheet (see 18m)		
18n Identifying playing cards (playing cards)		

19. Judgement/Decision Making Skills		
Does the student think on their own?		
19a Responding to judgement/decision making questions (see 19a)		

20. Organizational Skills		
20a Deciding where to begin when looking at pictures (see 20a)		
20b Organizing stapling, folding, and stuffing envelopes (envelopes-light green)		
20c Organizing setting a table (setting table bag)		
20d Counting a pile of money (box of money)		
20e Deciding what cleaning supplies to use when cleaning windows, dishes, bathrooms, etc. (see 20e)		
20f Filing number 1-100 (small orange cards)		
20g Putting a puzzle together (puzzle of U.S.)		

*Instructions Provided

Transition to Work Project - Ohio RSC - September, 1987

COGNITIVE PERCEPTION (Continued)

	+/-	Comments
21. Compulsivity		
21a Observing		
22. Impulsivity		
22a Observing		
23. Perserveration		
23a Observing		
24. Short Term Memory		
24a Responding to questions recalling recent events (these activities)		
25. Long Term Memory		
25a Responding to questions recalling events that took place awhile ago		
26. General Skills		
26a Using money – Adding		
– Making change		
26b Measuring – ruler		
– liquid cup (cups)		
26c Telling Time – calendar (see 26c)		
– lapsed		
– digital watch		
– regular watch (paper clocks)		
– lapse watch (paper clocks)		
– schedules (see 26c)		
26d Understanding Number Concepts (puzzles up to 10)		
26e Adding (worksheets and flashcards)		
Subtracting (worksheets and flashcards)		
26f Using a telephone – rotary		
– digital		
– emergency calls		
– read phone numbers accurately		

One of my first questions before getting started is to ask the client if he **wears glasses** and if he ever had his eyes examined. I once worked with a client who was not wearing glasses. I did not ask the question until he had completed one of the pages of the visual portion of the assessment, and the data showed some severe visual problems. When I asked him if he wore glasses, he said no but that he used to. I asked him if his eyes got better and he replied, "Not really," adding that he had left his glasses on the bus. When I asked him if he had any difficulty seeing, he responded by telling me that sometimes one eye saw green and the other purple. He added that things were fuzzy far away and not too good close up! I stopped the visual assessment and requested that he have his eyes examined. The eye exam showed that he was legally blind, but his sight could be improved with correction.

I also worked with a client who had been given bi-focals but had not been taught how to use them. I taught her to move her eyes from the top lens for distance to the bottom lens for reading, instead of her head. After practicing this technique, she gained an understanding of the concept and used the glasses properly.

As with the glasses, it is wise to ask about **hearing aids.** It is not unusual for a client who is hearing impaired to wear his aid without batteries. It is necessary to question the client as to whether his batteries are in his aid, if they are good, and if the aid is turned on.

It is important that you try to keep the **atmosphere positive.** If the client is struggling and clearly unable to complete a task without success, discontinue what you are doing and go on to another exercise. I sometimes say to my client that I am running out of time and would rather have him complete another task. If the client appears frustrated because the task was difficult, I acknowledge his frustration by saying, "That was hard wasn't it? I was pleased with how hard you tried." Giving him positive feedback for his work is helpful in building his confidence. I think this is extremely important when working with anyone.

Remember that this is an **informal assessment.** That is, the person administering the exercises is not bound to read and follow all instructions without deviating, as is necessary when administering a standardized test. Because this is informal, the trainer may make modifications to assist the client to learn at any time throughout the assessment. For example, the client is having difficulty drawing a figure the way it should be drawn. The trainer may try any number of modifications, or techniques, in order to learn how to teach the client. (Examples of modifications are listed on the instruction sheet later in this chapter.) On a standardized test, the evaluator would report that the client was unable to perform the task. On this assessment, the trainer will report that the client was able to perform the task when a specific modification was used.

It is sometimes necessary for the trainer to modify the actual assessment exercises, as the person may be functioning at either a much lower level and is unable to understand much of what you are presenting, or the person is higher functioning and is feeling **put down** by doing these childish activities. Sometimes the client may be either visually impaired or hearing impaired. Obviously, if a person has no sight, it is pointless to ask him to read a passage or copy a figure on paper. If the person has some sight, it is sometimes helpful to give some exercises in which the eyes are needed, to give you a feeling for how much sight the person has and how he uses it. You may enlarge the written materials on a copy machine to make it easier for the visually impaired person to see the material. The same principles apply to the hearing impaired.

WARNING!

The danger of allowing people who have not been trained to give this assessment cannot be stressed enough. **Practice** before giving it. **Ask questions** if you are unsure of what you are seeing. And lastly, BECAUSE YOU GIVE THIS ASSESSMENT, YOU ARE NOT TO CONSIDER YOURSELF AN EVALUATOR!

Be sure you are familiar with all learning modalities and everything in this chapter before administering an assessment!

VISUAL SPATIAL PERCEPTION
VISUAL-MOTOR PERCEPTION
FINE FINGER DEXTERITY

Copy Pictures

Major Objectives

1. To determine if the client is able to reproduce shapes in a reasonable likeness (i.e. size, shape, details). (visual spatial perception, visual-motor perception, fine finger dexterity)

2. To determine if the client is able to identify similarities and differences between the original and the reproduction. (visual spatial and visual-motor perception)

3. To determine if the client is able to both identify differences and correct errors. (visual-motor perception)

Secondary Objectives. To determine strengths/limitations in the following areas: visual acuity, visual discrimination, handedness, visual figure-ground, language level, auditory memory, directionality, planning, organization, distractibility, impulsivity, compulsivity, perseveration.

Considerations for Administration

1. Be aware of how you give instructions. **Make sure the client is able to understand the language used in the instructions.**

2. The work area should consist of a table, chair, adequate lighting, as well as assorted writing instruments, figures to be copied (see Figure 2), and extra plain paper.

3. **Observe the client** (see "Observations" section at the end).

4. If the client experiences difficulty with the task:

    a. **Never assume the client has a problem.**

    b. Question the client first (e.g. DO YOU UNDERSTAND WHAT YOU ARE TO DO?).

    c. Try modifications to help teach the task (see "Suggested Modifications" below). If you do this, be sure to document what you did and the outcome.

    d. The problem must appear on **at least** three separate tasks to be verified. You are looking for consistency.

Instructions (Actual words the examiner uses are in capitals. Notes to the examiner are in lowercase letters.)

WOULD YOU PLEASE COPY THESE SHAPES IN THE EMPTY BOX NEXT TO THEM? MAKE THEM THE SAME SIZE AND SHAPE.

FIGURE 2

The client copies that shape in the adjacent space. (See "Copy Pictures")

FIGURE 2 (CONT.)

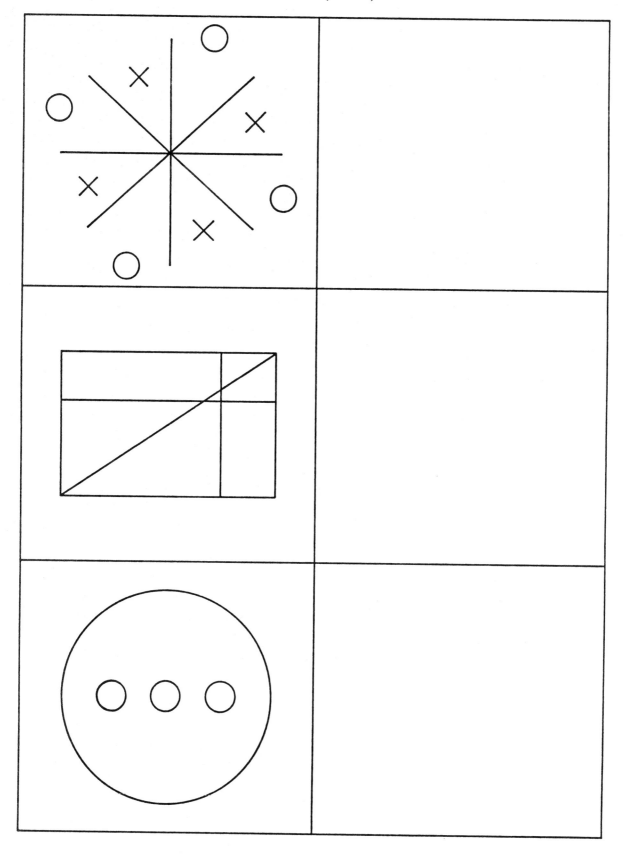

Suggested Modifications

If the client is having obvious difficulties and is unable to complete the task, some of these modifications may assist you. These are merely ideas to prompt your imagination. **If you use modifications, be sure you document the methods you use and the success of the various modifications.**

1. If the client is having difficulty focusing his attention on the figure to be copied, take two plain papers and cover all except the figure he is to be copying. (visual overloading)

2. If he is having difficulty beginning his drawing or making the shape correctly, **demonstrate** the task on a separate paper, then have him try to draw the figure. If the client is successful, have him duplicate it without assistance. (visual sequencing, visual memory, planning, organization)

3. If he is still having difficulty, demonstrate **each step individually** and have him reproduce each step in turn. If he is successful, have him draw the figure without assistance. (visual-motor sequencing)

4. If he was unable to master step 3, have him trace each portion of the picture with a marker. (You may wish to use several different-colored markers.) Then have him try drawing the figure. (visual-motor)

5. If necessary, add talking to number 4. (visual-motor and auditory sequencing)

6. If the client is unable to master this task, go on to another.

Observations

1. Did the client reproduce the shapes so they appeared similar to the original? (visual-motor perception, visual spatial perception)

2. If there were differences, could the client identify them? If yes, the problem is visual-motor; if not, the problem is visual spatial perception.

3. Could he correct his errors? Did he need assistance? (visual-motor)

4. Did he hold his head close to the paper or have difficulties actually seeing the items? (visual acuity)

5. Did he have difficulties determining differences between similar objects? (visual discrimination)

6. With which hand did he hold the pencil or pen? (handedness)

7. Did he have difficulties picking out a figure or portion of it from its background? (visual figure-ground)

8. Was he able to understand the language used? (language level)

9. Was he able to retain the verbal instructions? (auditory memory)

10. Did he work from top to bottom and left to right? (directionality)

11. Did he work in an organized manner? (organization)

12. Did a noise or person walking in the room cause him to stop working and look up? (distractibility)

13. Did he jump into the task before the instructions were completed? (impulsivity)

14. Was he intent on completing the task **exactly** as you requested to the detriment of his speed? (compulsivity)

15. Did he want to continue the exercise even after you asked him to stop? (perseveration)

VISUAL DISCRIMINATION

Pictures

Major Purpose. To determine if the client is able to perceive differences in similar shapes.

Secondary Observations. To determine strengths/limitations in the following areas: visual-motor integration, visual overloading, auditory memory, language level, handedness, visual acuity problems, directionality, organizational ability, distractibility, impulsiveness, compulsiveness, ability to reason.

Considerations for Administration

1. Beware of how you give instructions. Written instructions are listed below. **Make sure the client is able to understand the language of the instructions.**

2. Supplies include: paper(s) with shapes (see Figure 3), writing instruments. (If the illustration is too difficult and for more ideas, check reading-readiness workbooks at teacher's supply stores. Letters or short words can also be used for this exercise.) The client should be seated comfortably facing the table or desk.

3. There should be plenty of light.

4. **Observe** the client (see "Observations" questions at the end).

5. If the client experiences difficulty with the task:

   a. **Never assume the client has a problem.**

   b. Question the client first (e.g. WOULD YOU HOLD YOUR HEAD UP WHILE WRITING? or SEE IF YOU CAN DO THIS WITHOUT SQUINTING YOUR EYES.)

   c. The problem must appear on **at least** three separate tasks to be verified. You are looking for consistency.

Instructions (Actual words the examiner uses are in capitals. Notes to the examiner are in lowercase letters.)

1. ON EACH LINE, THERE IS ONE THAT DOES NOT BELONG. PUT A CIRCLE AROUND IT.

2. If the client does not understand the verbal instructions alone, reword the instructions and point to the picture. SEE THIS PICTURE? The first one, on the far left. TELL ME ABOUT IT. His answer should include that it has a circle and a square. Continue asking this question for each item on the line.

NOTE: There may be more than one answer. For example, on the third line, the client may answer the second shape because it has more dots. He may also answer the middle one because there are no dots on the top. **Always** ask why an answer has been chosen. (language and visual discrimination)

3. If he is still having difficulties, take two plain papers and block out all writing on the page **except** the line on which you are working. (visual overloading)

FIGURE 3

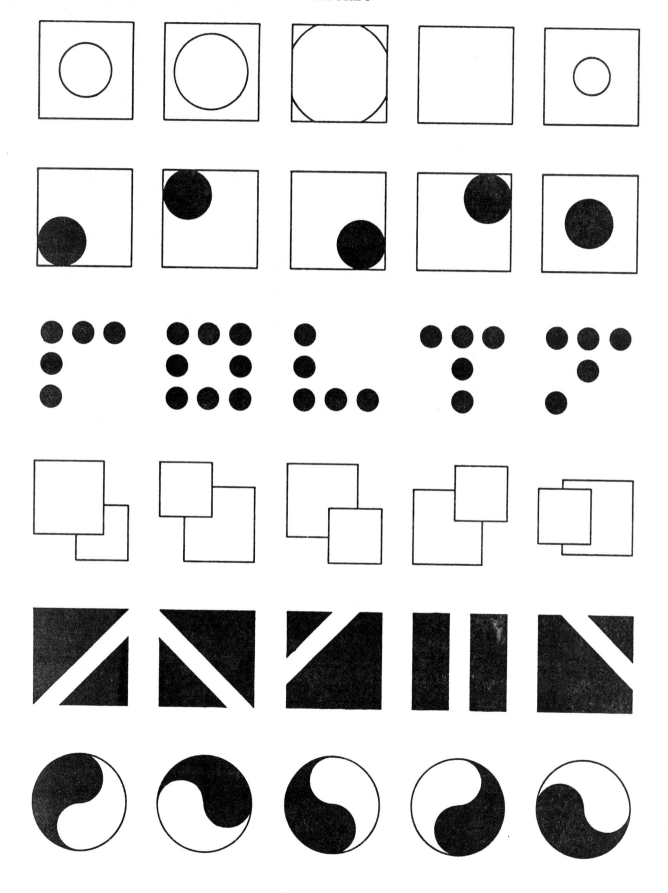

4. If the client still does not understand, do not pursue the task.

Observations

1. Did the client identify the correct pictures? (visual discrimination)

2. Was the client able to draw circles **around** the figures? (visual-motor integration)

3. Was it necessary to cover extraneous visual stimuli? (overloading)

4. Was he right- or left-handed?

5. Did he squint or look closely at the paper? When you asked him, did it seem like a habit or because he had difficulty seeing? (visual acuity)

6. Did he work from the top to bottom and left to right? (directionality)

7. Could he remember the instructions? (auditory memory)

8. Could he understand the language used? (language level)

9. Did a noise or a person walking in the room cause him to stop working and look up? (distractibility)

10. Did he approach the task in an organized manner? (planning, organization)

11. Did he jump into the task before the instructions were completed? (impulsivity)

12. Was he intent on completing the task **exactly** as you requested to the detriment of his speed? (compulsivity)

13. Did he want to continue the exercise, even after you asked him to stop? (perseveration)

14. Was he able to give a valid reason for choosing his answer? (reasoning and language)

VISUAL DISCRIMINATION
IDENTIFYING REVERSALS

Instructions for
Can You Find the Words and Numbers that Match?

Major Purpose. To determine if the client has visual discrimination problems and tends to reverse letters and or numbers.

Secondary Observations. To determine strengths/limitations in the following areas: visual figure-ground, visual-motor perception, auditory memory, language level, ability to identify several words, handedness, visual acuity problems, directionality, impulsiveness, compulsiveness.

Considerations for Administration

1. Be aware of how you give instructions. Sample instructions are listed below. **Make sure that the client is able to understand the language of the instructions.**

2. The work area should consist of a table, chair and writing utensils, in addition to the word page (see Figure 4). Lighting should be adequate for reading.

3. If the client experiences difficulty with the task:

    a. **Never assume the client has a problem.**

    b. Question the client before assuming that he cannot complete the exercise. Some clients will think that they must be able to read in order to complete this exercise. Observe the client closely to determine if the client is having difficulties because he is trying to sound out the words. If he is attempting to read the words, assure him that it is not necessary.

    c. If necessary, see if you can make modifications (see below). Be sure to document the techniques you used and the outcome.

    d. In order to be considered a problem, the difficulty/errors must appear on at least three separate tasks to be verified. You are looking for consistency.

4. Observe the client (see "Observations" questions at the end).

Instructions (Actual words the examiner uses are in capitals. Notes to the examiner are in lowercase letters.)

1. ON THIS PAGE YOU WILL FIND WORDS, AND NUMBERS WITH LINES UNDER THEM. YOU WILL ALSO SEE WORDS OR NUMBERS UNDER THEM. I WANT YOU TO FIND THE WORD OR NUMBER UNDER THE ONE WITH THE LINE THAT LOOKS EXACTLY THE SAME. If the client has difficulty with the language, try substitutes for the word "same," such as alike or twin.

2. If the client has difficulty understanding the verbal instructions, then demonstrate with the client. LOOK AT THIS WORD. DOES THIS ONE LOOK THE SAME? (Point to each word under the one at the top.)

3. Sometimes it is necessary to cross the wrong ones out as you go.

FIGURE 4

CAN YOU FIND THE WORDS AND NUMBERS THAT MATCH?

<u>dog</u>	<u>walk</u>	<u>broad</u>	<u>fight</u>	<u>orange</u>	<u>bread</u>
deg	wakl	droad	fihgt	orange	dread
god	wake	broad	tight	roange	dreab
dog	malk	braod	fight	oronge	bread
dob	walk	bread	fighF	oragne	broad

<u>seat</u>	<u>battle</u>	<u>minus</u>	<u>because</u>	<u>although</u>
seet	dattle	nimus	becuase	althuugh
teas	batlte	minus	decause	althouhg
seat	battel	munus	because	althouht
saet	battle	minns	beacuse	although

<u>351</u>	<u>427</u>	<u>380</u>	<u>0196</u>	<u>6534</u>	<u>9669</u>
531	427	038	3196	6354	9660
351	472	830	0169	6534	6996
135	274	380	0196	4536	9669
513	724	330	9196	4356	9659

The client finds the one that matches. (See "Can You Find the Words and Numbers that Match?")

Suggested Modifications

If the client is having obvious difficulties and is unable to complete the task, some of these modifications may assist you. These are merely ideas to prompt your imagination. **If you use modifications, be sure you document the methods you used and the success of the various modifications.**

1. Using plain paper, block out all the extra writing by placing the paper over all the items on the paper that you will not be viewing immediately. Sometimes clients become overloaded with extra items in their visual field and perform better when they see only one or two words or lines. (visual overloading)

2. The client may need to say the letters/numbers aloud to help him remember what he is seeing. (auditory memory)

3. The client may need to trace over the letters/numbers. (visual-motor perception)

4. It may be necessary to print each set on another paper so it is larger on the page and the letters/numbers are spaced farther apart. It may also be helpful to draw vertical lines between the letters in order to help separate them. (visual spatial perception)

5. After attempting various modifications, if the client does not understand the concept, end this task and go to another.

Observations

1. Did the client reverse any letters/numbers? (visual discrimination)

2. Did the client have difficulty differentiating the letters/numbers from the background? (visual figure-ground)

3. Did he have difficulty placing lines under the words where he intended? (visual-motor)

4. Did he have difficulty retaining the instructions? (auditory memory)

5. Could he understand the language used? (language level)

6. Was he able to identify any words?

NOTE: The ability to identify words does not mean that the client understands their meanings or would be able to comprehend them in sentences! (rough estimate of reading ability)

7. Which is the client's dominant hand? (handedness)

8. Did the client have to look at the paper closely in order to see? Did he complain of eye strain? (visual acuity)

9. Did the client work from left to right and top to bottom? (directionality)

10. Did he jump into the task before the instructions were completed? (impulsivity)

11. Did a noise or person walking in the room cause him to stop working and look up? (distractibility)

12. Was he intent on completing the task **exactly** as you requested to the detriment of his speed? (compulsivity)

13. Did the client underline or circle each word on the page, not stopping if you requested? (perseveration)

VISUAL SEQUENCING
VISUAL SPATIAL PERCEPTION
VISUAL-MOTOR PERCEPTION
FINE FINGER DEXTERITY

What Comes Next?

Major Objectives

1. To determine if the client is able to identify the next shape in a series of different shapes. (visual sequencing)

2. To determine if the client is able to reproduce shapes in a reasonable likeness (i.e. size, shape, details). (visual spatial perception, visual-motor perception, fine finger dexterity)

3. To determine if the client is able to identify similarities and differences between the original and the reproduction. (visual spatial and visual-motor perception)

4. To determine if the client is able to both identify differences and correct errors. (visual-motor perception)

Secondary Objectives. To determine strengths/limitations in the following areas: visual acuity, visual discrimination, handedness, visual figure-ground, language level, auditory memory, directionality, planning, organization, distractibility, impulsivity, compulsivity, perseveration.

Considerations for Administration

1. Be aware of how you give instructions. **Make sure the client is able to understand the language for the instructions.**

2. The work area should consist of a table, chair, adequate lighting, as well as assorted writing instruments, figures to be used (see Figure 5) and extra plain paper.

3. **Observe the Client** (see "Observations" section at the end).

4. If the client experiences difficulty with the task:

    a. **Never assume the client has a problem.**

    b. Question the client first (e.g. DO YOU UNDERSTAND WHAT YOU ARE TO DO?).

    c. Try modifications to help teach the task (see "Suggested Modifications" section below). If you do this, be sure to document what you did and the outcome.

    d. The problem must appear on **at least** three separate tasks to be verified. You are looking for consistency.

Instructions (Actual words the examiner uses are in capitals. Notes to the examiner are in lowercase letters.)

ON EACH LINE YOU WILL SEE A PATTERN OF SHAPES. I WANT YOU TO LOOK CLOSELY AT THE SHAPES AND ADD THE NEXT THREE PARTS ON EACH ROW.

FIGURE 5

The client completes the sequence. (See "What Comes Next")

Suggested Modifications

If the client is having obvious difficulties and is unable to complete the task, some of these modifications may assist you. These are merely ideas to prompt your imagination. **If you use modifications, be sure you document the methods you used and the success of the various modifications.**

1. If the client is having difficulty understanding the directions, you may want to change the directions. DID YOU EVER STRING BEADS AS A CHILD? THIS IS LIKE THAT, ONLY THE SHAPES ARE ON PAPER. WOULD YOU PUT THREE MORE SHAPES ON EACH ROW?

2. If the client is still having difficulty grasping the idea, you may do the first one with him. LET'S LOOK AT THE TOP ROW. BIG, LITTLE, BIG, LITTLE, BIG. WHAT COMES NEXT? Point to the shapes as you say them.

3. If he is still unable to understand the concept, you may want to use colored markers to trace around the shapes, assigning, for example, red to the big boxes and blue to the small. Then use instructions as in number 2 using the color words.

4. If he is clearly unable to understand the concept of this exercise, terminate this one and go to another exercise.

5. If the client is having difficulty focusing his attention on the figure to be copied, take two plain papers and cover all except the figure he is to be copying. (visual overloading)

6. If he is having difficulty beginning his drawing or making the shape correctly, **demonstrate** the task on a separate paper, then have him try to draw the figure. If the client is successful, have him duplicate his without assistance. (visual sequencing, visual memory, planning, organization)

7. If he is still having difficulty, demonstrate **each step individually** and have him reproduce each step in turn. If he is successful, have him draw the figure without assistance. (visual-motor sequencing)

8. If he was unable to master step 3, have him trace each portion of the picture with a marker. (You may wish to use several different-colored markers.) Then have him try drawing the figure. (visual-motor)

9. If necessary, add talking to number 4. (visual-motor and auditory sequencing)

10. If the client is unable to master this task, go on to another.

Observations

1. Was the client able to determine the next shape in the pattern? (visual sequencing)

2. Did the client reproduce the shapes so they appeared similar to the original? (visual-motor perception, visual spatial perception)

3. If there were differences, could the client identify them? If yes, the problem is visual-motor; if not, the problem is visual spatial perception.

4. Could he correct his errors? Did he need assistance? (visual-motor)

5. Did he hold his head close to the paper or have difficulties actually seeing the items? (visual acuity)

6. Did he have difficulties determining differences between similar objects? (visual discrimination)

7. With which hand did he write? (handedness)

8. Did he have difficulties picking out a figure or portion of it from its background? (visual figure-ground)

9. Was he able to understand the language used? (language level)

10. Was he able to retain the verbal instructions? (auditory memory)

11. Did he work from top to bottom and left to right? (directionality)

12. Did he work in an organized manner? (organization)

13. Did a noise or a person walking in the room cause him to stop working and look up? (distractibility)

14. Did he jump into the task before the instructions were completed? (impulsivity)

15. Was he intent on completing the task **exactly** as you requested to the detriment of his speed? (compulsivity)

16. Did he want to continue the exercise even after you asked him to stop? (perseveration)

VISUAL FIGURE-GROUND PERCEPTION
VISUAL DISCRIMINATION
VISUAL SEQUENTIAL MEMORY
VISUAL-MOTOR PERCEPTION

Can You Find the Hidden Words and Numbers?

Major Objectives

1. To determine if the client is able to separate letter/words/numbers from a group. (visual figure-ground)

2. To determine if the client is able to identify specific letters/words/numbers from a group. (visual discrimination)

3. To determine if the client is able to retain what he sees in the correct order. (visual sequential memory)

4. To determine if the client is able to coordinate his eye and hand movements in order to circle the correct data. (visual-motor perception)

Secondary Objectives. To determine strengths/limitations in the following areas: visual acuity, visual spatial perception, handedness, language, auditory memory, directionality, planning, organization, distractibility, impulsiveness, compulsiveness, perseveration.

Considerations for Administration

1. Be aware of how you give instructions. **Make sure the client is able to understand the language of the instructions.**

2. The work area should consist of a table, chair, adequate lighting, as well as writing instruments and the "Can You Find the Words and Numbers?" sheet (see Figure 6). You may also want to have two pieces of plain paper handy for possible modifications.

3. **Observe the client** (see "Observations" section at the end).

4. If the client experiences difficulty with the task:

   a. **Never assume the client has a problem.**

   b. Question the client first (e.g. DO YOU UNDERSTAND WHAT YOU ARE TO DO?)

   c. Try modifications to help teach the task (see "Suggested Modifications" below). If you do, be sure to document what you did and the outcome.

   d. The problem must appear on **at least** three separate tasks to be verified. You are looking for consistency.

Instructions (Actual words the examiner uses are in capitals. Notes to the examiner are in lowercase letters.)

THERE ARE 12 WORDS HIDDEN IN THIS PUZZLE. THE LIST OF THOSE WORDS IS BELOW. WOULD YOU PUT A CIRCLE AROUND EACH WORD? WHEN YOU FINISH WITH THE WORDS, YOU MAY DO THE SAME WITH THE NUMBERS.

FIGURE 6

CAN YOU FIND THE WORDS AND NUMBERS?

t	a	b	o	s	s	b	t		time clock
i	o	f	s	p	a	z	e		on time
m	n	b	r	e	a	k	a		boss
e	t	e	a	e	b	e	m		break
c	i	g	b	d	e	x	l		speed
l	m	n	o	f	f	i	e		exit
o	e	n	t	e	r	t	a		team
c	o	w	o	r	k	e	r		learn
k	l	i	s	t	e	n	n		enter
									coworker
									listen
									off

4	8	9	2	3	6	5		346
7	1	0	8	4	4	6		541
2	5	9	9	6	3	5		412
8	7	5	4	1	0	9		9732
6	6	3	5	9	8	7		1576
1	1	9	7	3	2	4		2599
5	4	1	2	3	6	8		43082
								89457
								63598

The client finds the hidden words and numbers. (See "Can You Find the Words and Numbers?")

Suggested Modifications

If the client is having obvious difficulties and is unable to complete the task, some of these modifications may assist you. These are merely ideas to prompt your imagination. **If you use modifications, be sure you document the methods you used and the success of the various modifications.**

1. If the client is having difficulty identifying the letters or numbers because of the clutter, take two plain papers and cover all information except one line, first horizontally, then vertically. (visual overloading)

2. If the above suggestion (see number 1) helps but he is still having problems, have him point to each letter and then read it aloud. (visual-motor-auditory channels combined)

3. If the client is having difficulty remembering the individual letters and numbers, have him point to the word with his non-dominant hand and then to the letters or numbers with the dominant hand. You may want to have him repeat the first two as he looks for them. (visual-motor-auditory channels combined)

4. It may be necessary to demonstrate the procedure of looking at a word then locating it. (visual sequential memory)

5. If the client is unable to master the task, then discontinue the exercise.

Observations

1. Was the client able to separate the letters or numbers from the group? (visual figure-ground perception)

2. Was the client able to correctly identify specific letters and numbers? Did he reverse some letters? (visual discrimination)

3. Was he able to retain the letters or numbers to be found in the correct order? (visual sequential memory)

4. Did he have difficulty placing a circle around the letters or numbers he intended? (visual-motor perception)

5. Did he hold his head close to the paper, or did he have difficulty actually seeing the letters or numbers? (visual acuity)

6. Did he have difficulty determining the placement of the letters or numbers in the space? (visual spatial perception)

7. With which hand did he write? (handedness)

8. Was he able to understand the language you used to instruct him? (language development)

9. Did he have difficulty reading left to right or top to bottom? (directionality)

10. Before he started working, did he plan how he would accomplish the task? (planning)

11. Was he organized in his approach to the task? (organization)

12. Did a noise or a person walking in the room cause him to stop working and look up? (distractibility)

13. Did he jump into the task before the instructions were completed? (impulsivity)

14. Was he intent on completing the task **exactly** as you requested to the detriment of his speed? (compulsivity)

15. Did he want to continue the exercise even after you asked him to stop? (perseveration)

VISUAL MEMORY

Identifying Items in Pictures Or on a Desk Top

Major Purpose. To determine if the client can remember what was presented to him visually.

Secondary Observations. To determine strengths/limitations in the following areas: visual discrimination, visual figure-ground, visual-motor perception, auditory memory, ability to read and comprehend, language levels, organizational ability, distractibility, impulsiveness, compulsiveness.

Considerations for Administration

1. Define what secondary observations you wish to make. For example, do you want to have the client **read the instructions** (if there are instructions written on the sheet or if you have written instructions for him) to determine if he is able to read and comprehend relatively easy words and sentences, or do you want to assess his ability to **comprehend auditory information?**

2. When giving instructions, **make sure the client is able to understand the language used.**

3. The work area should consist of a table and chair, the pictures, and a writing instrument or familiar objects to be identified (e.g. paper clip, comb, rubber band, eraser, etc.). Pictures may be obtained in a child's reading-readiness workbook which may be purchased at a teacher's supply store or toy store.

4. Observe the client (see "Observations" questions at the end).

5. If the client experiences difficulty with the task:

   a. **Never assume the client has a problem.**
   b. Question the client first (CAN YOU TELL ME WHAT THE INSTRUCTIONS SAID? WHAT ARE YOU SUPPOSED TO DO?)
   c. See if you can make modifications. If so, be sure that you document what you did and the outcome.
   d. The problem must appear on **at least** three separate tasks to be verified. You are looking for consistency.

Instructions (Actual words the examiner uses are in capitals. Notes to the examiner are in lowercase letters.)

Written Instructions

1. WOULD YOU PLEASE READ THE INSTRUCTIONS AND DO WHAT IT TELLS YOU TO DO?

2. If the client is unable to comprehend the instructions, then you will need to proceed with the verbal instructions listed below.

Verbal Instructions

1. **Pictures** — Cover the bottom picture. SEE THIS PICTURE? I WANT YOU TO LOOK AT IT CAREFULLY. IN A MINUTE, I WILL COVER IT AND ASK YOU TO REMEMBER WHAT WAS IN THE PICTURE.

2. Cover the original picture and show him the pictures with items from which to choose. I WOULD LIKE YOU TO CIRCLE AS MANY THINGS IN THIS PICTURE AS YOU SAW IN THE OTHER ONE.

3. If the client is unable to remember any, then show him the first picture again. CAN YOU TELL ME WHAT YOU SEE IN THIS PICTURE? As he tells you, you may have him circle the item or write down the name (visual-motor). Then have him look at the second picture and see if he can identify it.

4. If he still has difficulty, go back to the first picture. NAME ONE THING YOU SEE IN THIS PICTURE. Then go back to the second picture. CAN YOU FIND THE SAME PICTURE ON THIS PAPER?

5. If he is unable to remember even one item, then show him both pictures together and see if he can match any pictures. CAN YOU FIND THE SAME THING IN BOTH PICTURES?

6. If the client still has difficulties, then go on to another task. You have learned quite a bit about some of his problems.

Objects on a Desk Top

1. Place items on a table top in random order (i.e. not in a circle, or paired with similar objects). **Do not allow the client to see the objects until you have given the instructions.** I AM GOING TO SHOW YOU SOME THINGS ON THE TABLE. I WANT YOU TO LOOK AT THEM AND REMEMBER WHAT YOU SEE. I WILL COVER THEM AND ASK YOU TO REMEMBER AS MANY THINGS AS YOU CAN. READY? Let the client look at the items for about 10 seconds. Cover them with a paper, book, or handy object. TELL ME WHAT YOU SAW. As the client tells you, write down the list. You may show the client the objects when he cannot remember any more.

2. If the client has difficulty, allow him to look at the items again. Then ask him if he can recall one, then another, etc., until he cannot remember any more.

3. If the client cannot remember even one, allow him to look at the objects. As you point to each one, ask CAN YOU TELL ME WHAT THIS IS? Then cover the items and ask him to remember one, then another, etc.. (visual and auditory memory)

4. If he still has difficulties, remove all but two objects and see if he can remember what those are using the instructions for number 1.

5. If he is unable to remember any, discontinue this exercise.

6. Have the client put the objects away when the exercise is completed. (take a look at his motor skills)

Observations

1. Was he able to remember what he saw? If so, how many items? (visual memory)
2. Was he able to identify items that looked similar? (visual discrimination)
3. Was he able to pick out an object from its background? (visual figure-ground)
4. Did he have difficulty placing a circle around the figure he wanted? (visual-motor perception)
5. Did he have difficulties remembering verbal instructions? (auditory memory)
6. Was he able to understand the language used in the instructions? (language level)
7. Was he able to read the instructions and understand the meaning? (reading and comprehension)
8. Did he work in an organized manner? Did he show a method to his approach of the task? (planning and organization)
9. Did a noise or a person walking in the room cause him to stop working and look up? (distractibility)
10. Did he jump into the task before the instructions were completed? (impulsivity)
11. Was he intent on completing the task **exactly** as you requested to the detriment of his speed? (compulsivity)
12. Did he want to continue the exercise, even after you asked him to stop? (perseveration)

VISUAL SPATIAL PERCEPTION
VISUAL FIGURE-GROUND PERCEPTION
VISUAL-MOTOR PERCEPTION
FINE FINGER DEXTERITY
COLOR DISCRIMINATION

Copy Exact Placement of Objects

Major Objectives

1. To determine if the client is able to identify the positioning of objects in space. (visual spatial perception)

2. To determine if the client is able to isolate an object from its background. (visual figure-ground perception)

3. To determine if the client is able to accurately coordinate eye and hand movements to copy designs. (visual-motor perception)

4. To determine if the client is able to manipulate small objects. (fine finger dexterity)

5. To determine if the client is able to discriminate between differences in color. (color discrimination)

Secondary Objectives. To determine strengths/limitations in the following areas: visual acuity, handedness, midline, language development, auditory memory, directionality, impulsivity, compulsivity, perseveration.

Considerations for Administration

1. Be aware of how you give instructions. **Make sure the client is able to understand the language of the instructions.**

2. The work area should consist of a table and chair, adequate lighting, and the items to be placed on the table and copied. (You must have at least two of each item you plan to use, one for your model and one for the client to use.) Suggested items include: desk top items such as papers, pens, pencils, paper clips, mugs, etc.; or assorted miscellaneous objects such as multicolored blocks of similar shapes (teacher-supply stores have a variety of objects), golf tees, nails, screws, etc..

3. **Observe the client** (see "Observations" section at the end).

4. If the client experiences difficulty with the task:

   a. **Never assume the client has a problem.**

   b. Question the client first (e.g. DO YOU UNDERSTAND WHAT YOU ARE TO DO?)

   c. Try modifications to help teach the task (see "Suggested Modifications" section below). If you do, be sure to document what you did and the outcome.

d. The problem must appear on **at least** three separate tasks to be verified. You are looking for consistency.

Instructions (Actual words the examiner uses are in capitals. Notes to the examiner are in lowercase letters.)

Before administering this exercise, place one set of objects to be duplicated on the table. **Do not allow the client to watch you position the items!**

I HAVE PLACED SOME THINGS ON THE TABLE. I WOULD LIKE YOU TO USE THESE THINGS AND PUT THEM ON THE TABLE SO THEY LOOK EXACTLY LIKE MINE.

Suggested Modifications

If the client is having obvious difficulties and is unable to complete the task, some of these modifications may assist you. These are merely ideas to prompt your imagination. **If you use modifications, be sure you document the methods you used and the success of the various modifications.**

1. If the client is having difficulty placing the items correctly, have him identify one item and place that in the correct position. Continue until the exercise is complete. Hopefully, the client will be able to continue the exercise on his own after placing several in this manner. (visual overloading)

2. If it is apparent that there are too many items, make a new model with fewer objects. This exercise can be done with as few as one item, although two or more will give you more information. (visual overloading)

Observations

1. Was the client able to place the objects exactly as you wanted? (visual spatial perception, figure-ground, visual-motor perception, fine finger dexterity, color discrimination)

2. Did he have difficulties placing the objects in the **exact** position? When asked about the difference (e.g. DOES YOURS LOOK EXACTLY LIKE MINE?) did he recognize that it was different (visual-motor perception) or not (visual spatial perception)?

3. Was he able to pick out each item from the group? (visual figure-ground)

4. Was he able to manipulate small objects? (fine finger dexterity)

5. Was he able to discriminate between differences in color? (color discrimination)

6. Did he have difficulty recognizing the object? (visual acuity)

7. Which hand did he use? (handedness)

8. When he picked up items to place them, was he able to cross midline? Or did he change hands at the center of his body or turn his body so it was not necessary to cross midline? (midline)

9. Was he able to understand the language of your instructions? (language development)

10. Could he remember the instructions? (auditory memory)

11. Did he have difficulty positioning his hands to pick up the objects? (directionality)

12. Before he started working, did he plan how he would accomplish the task? (planning)

13. Was he organized in his approach to the task? (organization)

14. Did a noise or a person walking in the room cause him to stop working and look up? (distractibility)

15. Did he jump into the task before the instructions were completed? (impulsivity)

16. Was he intent on completing the task **exactly** as you requested to the detriment of his speed? (compulsivity)

17. Did he want to continue the exercise even after you asked him to stop? (perseveration)

VISUAL DISCRIMINATION
FINE FINGER DEXTERITY

Sorting Plastic Utensils

Major Purposes

1. To determine if the client is able to perceive differences in similar shapes.
2. To determine if the client is able to manipulate familiar objects.

Secondary Observations. To determine strengths/limitations in the following areas: visual figure-ground, visual-motor perception, fine finger dexterity, bi-manual coordination, auditory memory, language level, handedness, visual acuity problems, directionality, organizational ability, distractibility, impulsiveness, compulsiveness.

Considerations for Administration

1. Define exactly what you want the client to do. Decide what the purpose is of this exercise. If the client is aiming toward a precision job, you will want to give **specific** instructions. If the client will have little supervision, give **general** instructions and see how the client handles the task. Do you want the utensils sorted into piles? If so, must they be neat? Does it matter? If not, do you want to give non-specific instructions and let the client work on his own without much direction? Do you want to give precise instructions?

2. Be aware of how you give instructions. Sample instructions are listed below. **Make sure the client is able to understand the language of the instructions.**

3. Make sure the utensils are thoroughly mixed up before the client starts working.

4. The work area should be comfortable for the client. He should not have to either reach up a great deal or down too far. Lighting should be adequate.

5. **Observe** the client (see "Observations" questions at the end).

6. If the client experiences difficulty with the task:

   a. **Never assume the client has a problem.**
   b. Question the client first (e.g. WHAT IS THIS CALLED? a fork, knife, or spoon)
   c. See if you can make modifications. If so, be sure to document what you did and the outcome.
   d. The problem must appear on **at least** three separate tasks to be verified. You are looking for consistency.

Instructions (Actual words the examiner uses are in capitals. Notes to the examiner are in lowercase letters.)

1. I HAVE A LOT OF KNIVES, FORKS AND SPOONS IN THIS BAG. I WOULD LIKE YOU TO SORT THEM…(you choose, depending on the data you are gathering):

> …ON THE TABLE
> …IN A STRAIGHT LINE
> …IN THREE PILES
> …IN THREE LINES

2. If the client does not understand the verbal instructions alone, then **demonstrate** by emptying the bag and picking out several utensils and placing them per your instructions.

3. If you instructed him to make lines and he is having difficulties, take three pieces of paper and place them on the table. Have him place the knives on one, the forks and spoons on the other two. If necessary, place marks or draw boxes or pictures on the paper to show where they should be placed.

4. After attempting various modifications, if the client does not understand the concept, end this task and go to another.

5. After the client completes the task, ask him to put the utensils away.

Optional Instructions

Purpose. To determine if the client is able to count accurately.

Instructions

WOULD YOU PLEASE COUNT THE FORKS? …KNIVES? …SPOONS? HOW MANY ARE THERE ALTOGETHER?

If the client is unable to count the forks, then stop this exercise.

Observations

1. Was he right- or left-handed?
2. Did the client have difficulty picking out the individual utensil from the background? (visual figure-ground)
3. Did he reach for a utensil and grab another unintentionally? (visual-motor)
4. Did he have difficulty grabbing the utensil? (fine finger dexterity)
5. Could he use both hands at once, or was he able to use only one? (bi-manual coordination)
6. Could he remember the verbal instructions? (auditory memory)
7. Could he understand the language used? (language level)
8. Before he started working, did he plan how he would accomplish the task? (planning)
9. Was he organized in his approach to the task? (organization)

10. Did a noise or a person walking in the room cause him to stop working and look up? (distractibility)

11. Did he jump into the task before the instructions were completed? (impulsivity)

12. Was he intent on completing the task **exactly** as you requested to the detriment of his speed? (compulsivity)

13. Did he want to continue the exercise, even after you asked him to stop? (perseveration)

VISUAL SPATIAL PERCEPTION
VISUAL-MOTOR INTEGRATION

Setting a Table

Major Purposes

1. To determine if the client is able to determine the positions of different objects in space.

2. To determine if the client is able to accurately place objects in a specific position on a table.

Secondary Observations. To determine strengths/limitations in the following areas: visual discrimination, visual figure-ground, fine finger dexterity, bi-manual coordination, auditory memory, language level, ability to count, handedness, visual acuity problems, directionality, organizational ability, distractibility, impulsiveness, compulsiveness.

Considerations for Administration

1. Define exactly what you intend to learn from this exercise. What are you interested in observing in addition to visual spatial perception? Do you want to evaluate his ability to handle **non-specific instructions** (i.e. SET THE TABLE FOR FOUR PEOPLE.)? His ability to **retain lengthy verbal instructions** (i.e. PLACE THE FORK ON THE FOLDED NAPKIN TO THE LEFT OF THE PLATE AND THE KNIFE TO THE RIGHT OF THE PLATE, WITH THE SHARP EDGE FACING THE PLATE. THE SPOON GOES NEXT TO THE KNIFE. ALL ITEMS SHOULD BE APPROXIMATELY ONE INCH FROM THE EDGE OF THE TABLE.)? Are you interested in **speed** (i.e. SEE IF YOU CAN SET THIS TABLE IN ___ MINUTES.)? **Counting** (i.e. Give the client more than the amount of items needed to set the table.)?

2. Be aware of how you give instructions. Sample instructions are listed above. **Make sure the client is able to understand the language of the instructions.**

3. The work area should consist of a table, chairs (optional), and items for setting a table (i.e. utensils, plates, napkins). Lighting should be adequate.

4. Make sure the utensils are thoroughly mixed up before the client starts working.

5. **Observe** the client (see "Observations" questions at the end).

6. If the client experiences difficulty with the task:

   a. **Never assume the client has a problem.**

   b. Question the client first (e.g. WHAT IS THIS CALLED? a fork, knife, or spoon)

   c. Try modifications to help teach the task (see "Suggested Modifications" below). If you do, be sure to document what you did and the outcome.

   d. The problem must appear on **at least** three separate tasks to be verified. You are looking for consistency.

Instructions (Actual words the examiner uses are in capitals. Notes to the examiner are in lowercase letters.)

   1. I WOULD LIKE YOU TO SET THE TABLE FOR FOUR PEOPLE. (See above for optional instructions.)

   2. If the client does not understand the verbal instructions alone, then **demonstrate** by emptying the bag and picking out several utensils and placing them per your instructions.

Suggested Modifications

If the client is having obvious difficulties and is unable to complete the task, some of these modifications may assist you. These are merely ideas to prompt your imaginations. **If you use modifications, be sure you document the methods you used and the success of the various modifications.**

   1. **Demonstrate** the task to the client. Be aware of how much verbal instruction you give, if any. (visual sequential memory)

   2. If the client is unable to profit from demonstration, **draw** the correct placements on a paper and have him place the utensils on top of the pictures. (visual cues — diagrams)

   3. Place the items on the table above where you want them to be placed. Have the client place his items between yours and the table edge or his stomach. (visual cues — models)

   4. If the client is unable to determine the appropriate space from the table's edge, have him place his thumb on the table as a guide. (visual-motor cue)

   5. Place the chair in front of the area in which the place setting is to be. Have the client place the plate directly in front of the chair. If he still has difficulties, use his stomach (or tummy or belly button) for a reference point. He should be familiar with one of those terms. Then you can proceed to teach him to place the napkin, fork and spoon using his dominant hand for reference.

   6. It may be necessary to utilize the **hands-on** approach. Place your hands on top of his and guide them. (kinesthetic or motor patterning)

   7. Sometimes numbering or naming the steps help (e.g. plate, napkin, fork, knife, spoon, or 1-2-3-4-5). (auditory sequencing)

   8. After attempting various modifications, if the client does not understand the concept, end this task and go to another.

   9. After the client completes the task, ask him to put the utensils away. (planning, organization, auditory memory, language level)

Observations

1. Was he right- or left-handed?

2. Did he have difficulty determining the difference between a fork and spoon, teaspoon and soupspoon, or one and two plates? (visual discrimination)

3. Did the client have difficulty picking out the individual utensil from the background? (visual figure-ground)

4. Did he reach for a utensil and grab another unintentionally? (visual-motor)

5. Did he have difficulty grabbing the utensil? (fine finger dexterity)

6. Could he use both hands at once, or was he able to use only one? (bi-manual coordination)

7. Could he remember the verbal instructions? (auditory memory)

8. Could he understand the language used? (language level)

9. Before he started working, did he plan how he would accomplish the task? (planning)

10. Was he organized in his approach to the task? (organization)

11. Did a noise or a person walking in the room cause him to stop working and look up? (distractibility)

12. Did he jump into the task before the instructions were completed? (impulsivity)

13. Was he intent on completing the task **exactly** as you requested to the detriment of his speed? (compulsivity)

14. Did he want to continue the exercise, even after you asked him to stop? (perseveration)

15. Did he have difficulty counting to four?

VISUAL SPATIAL PERCEPTION
BI-MANUAL FINE AND GROSS MOTOR PERCEPTION

Folding a Tablecloth, Sheet, Towel, or Pillowcase

Major Purposes

1. To determine if the client is able to position different objects in space.

2. To determine the client's ability to work quickly and accurately utilizing bi-manual fine and gross motor skills.

Secondary Observations. To determine strengths/limitations in the following areas: visual discrimination, visual figure-ground, visual-motor perception, auditory memory, language level, visual acuity problems, directionality, organizational ability, distractibility, impulsiveness, compulsiveness.

Considerations for Administration

1. Define exactly how you want the client to perform this task. Do you want the item folded in a specific manner? Do you want to evaluate the client's ability to fold without specific instructions? Does neatness count? Should the edges meet exactly?

2. Be aware of how you give instructions. **Make sure the client is able to understand the language of the instructions.**

3. The work area should consist of a table and items to be folded.

4. **Observe** the client (see "Observations" questions at the end).

5. If the client experiences difficulty with the task:

    a. **Never assume the client has a problem.**

    b. Question the client first (e.g. DO THESE EDGES MEET? DOES THIS ONE STICK OUT? ARE THEY EVEN?).

    c. See if you can make modifications. If so, be sure to document what you did and the outcome.

    d. The problem must appear on **at least** three separate tasks to be verified. You are looking for consistency.

Instructions (Actual words the examiner uses are in capitals. Notes to the examiner are in lowercase letters.)

I WOULD LIKE YOU TO FOLD THESE. (See below for optional instructions and modifications.)

Suggested Modifications

If the client is having obvious difficulties and is unable to complete the task, some of these modifications may assist you. These are merely ideas to prompt your imagination. **If you use modifications, be sure you document the methods you used and the success of the various modifications.**

1. **Demonstrate** the task to the client. Be aware of how much verbal instruction you give, if any. I WANT YOU TO DO WHAT I DO. (visual sequential memory)

2. In addition to the demonstration, you may want him to watch you and perform each step after you do it. Give the same instructions as above, except stop after each step. (visual-motor cues)

3. It may be necessary to utilize the **hands-on** approach. Place your hands on top of his and guide them. I AM GOING TO SHOW YOUR HANDS WHAT TO DO. (kinesthetic or motor patterning)

4. Sometimes numbering or naming the steps help (e.g. ENDS, FOLD, ENDS, FOLD or 1-2-3-4-5). (auditory and visual sequencing)

5. After attempting various modifications, if the client does not understand the concept, end this task and go to another.

6. After the client completes the task, ask him to put his supplies away.

Observations

1. Did he have difficulty determining when two ends were exactly together? (visual discrimination)

2. Did the client have difficulty picking out each individual end from the one under it? (visual figure-ground)

3. Did he reach for an end and grab another unintentionally? (visual-motor)

4. Did he have difficulty grabbing the ends? (fine finger dexterity)

5. Could he use both hands at once, or was he able to use only one? (bi-manual coordination)

6. Could he remember the verbal instructions? (auditory memory)

7. Could he understand the language used? (language level)

8. Before he started working, did he plan how he would accomplish the task? (planning)

9. Was he organized in his approach to the task? (organization)

10. Did a noise or a person walking in the room cause him to stop working and look up? (distractibility)

11. Did he jump into the task before the instructions were completed? (impulsivity)

12. Was he intent on completing the task **exactly** as you requested to the detriment of his speed? (compulsivity)

13. Did he want to continue the exercise, even after you asked him to stop? (perseveration)

AUDITORY DISCRIMINATION

General Instructions for Administering Exercises

1. All instructions to the examiner will be written in lowercase letters. ALL IN-STRUCTIONS TO THE CLIENT WILL BE WRITTEN IN CAPITAL LET-TERS.

2. Always give instructions while **facing** client except when stated otherwise. If it is evident that the client is not hearing you correctly and you suspect that he may have a hearing loss, **discontinue** the exercises until his hearing acuity is checked. If his hearing acuity is fine and he is having difficulty understanding the language, then face the client and instruct him to look at your lips. Note this on your paper, and note also any improvement or lack of improvement.

3. Speak rather slowly and distinctly, but do not make your voice sound affected.

4. It is fine to repeat any part of this exercise. If you do repeat, **be sure to document that you did.** You may decide to place the letter R on your lists in front of the portion repeated.

If you find the client asks for **each** word/phrase/number to be repeated, then discontinue that portion of the exercise and go on to the next.

5. Stand behind your client when you administer the auditory discrimination section. **Be sure to inform your client you will be standing behind him,** as some people do not like anyone to stand where they cannot see the person.

Direct approximately ⅓ of each exercise to the left ear, ⅓ to the middle back (both ears), and ⅓ to the right ear. **Note any difficulty and which ear appears to be affected** (i.e. hesitation before answering, turning of the head to follow your voice, inability to hear).

6. When presenting verbal information to the client, speak in even intervals. Do not group the information. For example, say 1-2-3-4-5-6-7, not 123-456-7. This is difficult to do and takes concentration and awareness on the part of the examiner.

7. **Mark all errors** the client makes by documenting the **exact answer** given.

8. When finished with a section, mark the last item given so you will know later how many items were administered.

FIGURE 7

AUDITORY DISCRIMINATION

Word List

sad - sag _____ _____   tip - tap _____ _____

cam - can _____ _____   tall - wall _____ _____

yell - well _____ _____   big - bid _____ _____

war - were _____ _____   sick - sick _____ _____

house - house _____ _____   bag - bog _____ _____

bean - beam _____ _____   hot - hat _____ _____

kit - kite _____ _____   bar - bore _____ _____

bought - brought _____ _____

REPEAT THESE SENTENCES AFTER ME EXACTLY LIKE I SAY THEM (or SAY WHAT I SAY.).

1. How well do you yell?

2. The sunbeam shone on the green bean.

3. The cam can stay where it is.

4. Were you ever a winner at war?

5. The dog fell in the bog.

6. His bridge bid was big.

7. It was too hot to wear a hat, mitts, and coat.

8. He brought the brown book he bought yesterday.

9. The boy was sad about the sag in his bed.

10. Tom had to put the tap on the tip of the stick.

11. The bear bore a hole in the bar.

12. That wall was so tall you could hardly throw a ball over it.

A Job Trainer's Manual

FIGURE 8

AUDITORY SEQUENTIAL MEMORY

Do not allow the client to see this paper, unless he is having extreme difficulties. If that is the case, he may look only at the letters, numbers, or words, not the instructions.

I AM GOING TO SAY SOME LETTERS, THEN NUMBERS, THEN WORDS, AND I WANT YOU TO REPEAT THEM EXACTLY AS I SAID THEM.

fc	64	hat, car, doll
rbq	352	cake, picture, box
amz	184	paper, truck, chair, dog
nomh	9923	pen, cat, boat, glue
toqm	8179	flower, door, spoon, lamp, cup
depsu	72405	staple, red, phone, book, tire
gipjx	69174	clip, tea, girl, plant, sugar, tape
kvlwaz	856496	pad, jar, bank, corn, man, frog
bfqmzo	943685	day, house, coat, desk, baby, zoo

FIGURE 9

AUDITORY MEMORY

I AM GOING TO READ A STORY TO YOU. WHEN I FINISH, I
WILL ASK YOU SOME QUESTIONS ABOUT THE STORY.

John decided to grow a carrot. To grow a carrot he
needs a cup, a seed, dirt, light and water. He filled the
cup with dirt. After he put the seed in the dirt, he
watered it. He put the cup in the sunshine. After a week,
a small leaf started to grow. He watered it once a week,
then planted it in the ground.

1. Tell me everything you can remember about the story.

2. Who was the story about?

3. What did he want to do?

4. What did he need in order to do it?

5. How long was it before the leaf grew?

6. What was the last thing he did with it?

AUDITORY DISCRIMINATION

Instructions (TO CLIENT, to examiner)

I AM GOING TO SAY TWO WORDS TO YOU. I WANT YOU TO TELL ME IF THEY ARE THE SAME WORDS OR **DIFFERENT** WORDS. LET'S DO AN EXAMPLE. ARE THE WORDS **BOOK** AND **CAR** THE SAME?

What to do With the Answer

a. If the client says NO, give a harder example: ARE THE WORDS **BOB** and **ROB** THE SAME? If the answer is NO, proceed with the word list. If the answer is YES, go to (b).

b. If the client answers YES, you may say, DO THE WORDS **BOOK** AND **CAR** SOUND ALIKE, ARE THEY TWINS? If the answer is NO, proceed to the word list and continue using the same words you used above. If the answer is YES, proceed to (c).

c. If the client answers YES, ask him to repeat the two words. SAY THESE WORDS AFTER ME. BOOK-CAR. MAKE YOURS SOUND JUST LIKE MINE. If the client is able to repeat the words correctly, then continue the exercise in this manner by having the client repeat the pairs of words. If the client is unable to repeat both words, then present them individually. If the client is unable to repeat them individually, then do not attempt any other form of instruction, as it will frustrate both you and your client.

d. If you are unsure if your results are precise, re-administer the exercise at a later date.

AUDITORY SEQUENTIAL MEMORY
ABILITY TO READ
LANGUAGE DEVELOPMENT
DIRECTIONALITY

Follow the Directions

Major Objectives

1. To determine the client's ability to retain single and multistep verbal or written instructions.

2. To determine the client's ability to understand basic language development.

3. To determine the client's ability to interpret and utilize directional terms.

Secondary Objectives. To determine strengths/limitations in the following areas: visual acuity, visual discrimination, visual-motor perception, visual spatial perception, fine finger dexterity, ability to count to five, planning, organization, distractibility, impulsivity, compulsivity, perseveration.

Considerations for Administration

1. Determine specifically what you wish to learn from this exercise. Do you want to assess the client's ability to remember information presented **verbally** (i.e. auditory sequential memory)? Or do you want to assess the client's ability to **read and follow directions** (i.e. ability to read, visual discrimination, visual memory)?

2. If you are reading the instructions, present them as they are written. As this is an informal exercise, you may repeat the instructions in order to assist the client. **Be sure to document when you repeat.**

3. The work area should consist of a table, chair, instructional sheet, and objects to maneuver. When utilizing the FOLLOW THE DIRECTION sheet, it is necessary to provide **at least** the following items:

> 6 coins
> rubber band
> paper clips
> plain paper (scratch paper is fine)
> pencil
> pen
> marker
> screws
> additional objects may be helpful

4. **Observe the client** (see "Observations" questions at the end).

5. If the client experiences difficulty with the task:

   a. **Never assume the client has a problem.**

   b. Question the client first (e.g. WHAT DO I WANT YOU TO DO?).

FIGURE 10

FOLLOW THE DIRECTIONS

1.   Place five coins in a straight line.

2.   Put a rubber band between two paper clips.

3.   Place an X in the middle of the paper.

4.   Draw a circle in the top right corner.

5.   In a row behind the box, place a pencil, coin, screw, rubber band, and paper clip.

6.   Fold the paper in half two times.

     c. See if you can make modifications. If so, be sure that you document what you did and the outcome.

     d. The problem must appear on **at least** three separate tasks to be verified. You are looking for consistency.

Instructions (Actual words the examiner uses are in capitals. Notes to the examiner are in lowercase letters.)

Verbal Instructions

I AM GOING TO ASK YOU TO DO SOME THINGS. THE ITEMS YOU WILL NEED ARE ON THE TABLE. PLEASE WAIT UNTIL I FINISH READING BEFORE STARTING.

Suggested Modifications

If the client is having obvious difficulties and is unable to complete the task, some of these modifications may assist you. These are merely ideas to prompt your imagination. **If you use modifications, be sure you document the methods you used and the success of the various modifications.**

1. If the client has difficulty retaining the instructions, repeat them. Document how many times you repeat. (You probably won't want to repeat more than twice, because the client will become frustrated.)

2. It may be necessary to give the instructions slowly and have the client touch the object as you read it.

3. If the client still has difficulty due to **auditory memory** problems, give him the paper and allow him to read the instructions (see below). If the problem is due to **language problems** (i.e. he does not know what a coin, paper clip, etc., is), then **terminate the exercise.**

Written Instructions

WOULD YOU DO WHAT THE DIRECTIONS ASK? YOU MAY USE THE THINGS ON THE TABLE.

Suggested Modifications

If the client is having obvious difficulties and is unable to complete the task, some of these modifications may assist you. These are merely ideas to prompt your imagination. **If you use modifications, be sure you document the methods you used and the success of the various modifications.**

1. If the client is unable to read all the words, help him or read it to him while pointing to the words.

2. If he is overloading with visual stimuli, cover all the sentences except the one on which he is working.

3. If he is unable to do the exercise due to a **language problem** (i.e. he does not know what a coin, paper clip, etc., is), then terminate the exercise.

Observations

1. Was the client able to remember single-step verbal instructions? Multistep? (auditory memory and sequential memory) Or was the client able to read the instructions? (ability to read and comprehend)

2. Was the client able to understand the language used? (language level)

3. Was he able to demonstrate an accuracy with directionality terms? (directionality)

4. Was it necessary for him to look closely at the objects or written instructions? (visual acuity)

5. Could he accurately determine the differences in objects? (visual discrimination)

6. Was he able to place the items exactly where he wanted? (visual-motor)

7. Did he have difficulty determining the correct position of the objects in a space? If he made an error, was he able to identify it? (visual spatial perception)

8. Was he able to manipulate the small objects? (fine finger dexterity)

9. Was he able to count to five accurately and without assistance? (ability to count to five)

10. Did he work in an organized manner? Did he show a method to his approach of the task? (planning and organization)

11. Did a noise or a person walking in the room cause him to stop working and look up? (distractibility)

12. Did he jump into the task before the instructions were completed? (impulsivity)

13. Was he intent on completing the task **exactly** as you requested to the detriment of his speed? (compulsivity)

14. Did he want to continue the exercise, even after you asked him to stop? (perseveration)

INTERPRETING THE CLIENT ASSESSMENT

Now that you have finished giving the assessment and you have information about each of the learning channels, it is necessary to interpret your information. In front of you sits a stack of information that seems to be overwhelming! This portion of the assessment is crucial to you and your client. If you interpret the data incorrectly, you could have a difficult time working with your client. So, before you begin, the first thing to do is take a big breath or two and try to relax. Make sure you have a block of uninterrupted time, some blank paper, and this manual.

Place a straight line down the middle of your paper. On one side of the line you will place the strengths and, on the other side, you will place the limitations or problem areas. This will be your working sheet.

Turn to the "Perceptual Modalities" section of this manual. The first is the "Visual Modality." Visual discrimination is the first area to examine. Look through all of the exercises you administered and decide if the client has the ability to determine differences in similar letters, words, numbers, or shapes. I would suggest placing the name of each exercise on the list, on whichever side it belongs. This will help you remember the exact task on which the client had difficulties and determine if there are inconsistencies. Then do the same thing for each area listed in Chapter 3, "Perceptual Modalities." **This is a time-consuming, but necessary task.**

When you finish, you will have a long list of information. Hopefully, the information will be grouped on one side or the other of the paper. Those are the easy ones. It should be fairly clear which learning channels are **blocked,** because most everything you did that utilized that channel created difficulties for the client. Likewise, the **open** channels should be clear, because the client had little difficulty within that area.

The difficulty interpreting comes when the information is divided across the page. It is then that you must become a detective to figure out what outside influences caused the client to exhibit either a strength or limitation in that area. For example, your client did fine on the auditory discrimination exercise when it was necessary to determine differences in words. However, when he had to repeat sentences that had similar sounds, he was unable to determine the differences. Think about the differences in the exercises. In the first exercise, he had only two words on which to focus, but on the second, he had to sort out the sounds from a group of sounds. If this theory was correct, he should have difficulties consistently throughout the assessment whenever he listened to a group of words together. (This example is very common with the rehabilitation clients with whom I have worked.)

Look closely at the modifications you made during the assessment. You should have written them down. Did the client respond consistently when you used visual demonstrations, for example? Was it because his auditory channel was blocked or unable to function as it should? You may want to write down all the modifications that you tried on another strength, limitation sheet. You could place the modifications on the corresponding side of the paper. You should see few inconsistencies.

Unfortunately, determining one's learning style is not always easy. Sometimes you will assess a client who has no strengths in any modality. You may have found that you will need to use a variety of methods of teaching him. For example, you may have used demonstrating step-by-step accompanied by short verbal instructions and hand-over-hand teaching to finish the task.

CAUTION: Over the years, I have seen professionals and trainers get into a rut. All of their clients seem to learn by demonstration or kinesthetic methods of learning. While it is true that many clients do learn by one of those methods, certainly not every client will fall into any one category. My advice to you is: **If you do not skip any of the steps listed above, your information should be accurate.**

I once worked with a young woman who was concerned because of memory problems. During the assessment, it was obvious that she had fairly severe auditory figure-ground problems. I gave her some earplugs to block out the excess noises, which helped her tremendously. Further into the assessment, I discovered that she had great difficulty remembering verbal information when she was unable to remember any facts of a short story. As the assessment proceeded, she informed me that she was proficient in sign language and was considering becoming an interpreter, which is a high-level skill. I asked her to sign, either to me or to herself by visualizing, the short story. She was able to retain every detail of the story. We then tried other verbal information such as multistep instructions, combined with the signing. She showed great success in remembering what was said. This example of a visual-motor learner is rather extreme. However, if I would have settled for demonstration as the way to teach her, she would have continued to have difficulties.

Factors That May Influence Performance on the Assessment

Anxiety is perhaps the most common reason for a client's performance on an assessment to be adversely affected. This is especially true if the client has been told that you will be **testing** him. Many clients become nervous at the sound of that word. It was mentioned earlier that you may want to divide the assessment into two sessions in case your client is highly anxious. **It is important to work with your client when he is in a state of anxiety,** because when he begins a new job, he will be even more nervous than he is with you for the assessment. You will learn how well he performs while nervous and how he responds to you. As you work with him later, you will also get to see how well he does when relaxed.

Clients with emotional problems will perform as if they have a perceptual problem or a problem paying attention. If the problem is due to an emotional difficulty, the client's performance may change with medication or cycles. Regardless of the reasons for a client's inability to function well, the problems are handled the same, with the same modifications.

Some clients display **behavior problems** during the assessment which may also surface on a job. During the assessment, the trainer is able to practice different methods of working with these behaviors (see Chapter 8).

Bringing It All Together

Once you have finished your strength and limitation papers, then try to condense it to a few sentences. For example, the job trainers in our program summarize the client's assessment on the **Client Analysis** form (see Figure 11).

Once you can identify the things listed on that form and feel that they are accurate, then you should be ready to go to a job match meeting and work with a client on a job. Chapter 8 will give you ideas of modifications that can be made on jobs to assist your client in learning.

Good luck! You're off to a good start! Stay relaxed and you will do fine!

FIGURE 11

<u>CLIENT ANALYSIS</u>

Job
Trainer:_____

Date:_____

_____ open learning channel(s) are_____

_____

Modifications to be utilized while teaching him/her new jobs are:

     1. _____

     2. _____

     3. _____

     4. _____

     5. _____

(Positive) Considerations when determining appropriate job site/duties/
environment include:

1. _____

2. _____

3. _____

4. _____

5. _____

(Negative) Considerations:

1. _____

2. _____

3. _____

4. _____

5. _____

Chapter 5

JOB ANALYSIS

THE JOB ANALYSIS is an extremely important part of the whole process of placing the client in the **right** job. The job analysis should tell you everything about the job, including all job tasks, the co-workers, the environment, accessibility by transportation, and more. There will not be a lot of explanation in this chapter, just some guidelines and a few examples at the end of this chapter (Figs. 13, 14, and 15) to help you along. Your first few analyses will probably seem easy while you are at the job site but may prove to be difficult when you prepare to write them down in the complete form. Don't worry, you can go back to the site and look at the job again. As in anything new, with practice you will improve. You will find your observation skills becoming sharper and it will be easier to write the analysis in the format you want.

The main thing that I tell the trainers with whom I work is that **when it is completed, anyone should be able to pick it up and be able to do the job.** What does this mean? Details, details, details! It does not help to write "turn on the dishwasher." There can be as many as thirty steps to starting a dishwasher to make it functional. Some are so sensitive that if you do the wrong thing at the wrong time, you could break it. When I read a job analysis, I want to know every step involved in turning on the dishwasher.

I am often asked what format we use in our program to do the job analysis. My answer is a yellow pad. We do have a cover sheet that asks pertinent information, and that is included in this chapter (see Figure 12). Other than that, the trainer writes down each step from the correct door to enter, to the **specific** job tasks, to the closing procedures. I like to have the trainers draw a floor plan (remember, I'm a visual person!) in order to help put things into perspective.

WHY DO A JOB ANALYSIS?

First, the more complete the assessment, the better understanding you will have of the job. Secondly, if you are sick and someone needs to fill in for you on the job,

FIGURE 12

<u>JOB DESCRIPTION</u>

DATE:_____

Company: _____

Address: _____

_____

Phone: _____

Job Trainer:_____ Job Developer:_____

Bus Route/Access (for trainer & client):_____

_____

Job Title: _____

Immediate Supervisor:_____

Other Supervisors/Manager:_____

Staff/Co-Workers (Underline one who is of assistance):_____

_____

Type of Business and clientele(No. employed, No. working with):_____

_____

General Overview of Tasks and Frequency:

Additional Tasks in case of downtime:

Transition to Work Project – Ohio RSC – March, 1988

JOB DESCRIPTION
Page 2

Description of Working Area (Include equipment and working order):

Working Atmosphere (ex: noise, people, area size, distractors, pressure):

Safety Hazards (include equipment):

Wages:_____Per_____ Benefits/Discounts:_____

Work Hours:_____ Lunch/Break times:_____

Probation Period:_____

Dress Code/Uniforms:_____

Company Goals for the Client:

Professional Terminology:

Essential skills necessary for the job (include learning styles and personality traits):

Additional Comments:

she should be able to step in with ease. Thirdly, you will gain a better perspective on the job as a whole, how it relates to the other jobs and how your client will have to relate to the co-workers.

HOW DOES THIS WORK?

I strongly suggest that you spend an **entire shift** at the job site. In most jobs, there are specific jobs to be done both at the beginning and the end of the work shift. Also, I strongly recommend that you actually **perform** the job duties. You will get a better feel for the job, including the pressures. One of our trainers did a job analysis at a croissant shop. In order to get a better idea of how the croissants were actually assembled, she asked if she could make a few. She learned quickly that there was a lot of skill involved in that particular job.

IS THAT ALL I DO, JUST GO AND WATCH?

No, you will want to talk to co-workers and supervisors, if possible, to ask questions about the job. You may want to know if a specific task is always performed in a certain manner, or if the job is routine, or if it changes according to the amount of customers or business the company has on a given day. Are there busy times of the year? An employer once asked the trainer to do the job analysis on the busiest day of the year. I encourage this because your client will be working under the same conditions, so you should see exactly what they are like.

WHAT DO I WRITE DOWN?

The write-up is extremely important. Besides writing down the specific tasks, I suggest that you figure out the learning skills involved in each task and write those with each task. You will need this for the job match meeting, which will be discussed in the next chapter. Until you get used to using the vocabulary used in Chapter 3, this will be time consuming but well worth the time spent in the end. In our program, we use the job analysis as a working document, and we evaluate the client's ability to do each aspect of the job on the analysis. If you know the learning skills necessary for each task, you will be able to make more appropriate modifications for the task (see Chapter 7).

HOW LONG SHOULD THE JOB ANALYSIS BE?

The job analysis should be as long as necessary to include every aspect of the job. I have seen some that are fifteen pages long. That may seem lengthy, but it was complete! I have seen some that were two pages long and not worth anything. It takes quite a bit of time to write out a good job analysis, probably no less than two hours, maybe more, especially for the first few that you do. Hopefully, your administrator will see the value in a complete job analysis and allow you the time necessary to complete it.

HOW DO I GET STARTED?

Before you contact the employer, I suggest you become familiar with at least the beginning of Chapter 8 on working with employers. Although the chapter discusses working with the employer while you are training, the principles are the same whenever you are in contact with him.

Most likely you were given the name and phone number of the manager of the company. You will need to call and make an appointment with him. Explain who you are and who asked you to call. Tell him that you want to observe someone working in the job in question for a whole shift, and would like to perhaps try to do some of the job so you can better evaluate the job for your client.

Before you go to your appointment, you will want to make sure you have a thick pad of paper and a good pen or pencil. You should take a lot of notes, because little details can become lost after only a short time.

When you go on the day of your appointment, be sure you dress according to the job you will be doing. You will not want to wear a skirt and heels (or a sport coat and tie) if you will be working in a job in which you may get dirty, for example, dishwashing, bussing, janitorial, or assembly. On the other hand, you will not want to wear clothes that are old and faded and full of holes, unless you were instructed to do so by the employer. If you are unsure, ask.

You will start observing from the minute you near the place of business. You will look for bus stops if your client rides the bus. You will want to see where the client would have to cross the street. Is it a busy street? Are there lights? We've turned down jobs because of this factor alone. We could not take the risk of the client getting hit by a car because there were no crosswalks.

Once you walk into the building, you will watch every detail. Where would your client hang his coat? Are there lockers provided for personal belongings? If so, do they provide the lock? How do you get to the locker area? You will need to write this in your analysis.

Where are the restrooms? Is there an employees' restroom? Note where that is, both the men's and women's restroom.

Where is the time clock, or where does the client clock in? If it is a time clock, where is it located? Is it high on the wall or low? This may affect a short client. What type of time clock is it? There are many ways of clocking in. The easiest is the type where the client inserts the card in the top and it clicks when the time is printed. A difficult type is where the client must align the space with a small red line and hold it there with his left hand while pushing down on a lever with his right hand. For clients with visual spatial problems, this can be a difficult task. Some places are using computers. You must punch in a code, which may be your Social Security number. Others use the old-fashioned method of writing the time. But it isn't always that easy. Some clients must compute the hours they worked on the job to the tenth of the hour. Teaching decimals and lapsed time to a client with poor receptive language skills is difficult at best! It may sound strange to spend so much time talking about time cards, but if your client can't clock in, he won't get paid.

WHAT DO I LOOK FOR ON THE JOB?

Every tiny detail of the job will be studied. First, you will most likely meet the person whom you will be observing. He may be nervous and not know quite what to expect. It is up to you to put him at ease. Explain that you will be observing for the shift to get a good idea of what the job duties are. While there, you will have many questions to ask him about his job. I'll give you hints of things to look for later in this chapter. Don't be bashful! Your client's job depends on your ability to complete an accurate job analysis. You can't afford to not ask questions. Always keep in mind that you should never keep the person from performing his job. You certainly don't want to get him in trouble! And you don't want to start with a negative experience.

Next, you will want to note the physical layout of the work area. You will want to note where the supplies are located, and you will also want to find a place to stand where you will not be in the way of the workers. As you gain experience in different environments, you will become more adept at fading into the walls. If you are in the way, don't make the workers ask you to move. Watch for them and move before they come near you. This will leave a good impression and they won't mind having you around.

You will also want to take note of the co-workers. I ask the trainers to indicate how many co-workers there are, whether they are male or female, and the general make up of the co-workers. These areas can all be issues with clients and may need to be looked at carefully before placement.

You will probably be asked why you are there. Remember client confidentiality at all times (see Chapter 8). I usually tell people who ask, that I am here to see a specific job and that I am trying to find out if a client of mine has the capability to do this job. If they ask where you work, tell them and give a general description of the clients and that they are handicapped or disabled. That usually satisfies them.

Information to Find for Every Job

There are some things to look for on every job that you will analyze. In order to assist you, I will list some questions to help you get started. You may choose to make up a checklist for yourself to take to the job site to help you remember all the questions to ask.

Breaks and Lunch

1. What time are they given and for how long?
2. How does the employee know that it is time to go to break and return?
3. Is there a buzzer or must he tell time?
4. Will co-workers have the same break time as your client?
5. Where is the break room?
6. Does the client bring his lunch?
7. If he does bring it, is there a refrigerator in which to store it?
8. Is there a place to purchase either coffee or soft drinks? If so, how much does it cost?
9. Do they have decaffeinated coffee?
10. Is smoking permitted? If so, where?

Uniforms

1. Will it be necessary for your client to wear a uniform? If so, what is it?
2. Does the employer furnish any or all of it? If so, what specific parts?
3. How many uniforms are given to each employee?
4. Who is responsible for cleaning the uniform? If it is the responsibility of the employer, what is the pickup and return schedule?
5. If uniforms aren't furnished, what is acceptable attire (e.g. shirt, pants, shoes)? Must the clothes be a specific color?

Co-Workers (Please see Chapter 8 for more information about co-workers.)

1. How many co-workers are there?
2. How close will your client be to the co-workers when at his job station?
3. Are they male or female?
4. What race are they? (Although sex and race ideally should not enter into a decision of whether to place a client into a job or not, at times it does. I have worked with numerous clients who responded better to one sex or race and I would not want to place them in a job situation with the opposite. I felt it was not fair to either the client or the potential co-worker. When a client feels strongly enough to allow his feelings to interfere with his job performance, he will most surely lose the job if placed in the wrong environment.)
5. What is the maturity level of the co-workers? They will be serving as role models for your client. Do you want your client working with them and learning their behaviors?
6. How do they communicate with each other? Do the co-workers tease, are they sarcastic, or are they formal?

7. Do the co-workers work as a team? If they do, then perhaps they will work with your client also.

8. Do the co-workers perform the job as you understood it to be, or are they doing as they please, using shortcuts that are not approved?

9. What is their attitude about your client? (Be aware that the co-workers are not always aware that the supervisor is considering hiring one of your clients. If this is the case, you won't be able to answer this question at the time of the job analysis.)

Supervision

1. Is there close supervision? Sometimes the worker might not see the supervisor for a shift or several days.

2. What is his style of supervision? Is he a supportive person who gives suggestions, or is he easily frustrated and raises his voice often?

3. Does the supervisor train new staff or does a co-worker? Sometimes, if the supervisor is to do the training, he is called away to perform his other duties and the training suffers.

4. What is the supervisor's attitude toward your client? Is he overprotective, is he willing to work with the co-workers to help them adjust, or is he overbearing? Do the co-workers respond positively to him, or ignore him and do what they want to do?

Cleanup

1. Are there cleanup duties to be performed? If so, what are they and what are the quality standards?

2. How much time should they take?

3. How do the employees know when to start to cleanup?

Specific Jobs

Obviously, you are going to watch the person performing the job duties. I will give you some hints on things to look for in specific jobs: janitorial, dishwashing, bussing, laundry, clerical, and assembly/packaging. (These same job areas will be discussed throughout this manual.)

Janitorial Work

When looking at a janitorial job, you will want to look at several areas: the items to be cleaned, the equipment, the chemicals, co-workers, and amount of supervision. These areas are extremely important to your client's success on a job. For your ease in reading and use for a reference, I will list suggested observations or questions to ask and the learning channels or behaviors critical to the task. Remember that these are just suggestions for a starting place. When you are actually at the job site, you will think of many more things to observe.

1. Is the geographical area large or small? (visual spatial, directionality)

2. Are there many steps to climb, or is there an elevator? If the client must carry his mop water up a flight of stairs, this may have a bearing on whether he is placed on that job. (gross motor—may affect persons with physical disabilities)

3. Will he be cleaning the same areas everyday, or will there be something new everyday? Many clients need a **routine** and would have difficulty with a job that changes everyday.

4. If he would be working with a crew, would he have to learn all the jobs, and if so, how quickly? Some crews give new employees only a couple of days to learn all of the jobs. They are usually broken down into areas like: dusting, vacuuming, bathrooms, kitchens. If the crew cleans houses, they usually divide the jobs and are in and out in 20 minutes. In the next house, the crew switches jobs. (visual discrimination, spatial perception, figure-ground perception, closure, visual and auditory memory, fine and gross motor, bi-manual dexterity, touch sensitivity, sequencing, planning/organization, judgment, able to get along with co-workers, accept supervision)

5. What kind of equipment do they use? If it is mechanical, is it difficult to operate? Does it seem to be in good repair? (see number 4 above)

6. How does the client carry his equipment? Is there a janitorial cart or a carrying caddy or bucket? Is it cumbersome or easy to handle? (gross and fine motor, visual discrimination, spatial perception, figure-ground perception, memorize items, visual-motor perception, planning/organization, judgment)

7. Do they have enough supplies? So many jobs I have seen have difficulty keeping adequate supplies. Some employers expect people to share. Is that difficult to do because the workers are working in different areas? (get along with co-workers)

8. What about the chemicals? How many are there? How dangerous are they? (memory, judgment)

9. Are they premixed, or does the client have to do it? (visual discrimination, spatial perception, figure-ground perception, visual memory, fine finger dexterity, bi-manual coordination, planning/organization, judgment, reading and/or mathematical ability to measure)

10. Are they clearly marked as to the chemical, the proper use, and emergency procedures if the client should get some in his eye, for example? (reading ability and comprehension, judgment)

11. If the client has to mix the chemicals, is there a measuring container? If not, that may have to be one of your first modifications. (see number 9 above)

12. If the chemicals come in large quantities (e.g. five-gallon drums), will he have to lift them? (gross motor, bi-manual, visual discrimination, visual spatial perception, figure-ground, directionality)

Dishwashing

When observing a dishwashing job, you will want to pay close attention to the equipment, the procedures and the duties. Every dishwashing job is different; don't assume you know the procedures that one company uses because you are familiar with another company's. The following are ideas of things to look for on a dishwashing job. Remember that these are ideas to start you and give you some direction. While at the job site, you will most likely see things that are not listed in this section that are extremely important for that particular job.

1. What kind of equipment does the company have? Is the dishwasher fully automatic, semi-automatic, or manual? Or is there a dishwasher at all. I have seen restaurants where the dishes are done by hand and then placed in a sterilizer. (visual discrimination, spatial, figure-ground, directionality, visual memory, visual motor, bi-manual, fine and gross motor, sequencing, planning/organization, judgment)

2. What about the controls? Are they placed within easy reach? Are they easy to use? In one restaurant in which I worked, the on/off switch was almost six feet off the floor and it was necessary to reach over the sink in order to reach it. The valves for the water to fill the machine had no knobs and were turned on by using a fork. Some clients would have difficulties in a situation like this. (see number 1 above)

3. How do you fill the soap dispenser? Does a buzzer ring or a light flash when the soap is low? Where is the soap kept? (visual discrimination, spatial, figure-ground, directionality, auditory discrimination, memory, figure-ground, visual-motor, bi-manual, sensitivity, sequencing, judgment, planning/organization)

4. What are the procedures for filling the machine? Be sure you have a detailed task analysis on paper. (see number 3 above)

5. Is there other set up involved? For example, are there clean dish carts that must be placed into specific areas? (auditory and visual discrimination, figure-ground, and memory, visual spatial perception, visual-motor perception, gross motor, directionality, bi-manual, sequencing, judgment, get along with supervisors and co-workers)

6. Is there usually a pile of dirty dishes when the shift starts? (visual discrimination, figure-ground, spatial perception, visual overloading)

7. Is the dishwasher responsible for the pots and pans? Some places hire a person just to do that job. (gross and fine motor, touch sensitivity, judgment, visual discrimination, spatial, and figure-ground perception)

8. If your client is to do pots and pans, did you learn how the sinks are to be filled? (memory, visual discrimination, spatial, figure-ground, touch sensitivity)

9. Some sinks have pot cleaners in them. I'm not too familiar with them, but my understanding is that they churn the water to help get the crusted food off. If this kitchen is equipped with that, what are the procedures to run it safely?

10. Where are the scratch pads kept? (visual memory)

11. Is there a squeegee to clean the work area? Is it in good shape? Where is it kept? (visual memory, fine motor, directionality, visual discrimination, spatial, figure-ground)

12. Where does the dishwasher scrape the food? (visual memory, fine and gross motor, spatial, figure-ground)

13. Is the dishwasher responsible for taking the garbage out to the dumpster? If so, how much garbage is placed in the garbage can? Is it to be filled halfway or three-quarters of the way? Garbage bags are extremely heavy when filled. (gross and fine motor, visual memory, discrimination, spatial, and figure-ground perception, planning/organization)

14. How is the job organized? Do the glasses, cups, etc. go into racks above the work table? If so, can your client reach at least the first two rows of the dishracks? (Once these are filled, he can turn the rack around and place the empty rows at the bottom where he can reach them.) (planning/organization, fine and gross motor, visual discrimination, spatial, and figure-ground)

15. How many times are the glasses washed? Most places will have the glasses washed at least twice. The board of health usually determines this. (memory)

16. Silverware is another issue. How is the silverware to be washed? (I must warn you that this procedure changes from time to time. I worked on a job with a client where the manager changed the procedure three times in one week.) Usually, the silver is soaked in a solution to loosen the food, then placed on a flat rack to be washed. After that it is sorted and placed in round containers then run through the machine two more times. Then the silver is considered clean. (sequencing, visual discrimination, spatial, figure-ground, fine and gross motor)

17. If there is a soaking solution for the silverware, how is it prepared? How often should it be changed? (planning/organization, judgment, visual discrimination, spatial, figure-ground, ability to measure)

18. Is the disposal working? If so, how do you operate it safely? (visual discrimination, directionality, fine motor, judgment)

19. Which way do the dishes go through the dishwasher? Sometimes there is a specific way that the manufacturer requests the dishes face for maximum cleanliness. Must the dishrack be turned a quarter turn before running it through? Are the dishes sprayed before turning or after? (visual discrimination, spatial, and figure-ground, gross motor, directionality)

20. Once clean, does the dishwasher have to put the clean dishes away? If so, take note of where things go. Does the client have to walk through a busy area? Are the floors slick? (visual discrimination, spatial, figure-ground, and memory, gross motor, directionality)

21. Is the client responsible for bussing tables? If so, see the next section.

22. Is the client responsible for bringing the bus pans to the kitchen, or do the waitresses or bussers do this? (visual discrimination, spatial, figure-ground, and memory, gross motor, directionality)

23. What other duties are involved in the dishwasher's job? Sweeping and mopping? Taking the garbage out? Some dishwashers are required to stock the new supplies that are delivered, wash and wrap potatoes, deliver food to patients, to name a few odd jobs. (Skills needed depend on the job task.)

24. If the client is required to take out the garbage, must he sort through it first for silver and napkins? This is a messy, gross job and some clients would refuse to do it. (visual discrimination, spatial, and figure-ground, strong stomach)

25. Is it necessary for the client to read? If so, at what level? Some of the odd jobs mentioned above require reading. (Reading level depends on the job requirements.)

Bussing

Sometimes the job of busser and dishwasher overlap. If this is the case in the job you will analyze, please look at the previous section for suggestions. As in the other jobs, there are some things that are particular to the job of table busser that you will want to observe. Remember that these are suggestions only and that you will see many other things at the job site that are not listed below.

1. How will the dishes be carried, bus pan or tray? (gross and fine motor, bi-manual)

2. What is the procedure for taking the things off the table? Some employers want the glasses removed from the table first. Others don't care. (sequencing, visual discrimination, spatial, figure-ground, and memory, visual-motor, bi-manual, directionality, planning/organization, judgment)

3. Are there specific locations to place the tableware as it is removed from the table? Some employers want things placed in certain areas in the bus pan. (visual discrimination, spatial, figure-ground, memory, fine motor, directionality, planning/organization)

4. Are the plates scraped at the table or are they scraped in the kitchen? (memory, visual discrimination, spatial, figure-ground, directionality, fine motor, bi-manual)

5. Once the pan or tray is full and are returned to the kitchen, does the bus person need to empty the pan? In some restaurants this is the case, however, my experience is that the dishwasher usually does this step.

6. Is it necessary for the busser to read? If so, at what level?

7. Are there other duties required of the busser? If so, look carefully at each duty. (Skills required depend on the assigned duty.)

Laundry

Laundry work varies as the jobs listed above. The duties depend on the volume of laundry and the equipment used. Listed below are some things to look for when you do your job analysis in a laundry. Remember that these are only suggestions and you will see much more than is listed here while observing at the job site.

1. How do the washers and dryers operate? Are they computerized, or do they have control knobs? If they are computerized, must the client memorize complex codes to put into it, or are there cards to be inserted into slots? If there are cards, is it difficult to determine which card goes into which machine? (visual discrimination, spatial, figure-ground, and memory, fine motor, reading level)

2. Are there folding machines? If so, what kind? Large laundries will have large machines that require one or two operators at each end, one to place the sheets in and the others to remove them. Many folding machines require two people to operate when sheets are being folded. Towel folders require one person to operate. (Skills depend on the type of machine. All folding jobs require gross motor movements, bi-manual coordination, visual discrimination, spatial, figure-ground, and memory)

3. If there is no folding machine, is there a **third arm?** That is a pole that can **hold** the corner of a sheet while the laundry worker stretches it out and folds it. (gross motor, bi-manual coordination, visual discrimination, spatial, figure-ground, and memory, directionality, eye/hand/foot coordination)

4. Are there specific methods used to fold each item? In some hospitals or nursing homes, they require the sheets to be folded lenghwise first. Be sure that you write down how the sheets are folded. (visual discrimination, spatial, figure-ground, and memory, directionality, fine and gross motor, bi-manual dexterity, planning/organization)

5. When the folding is completed, does the laundry worker take the clean items to the closets and put them away? Do they have carts, or must they carry them? Are there steps or is there an elevator? (gross and fine motor, bi-manual coordination, visual discrimination, spatial, figure-ground, and memory, directionality, ability to count and perhaps read numbers, may need to read)

6. Must the laundry operator read? If so, at what level?

7. Are there other duties that may be performed by the laundry worker? In some jobs, the laundry worker also performs housekeeping duties. (Skills required depend on the assigned job tasks.)

Clerical

There are many types of clerical jobs. Because of the wide variety and the inconsistencies, I do not have many specific suggestions. You will need to watch everything carefully and write it down.

1. If the job requires the use of equipment (a copy machine, for example), will your client have to know how to make minor adjustments in addition to making copies? Will he need to know how to clear a jam and add toner? (visual discrimination, spatial, figure-ground, and memory, fine motor, directionality, bi-manual, ability to read instructions, judgment, planning/organization)

2. What reading level is required?

3. Are there numerous forms to fill out, or only a few? (reading level, visual discrimination, spatial, figure-ground, judgment)

4. Does the client need to know math? At what level?

5. Are there additional duties about which you were unaware? (Skills required depend on the assigned tasks.)

Assembly/Packaging

As in the clerical field, the type of assembly or packaging jobs are numerous. I have only a few suggestions, as it is impossible to try to guess the type of job you would be observing. It will be necessary to look at each task carefully to determine the skills necessary for the job.

1. Does the job require the use of equipment? If so, does it appear to be safe? Would your client need to make adjustments to the machine, repair and/or maintain it?

2. Is reading or math required? If so, at what level?

3. Look at each step of the job carefully. Write down each step, even if it takes all your paper. A pad of paper is cheap when compared with placing the client in the right job.

SUMMARY

The job analysis is an extremely important part of the whole process of working with a client. In our program, we perform the job analysis before the client commits to the job. We do this so we can determine during the job match meeting if the job is one in which the client can succeed (see Chapter 6).

Not all programs use the job match process. Whether or not your program uses the process, the job analysis is still important. This chapter gave hints to look for during the job analysis on six traditional jobs for rehabilitation clients. No matter when you perform your job analysis, before the client is placed, or on the first day of the job, the hints in this chapter should help the new trainer.

FIGURE 13

JOB DESCRIPTION

DATE: ____________

Company: Apartment Complex

Address: ____________

Cincinnati, Ohio

Phone: ____________

Job Trainer: ____________ **Job Developer:** ____________

Bus Route/Access (for trainer & client): Bus routes ----- on ----- Avenue

3/10 of mile walk from apartments to --------- Avenue

Job Title: Janitor

Immediate Supervisor: Resident Manager

Other Supervisors/Manager: None

Staff/Co-Workers (Underline one who is of assistance): Two tenants have been identified who could assist in an emergency

Type of Business and clientele (No. employed, No. working with): Apartment buildings. Worker is unsupervised, but will see tenants in the hallways.

General Overview of Tasks and Frequency:

Sweep and mop hallways. Clean laundry rooms (i.e. washer, dryer, clean out sink, wipe pipes, remove cob webs), wash entry doors and windows, dust handrails on stairs.

Additional Tasks in case of downtime:

Check work

Transition To Work Project - Ohio RSC - March, 1988

FIGURE 13 (CONT.)

JOB DESCRIPTION
Page 2

Description of Working Area (Include equipment and working order):
Two large buildings, each with three entrances. There are three floors to
each building, thus there are nine (9) hall areas. Each section has two
laundry rooms for a total of twelve (12) (six (6) in each building).

Working Atmosphere (ex: noise, people, area size, distractors, pressure):
Tenants enter and leave their apartments throughout the day. Occasional
noises from within the apartments. Worker is unsupervised.

Safety Hazards (include equipment): Constantly walking up and down stairs
with equipment.

Wages: ___$3.75___ **Per** ___hour___   **Benefits/Discounts:** ___N/A___

Work Hours: ___15 hrs./wk. - to be arranged___

Lunch/Break times: ___Depend on working hours___

Probation Period: ___30 days, salary increases to $4.00/hr.___

Dress Code/Uniforms: ___-----___

Company Goals for the Client:
Clean the buildings once a week.

Professional Terminology: N/A

**Essential skills necessary for the job (include learning styles and
personality traits):**

Visual discrimination   Stamina
Visual-motor and spacial   Fine & gross motor
Auditory discrimination and memory   Bi-manual coordination
Visual memory

Additional Comments:

FIGURE 13 (CONT.)

INSTRUCTIONS FOR COMPLETING TASK ANALYSIS

The following Key is to be used when working with a student/client on a particular job. At the end of each work week, the student is evaluated as to their ability to successfully complete each job task.

Should a student receive a rating of 0, 1, or 2, a Problem/Modification/Outcome Form should be completed. That form should be updated weekly, to correspond with the task analysis sheet.

Key: X = Task assigned to co-worker during training period.

0 = Task not yet presented, is being completed by job trainer

1 = Task not yet mastered (must have problem/modification/outcome sheet for this area)

2 = Task mastered, with supervision by job trainer

3 = Task mastered, retains without constant supervision (job trainer is on the premises)

4 = Task mastered, job trainer is not on premises. Must have phase out meeting with job developer and employer before this step! (Job trainer works with client on tasks not yet mastered.)

5 = Total phase out. Have had meeting with job developer and employer.

If the job duties change, note that on the Task Analysis Form by placing a line through the description and dates. If new duties replace the old, note that on the original by referring to the ammended section on page - attached to this form. If indicated Problem/Modification/Outcome Form(s) should be written.

In order to accurately track the student/client's progress both before and after phase out meetings, place a red line along the date column to indicate the week in which a phase out meeting was held. The INITIAL PHASE OUT MEETING MUST BE HELD (employer, job developer, job trainer) BEFORE THE TRAINER'S PHASE OUT FROM THE JOB SITE BEGINS. Until this meeting, the trainer is expected to be on the premisis the total work shift.

FIGURE 13 (CONT.)

Client's Name: _____

TASK ANALYSIS/PERFORMANCE RATING

Page __01__

Job Title: Janitorial
Company:
Job Trainer:

Dates:

Task Analysis		
1. Place belongings in empty apartment used for break.		
2. Collect materials from Building ____, middle floor storage. Materials include:		
Golf Bag		
Narrow Broom		
Wide Broom		
Squeegie		
Windex		
Ammonia		
Two (2) Rags		
Garbage Bags		
Mop		
Mop Bucket		
3. Go to first building to be cleaned.		

Transition To Work Project – Ohio RSC – March, 1987

FIGURE 13 (CONT.)

TASK ANALYSIS/PERFORMANCE RATING

Client's Name: _____

Job Title: Janitorial
Company:
Job Trainer:

Dates:

Task Analysis

FOLLOWING INSTRUCTIONS APPLY TO EACH UNIT CLEANED:

4. Go to top floor (Record on checklist).

5. Put materials on the floor in front of the rail on the left.

6. Prepare mop water with ammonia and HOT water.

7. Look at picture checklist to determine task.

Laundry Room (Record)

8. Get a trash bag from golf bag.

9. Take out dirty trash bag in laundry room.

10. Insert new bag into wastebasket.

11. Take garbage bag and place next to golf bag.

12. Check off trash on check list.

13. Look at check list for next duty.

14. Get rag from golf bag.

15. Wipe off top of washer moving rag from left to right from back to front.

16. Lift lid of washer and wash underside, making sure all soap is removed from the edges.

17. Wipe off dryer using same method as washer.

Transition To Work Project – Ohio RSC – March, 1987

FIGURE 13 (CONT.)

TASK ANALYSIS/PERFORMANCE RATING

Client's Name: _____

Page 03 _____

Job Title: Janitorial
Company:
Job Trainer:

Dates: _____

Task Analysis

18. Clean side of washer from top to bottom.

19. Clean side of dryer from top to bottom.

20. Wipe off all pipes behind washer and dryer.

21. Wipe off faucet and handles.

22. Wipe off splash trays on sink.

23. Check off completed task on check list.

24. Look at check list for next step.

25. Place supplies on landing.

26. Check off completed task on check list.

27. Look at check list for next step.

28. Shake out mats and place on railing.

29. Check off completed task on check list.

30. Look at check list for next step.

Floors (Record)

31. Get brooms and dust pan.

32. Sweep laundry room from back to front, moving from window to door. Sweep left to right.

Transition To Work Project – Ohio RSC – March, 1987

FIGURE 13 (CONT.)

TASK ANALYSIS/PERFORMANCE RATING

Client's Name:

Page 04

Job Title: Janitorial
Company:
Job Trainer:

Dates:

Task Analysis

33. Sweep hallway starting at laundry door. Sweep from back left side to middle, moving toward railing.

34. Sweep other half of floor from back right to middle, toward steps.

35. Sweep dirt in middle of hall into one pile, starting at back toward stairs.

36. Sweep dirt into dust pan using smaller broom.

37. Place dirt into trash bag on landing.

38. Put brooms and dust pan away in/on golf bag.

39. Check off completed task on check list.

40. Look at check list for next task.

41. Wring out mop in bucket.

42. Start mopping in back of laundry room, left to right, window to door.

43. Rinse mop in water.

44. Mop hall floor starting at rail, moving backwards toward door, mopping side to side. When you reach the door, turn ½ turn and mop walking backwards to apartment door and across the door, turn ½ turn and mop walking backwards to stairs.

45. Put materials away, replace door mats.

46. Check completed task off check list.

Transition To Work Project - Ohio RSC - March, 1987

FIGURE 13 (CONT.)

TASK ANALYSIS/PERFORMANCE RATING

Client's Name: _____

Page __05__

Job Title: Janitorial
Company:
Job Trainer:

Dates:

Task Analysis

47. Look for next task on check list.

48. Move materials to Tape.

49. Check completed task off check list.

Stairs (Between Record and Tape)

50. Get small broom and dust pan.

51. Check to see if anyone is on stairway below.

52. Starting on top step, sweep each step left-right-left. Have him count "1, 2", until he sweeps as instructed.

53. Sweep landing from stairs to next flight.

54. Pick up dirt with dust pan.

55. Place dirt in trash bag.

56. Sweep remaining stairs as above.

57. Pick up dirt and place in garbage bag.

58. Check completed task off check list.

59. Look for next step on check list.

60. Get rag with ammonia and water.

61. Squeeze water out of rag until damp, but not wet.

Transition To Work Project — Ohio RSC – March, 1987

FIGURE 13 (CONT.)

Client's Name: _____

TASK ANALYSIS/PERFORMANCE RATING

Dates:

Page 06

Job Title: Janitorial
Company:
Job Trainer:

Task Analysis

62. Wipe all railing.

63. Check completed task off check list.

64. Look at next task on check list.

65. Shake out mats and place on railing.

66. Check off completed task on check list.

67. Look at check list for next step.

68. Go to Utility Room (Tape).

69. Remove materials from floor.

Floors (Tape)

70. Get brooms and dust pan.

71. Sweep utility room from back to front, moving from window to door. Sweep left to right.

72. Sweep hallway starting at utility door. Sweep from back left side to middle, moving toward railing.

73. Sweep other half of floor from back right to middle, toward steps.

74. Sweep dirt in middle of hall into one pile, starting at back toward stairs.

Trainsition To Work Project – Ohio RSC – March, 1987

FIGURE 13 (CONT.)

Client's Name: _____

TASK ANALYSIS/PERFORMANCE RATING

Page _07_

Job Title: Janitorial
Company:
Job Trainer:

Dates:

	Task Analysis
75.	Sweep dirt into dust pan using smaller broom.
76.	Place dirt into trash bag.
77.	Put brooms and dust pan away in/on golf bag.
78.	Check off completed task on check list.
79.	Look at check list for next task.
80.	Wring out mop in bucket.
81.	Start mopping in back of laundry room, left to right, window to door.
82.	Rinse mop in water.
83.	Mop hall floor starting at rail, moving backwards toward door, mopping side to side. When reach the door, turn ¼ turn and mop walking backwards to apartment door and across the door, turn ¼ turn and mop walking backwards to stairs.
84.	Put materials away, replace door mats.
85.	Check completed task off check list.
86.	Look for next task on check list.
87.	Move materials to Radio.
88.	Check completed task off check list.

FIGURE 13 (CONT.)

TASK ANALYSIS/PERFORMANCE RATING

Page 08

Job Title: Janitorial
Company:
Job Trainer:

Client's Name: _____

Dates: _____

Task Analysis												

89. Look at next task on check list.

90. Remove door mat and shake outside.

91. Hang doormat on rail outside.

92. Check completed task off check list.

93. Look at next task on check list.

94. Get small broom and dust pan.

95. Check to see if anyone is on stairway below.

96. Starting on top step, sweep each step left-right-left. Have him count "1, 2", until he sweeps as instructed.

97. Pick up dirt with dust pan.

98. Place dirt in trash bag.

99. Check completed task off check list.

100. Look for next step on check list.

101. Get rag with ammonia and water.

102. Squeeze water out of rag until damp, but not wet.

103. Wipe all railing.

Transition To Work Project — Ohio RSC — March, 1987

FIGURE 13 (CONT.)

TASK ANALYSIS/PERFORMANCE RATING

Page 09

Job Title: Janitorial
Company:
Job Trainer:

Client's Name: _____

Dates: _____

Task Analysis												
104. Check completed task off check list.												
105. Look at next task on check list.												
106. Gather materials needed to clean windows:												
<u>Windex</u> <u>Squeegie</u> <u>Clean dry cloth</u>												
107. Wash inside windows first. Spray top of window on <u>left</u>.												
108. Wipe window, top to bottom, with squeegie.												
109. Dry window with cloth.												
110. Inspect window for smudges.												
111. Wash outside of window next. Spray top of window.												
112. Use squeegie to wipe window.												
113. Dry window with cloth.												
114. Inspect window for smudges.												
115. Spray door on inside.												
116. Wipe door with squeegie.												
117. Dry door with cloth.												

Transition To Work Project – Ohio RSC – March, 1987

Page 10

FIGURE 15 (CONT.)

TASK ANALYSIS/PERFORMANCE RATING   Client's Name: ___

Job Title: Janitorial
Company:
Job Trainer:

Dates:

Task Analysis

118. Spray door on outside.

119. Wipe door with squeegie.

120. Dry door with cloth.

121. Wash inside windows on right. Spray top of window on <u>right.</u>

122. Wipe window, top to bottom, with squeegie.

123. Dry window with cloth.

124. Inspect window for smudges.

125. Wash outside of window next. Spray top of window.

126. Use squeegie to wipe window.

127. Dry window with cloth.

128. Inspect window for smudges.

129. Check completed task off check list.

130. Look for next task on check list.

Mailboxes (Radio)

131. Get wet rag.

132. Wipe mailboxes with wet rag.

FIGURE 13 (CONT.)

TASK ANALYSIS/PERFORMANCE RATING

Client's Name: _____

Page 11

Job Title: Janitorial
Company:
Job Trainer:

Dates:

Task Analysis

133. Check completed task off check list.

134. Look for next task on check list.

Laundry (Radio)

135. Get a trash bag from golf bag.

136. Take out dirty trash bag in laundry room.

137. Insert new bag into wastebasket.

138. Take gargage bag and place next to golf bag.

139. Check off trash on check list.

140. Look at check list for next duty.

141. Get rag from golf bag.

142. Wipe off top of washer moving rag from left to right from back to front.

143. Lift lid of washer and wash underside, making sure all soap is removed from the edges.

144. Wipe off dryer using same method as washer.

145. Clean side of washer from top to bottom.

146. Clean side of dryer from top to bottom.

147. Wipe off all pipes behind washer and dryer.

Transition To Work Project – Ohio RSC – March, 1987

FIGURE 13 (CONT.)

TASK ANALYSIS/PERFORMANCE RATING

Client's Name: _____

Page ___12___

Job Title: Janitorial
Company:
Job Trainer:

Dates:

Task Analysis

148. Wipe off faucet and handles.

149. Wipe off splash trays on sink.

150. Check off completed task on check list.

151. Look at check list for next step.

152. Place golf bag by door, mop bucket in laundry room.

153. Check off completed task on check list.

154. Look at check list for next step.

155. Shake out mats and place on railing.

156. Check off completed task on check list.

157. Look at check list for next step.

Floors (Radio)

158. Get brooms and dust pan.

159. Sweep laundry room from back to front, moving from window to door. Sweep left to right.

160. Sweep hallway starting at laundry door. Sweep from back left side to middle, moving toward railing.

161. Sweep other half of floor from back right to middle, toward steps.

Transition To Work Project - Ohio RSC - March, 1987

FIGURE 13 (CONT.)

TASK ANALYSIS/PERFORMANCE RATING

Page 13

Job Title: Janitorial
Company:
Job Trainer:

Client's Name: _____

Dates: _____

Task Analysis

162. Sweep dirt in middle of hall into one pile, starting at back toward stairs.

163. Sweep dirt into dust pan using smaller broom.

164. Place dirt into trash bag on landing.

165. Put brooms and dust pan away in/on golf bag.

166. Check off completed task on check list.

167. Look at check list for next task.

168. Wring out mop in bucket.

169. Start mopping in back of laundry room, left to right, window to door.

170. Rinse mop in water.

171. Mop hall floor starting at rail, moving backwards toward door, mopping side to side. When reach the door, turn ¼ turn and mop walking backwards to apartment door and across the door, turn ¼ turn and mop walking backwards to stairs.

172. Put materials away, replace door mats.

173. Check completed task off check list.

174. Look for next task on check list.

Clean-Up

175. Replace floor mats.

Transition To Work Project - Ohio RSC - March, 1987

FIGURE 13 (CONT.)

TASK ANALYSIS/PERFORMANCE RATING

Client's Name: _____

Page 14

Job Title: Janitorial
Company:
Job Trainer:

Dates:

Task Analysis

176. Wash out mop under faucet in laundry room with HOT water.

177. Empty mop water in sink.

178. Rinse out mop bucket with HOT water.

179. Rinse out rag with very warm water.

180. Clean out sink.

181. Put supplies away.

182. Call Mom.

Transition To Work Project — Ohio RSC — March, 1987

FIGURE 13 (CONT.)

FIGURE 13 (CONT.)

FIGURE 14

JOB DESCRIPTION

DATE: _____

Company: __Hotel Laundry_____

Address: _____

_____Cincinnati, Ohio_____

Phone: _____

Job Trainer: _____ Job Developer: _____

Bus Route/Access (for trainer & client): __Routes ------- and -------.___

_Route ------- bus stop is closer._____

Job Title: ___Laundry worker code #_____

Immediate Supervisor: __Housekeeping Supervisor_____

Other Supervisors/Manager: __General Manager_____

Staff/Co-Workers (Underline one who is of assistance): Two co-workers in__

laundry_____

Type of Business and clientele (No. employed, No. working with): Hotel_____

and Restaurant_____

General Overview of Tasks and Frequency:

Operate washers, dryers, presser.
Fold all laundry - sheets, towels, table linens

Additional Tasks in case of downtime:

Clean area at the end of the day.

Transition To Work Project - Ohio RSC - March, 1988

FIGURE 14 (CONT.)

JOB DESCRIPTION
Page 2

Description of Working Area (Include equipment and working order):
One large and one smaller washer, three dryers, presser, shelves, sink
storage racks, soft drink machine, and large folding table are in the
laundry room. The dirty linens are outside the room to the right of the
door.

Working Atmosphere (ex: noise, people, area size, distractors, pressure):
The area is large and relatively cool and comfortable. The noise from the
equipment is constant. No heavy people traffic or stress factors were
noted. The worker works in laundry room only. Two workers presently
employed are helpful and congenial.

Safety Hazards (include equipment): Presser has safety controls so the
employee will not get hurt. Employee must be alert for occasional
utensils in the dining room linens.

Wages: $3.70 **Per** hour   **Benefits/Discounts:** After 6 months or 1,000 hrs.,
health benefits and 6 paid holidays; after 1 yr. – 2 weeks vacation

Work Hours: 8:00–4:30 M–F, 9:00–5:30 Sat. & Sun.; work every 4th weekend

Lunch/Break times: 11:00–11:30 M–F, 12:00–12:30 Sat., Sun.; 2 15 min. breaks

Probation Period: 90 days

Dress Code/Uniforms: Two uniforms provided; comfortable shoes (employee
provides); name tags and lockers are furnished.

Company Goals for the Client:
Work into full time worker who can assume all duties required of the
laundry workers.

Professional Terminology: Presser, names of items to be folded.

**Essential skills necessary for the job (include learning styles and
personality traits):**

Visual discrimination and memory	Fine & gross motor
Visual-motor and spacial perception	Speed
Auditory discrimination and memory	Bi-manual coordination

Addition Comments:
Lunches are free, soft drinks are in the laundry room and cost 40 cents.
Orientation: The first day is an orientation day. Worker should wear
jeans, a uniform will be given to worker that day. If the worker is late
he/she must call in one (1) hour ahead of time and inform Laundry
Supervisor, _____ .
Forms: The forms that need to be filled out and returned are:
      Medical History Record   _____ Payroll
      New Employee Orientation Check List   W-4 Form
      House Rules – bottom slip   New Hiring Information
      Employee Handbook – return last page

Note: (The handbook and houserules must be read to new employee and he
must sign, acknowledging that he was informed of rules and regulations.)

128   *A Job Trainer's Manual*

FIGURE 14 (CONT.)

INSTRUCTIONS FOR COMPLETING TASK ANALYSIS

The following Key is to be used when working with a student/client on a
particular job. At the end of each work week, the student is evaluated as
to their ability to successfully complete each job task.

Should a student receive a rating of 0, 1, or 2, a Problem/Modification/
Outcome Form should be completed. That form should be updated weekly, to
correspond with the task analysis sheet.

Key: X = Task assigned to co-worker during training period.

         0 = Task not yet presented, is being completed by job trainer

         1 = Task not yet mastered (must have problem/modification/outcome
             sheet for this area)

         2 = Task mastered, with supervision by job trainer

         3 = Task mastered, retains without constant supervision (job
             trainer is on the premises)

         4 = Task mastered, job trainer is not on premises. Must have phase
             out meeting with job developer and employer before this step!
             (Job trainer works with client on tasks not yet mastered.)

         5 = Total phase out. Have had meeting with job developer and
             employer.

If the job duties change, note that on the Task Analysis Form by placing a
line through the description and dates. If new duties replace the old,
note that on the original by referring to the ammended section on page -
attached to this form. If indicated Problem/Modification/Outcome Form(s)
should be written.

In order to accurately track the student/client's progress both before and
after phase out meetings, place a red line along the date column to
indicate the week in which a phase out meeting was held. The INITIAL PHASE
OUT MEETING MUST BE HELD (employer, job developer, job trainer) BEFORE THE
TRAINER'S PHASE OUT FROM THE JOB SITE BEGINS. Until this meeting, the
trainer is expected to be on the premisis the total work shift.

FIGURE 14 (CONT.)

TASK ANALYSIS/PERFORMANCE RATING

Client's Name: _____

Page __01__

Job Title: Laundry Worker
Company:
Job Trainer:
Date: _____   Dates: _____

Task Analysis

Work Procedures:

The worker comes into the establishment from the rear parking lot and enters at Entrance B.

The numbers "   " are on the left side next to the door.

The worker proceeds straight for 20 feet and turns right to go down a flight of stairs. He enters through folding doors. The ladies locker room is on the right side of the hall (corner). He/she will have a locker of his/her own. In this room he/she may wait for clocking in or clocking out after work is completed.

Walk straight along the hall to office, turn into left hallway. The time cards are right next to office entrance. He/she may clock in no earlier than 10 til 8:00 A.M.

From the office turn left into the hall and the next door to the left is the laundry room, just beyond storage bins.

The dirty clothes bins are in the hall just outside the laundry room (left side). They are taken into the room as needed for filling washers.

Three (3) plastic bins in laundry room are for clean washed clothes to transport to the dryer.

Three (3) cloth bins are for clean dry clothes or linens for folding.

No use of chemicals or dispursement of such is expected or permitted. An assigned co-worker or the Supervisor is in charge of chemicals.

Transition To Work Project — Ohio RSC — March, 1987

FIGURE 14 (CONT.)

Client's Name: _____

TASK ANALYSIS/PERFORMANCE RATING

Page 02

Job Title: Laundry Worker
Company:
Job Trainer:
Date:

Dates:

Task Analysis

CHORES:

Washing Table Linens, 2nd Sheets & Other Items: Fill both washers. Usually one bin full is one washer load for small washer. Two (2) bins full is one washer load for big washer. (Leave space for tumbling.) Set buttons on top.

Small Washer: Put computer card into slot at right top corner (card indicates for what item the washer is used). Push starter button on right button panel (red).

Large Washer: Turn knob on left side (top) until item to be washed shows on roller on top instrument box. Flick switch at left top corner and push button on right top corner at same time.

To open door flick up switch (up), push inspect button down (on top of flick switch) and open door at handle.

Dryers: Set dryers according to temperature chart on left wall behind the shelving (just past room entrance).

Pressing: To start presser; switch on at rear of presser (black), top left corner of Hot Shot box. Push in (ON) button in front of press machine. Wait until the light comes on or Temperature is at 80 degrees. Then machine is ready for use. Place items to be pressed in center of Press Table.

Napkins 25-30 in stack - press a stack at a time and make another stack.
Table Cloths - one at a time.
Sheets (regular) - 3 sheets at a time.
Sheets (king) - 4 sheets at a time.
Pillow cases - 1 at a time (2 stacks)

Transition To Work Project - Ohio RSC - March, 1987

FIGURE 14 (CONT.)

Client's Name: _____

TASK ANALYSIS/PERFORMANCE RATING

Page __03__

Job Title: Laundry Worker
Company:
Job Trainer:
Date:

Dates: _____

Task Analysis

Pressing (continued)

To Press: Pull drawer out (to the right of power panel) and place items on center, push drawer in. When "In Operation" light (2nd button from the right) goes off pressing is finished.

Remove item from the table and place on shelves on the left side of room as you enter laundry (napkins and table cloths).

On rear wall regular sheets.

On rear left wall King sixed sheets, wash cloths, hand towels and pillow cases are to be stacked (shelves are marked).

Note: Doing table linens is first priority in the morning. Table linens come down in A.M., bed linens in P.M.

Folding Procedures:

1. Napkins – Lay napkins flat on top of each other and make stacks approximately 18 inches high.

2. Table Cloths – With seam on outside, fold in half and in half again, fold down once in center and once again. Make stacks.

3. Large Table Cloths – Fold the same way but make a separate stack.

4. Banquet Table Cloths – These are folded by 2 employees together. With seam on the outside fold twice longways and twice shortways.

5. Round Table Cloths – These are folded twice one way and three times the other side (they are a square cloth).

6. Short Banquet Table Cloths – 2 folds plus 2 folds.

7. Sheets – Fold sheets lengthwise once and width once and length twice again.

8. Pillowcases – Put two pillowcases together and fold lengthwise twice and fold over once and make stacks.

Transition To Work Project – Ohio RSC – March, 1987

FIGURE 14 (CONT.)

TASK ANALYSIS/PERFORMANCE RATING

Client's Name: _____

Dates: _____

Page 04

Job Title: Laundry Worker
Company:
Job Trainer:
Date:

Task Analysis

Folding Procedures (continued)

9. King Sized Sheets - Fold these the same as regular sheets except last fold over twice.

Stained Items: Stained items are put into sink at rear left corner for soaking. It is a co-worker's job to complete the task and rewash this laundry.

Clean up Duties: At 4:00 P.M. laundry duties stop and clean-up begins.

Clean all lint boxes of dryers. (Pull out drawers at bottom of machine)

Clean all drains of debris.

Wipe Machines with damp cloth.

Sweep and mop floors.

After completion of tasks go to locker room until clocking out time.

Learning capacities Required are:

Stamina & strength	Some verbal skills
Motor	Directionality
Endurance	Visual discrimination
Standing all day	Auditory discrimination
Spacial awareness	Able to work in noise & closed area
Sequencing	Memory
Eye & hand coordination	Judgement

Transition To Work Project - Ohio RSC - March, 1987

FIGURE 14 (CONT.)

Client's Name: _____

TASK ANALYSIS/PERFORMANCE RATING

Page 05 - Addendum

Job Title: Laundry Worker
Company:
Job Trainer:
Date: Dates: _____

Task Analysis

1.) Pull out Dietary-Kitchen linens one at a time and shake.

2.) Pull sheets out of washer one at a time.

3.) Put sheets into washer one at a time.

4.) Put sheets into dryer one at a time.

5.) Pull sheets out of dryer one at a time.

6.) Make nice, neat stacks of hand towels,
   washcloths,
   bath towels,
   bath sheets,
   bath mats,
   sheets (regular),
   pillowcases (regular),
   pillowcases (king),
   sheets (king),
   rugs.

Transition To Work Project - Ohio RSC - March, 1987

FIGURE 14 (CONT.)

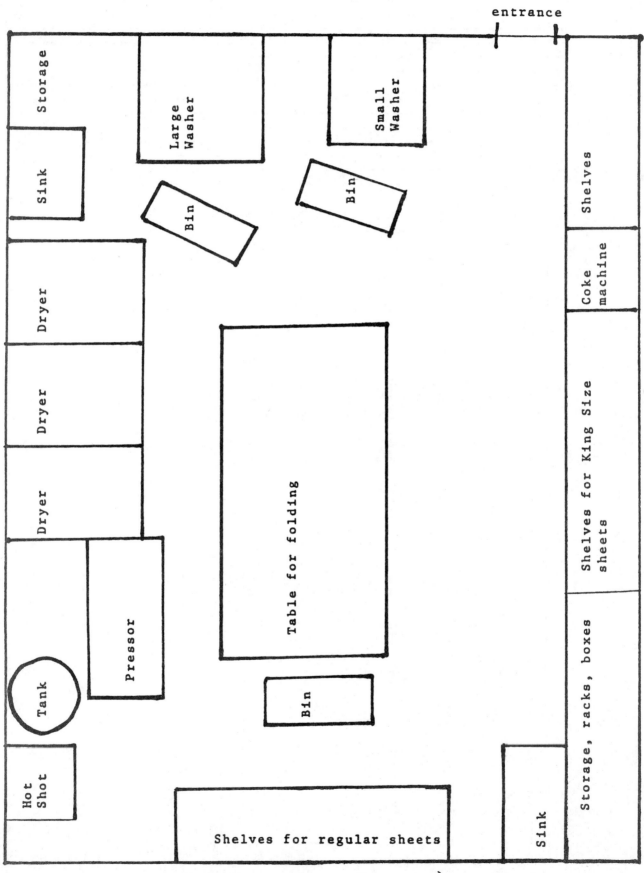

(Job Trainer drew this map.)

FIGURE 15

JOB DESCRIPTION

DATE:_____

Company: Department Store _____

Address: _____

          Cincinnati, Ohio _____

Phone: _____

Job Trainer:_____ **Job Developer:**_____

Bus Route/Access (for trainer & client): Routes ----- and ----- go to the

mall _____

Job Title: Housekeeper _____

Immediate Supervisor: Personnel Manager _____

Other Supervisors/Manager: Superintendent _____

Staff/Co-Workers (Underline one who is of assistance): Two other house-

keepers _____

Type of Business and clientele (No. employed, No. working with): Large

department store in a suburban mall. Many employees and customers

General Overview of Tasks and Frequency:

Major job is to stock and clean four (4) restrooms, especially the first
floor. This involves filling paper towel and toilet paper, checking soap
dispensers and feminine products, wiping excess water off counters. Sweep
and mop only as needed. Spot clean every mirror in the store, dust the
escalator rails, and clean the employee lounge, including defrosting the
refrigerator. Wash and dry rags using laundry facilities in hair salon.

Additional Tasks in case of downtime:

Always re-check the restrooms or start the routine again

FIGURE 15 (CONT.)

JOB DESCRIPTION
Page 2

Description of Working Area (Include equipment and working order):
Large, high volume department store. Constant contact with customers.
Worker stores supplies in designated areas at the beginning of the shift.
Women's restrooms are top priority and are checked every twenty (20)
minutes. It is not unusual for women to stand in line waiting for an
empty stall.

Working Atmosphere (ex: noise, people, area size, distractors, pressure):
Many people, some ask questions, some are not pleasant. Restrooms can
become crowded. Worker must listen for paging bells and leave the job to
take care of problems.

Safety Hazards (include equipment): Slippery floors. Gloves should be
worn when cleaning toilets, vomit, or other excrements.

Wages: $3.75 **Per** hour   **Benefits/Discounts:**   20% discount, plus other
benefits

Work Hours: 10-5 Monday - Saturday, 11-5 Sunday

Lunch/Break times: 1/2 hour, clock out

Probation Period: 90 days

Dress Code/Uniforms: neat, clean. Slacks and comfortable no-skid shoes.

Company Goals for the Client:
Do the best possible job.

Professional Terminology:
Areas of the store.

**Essential skills necessary for the job (include learning styles and
personality traits):**

Friendly, pleasant   Auditory sequential memory
Visual discrimination   Fine & Gross Motor
Visual motor & spacial perception   Bi-manual coordination
Visual memory   Directionality
Auditory discrimination
Able to be interrupted and return to task

Additional Comments:
Orientation is first half of first day. Handbook will be reviewed and
signed to show understanding.

FIGURE 15 (CONT.)

INSTRUCTIONS FOR COMPLETING TASK ANALYSIS

The following Key is to be used when working with a student/client on a particular job. At the end of <u>each</u> work week, the student is evaluated as to their ability to successfully complete each job task.

Should a student receive a rating of 0, 1, or 2, a Problem/Modification/ Outcome Form should be completed. That form should be updated <u>weekly</u>, to correspond with the task analysis sheet.

Key: X = Task assigned to co-worker during training period.

0 = Task not yet presented, is being completed by job trainer

1 = Task not yet mastered (must have problem/modification/outcome sheet for this area)

2 = Task mastered, with supervision by job trainer

3 = Task mastered, retains without constant supervision (job trainer is on the premises)

4 = Task mastered, job trainer is not on premises. <u>Must have phase out meeting with job developer and employer before this step!</u> (Job trainer works with client on tasks not yet mastered.)

5 = Total phase out. <u>Have had meeting with job developer and employer</u>.

<u>If the job duties change</u>, note that on the Task Analysis Form by placing a line through the description and dates. If new duties replace the old, note that on the original by referring to the ammended section on page - attached to this form. If indicated Problem/Modification/Outcome Form(s) should be written.

In order to accurately track the student/client's progress both before and after phase out meetings, place a red line along the date column to indicate the week in which a phase out meeting was held. The INITIAL PHASE OUT MEETING MUST BE HELD (employer, job developer, job trainer) <u>BEFORE</u> THE TRAINER'S PHASE OUT FROM THE JOB SITE BEGINS. Until this meeting, the trainer is expected to be <u>on the premisis</u> the <u>total</u> work shift.

FIGURE 15 (CONT.)

Page 02

Client's Name: _____

TASK ANALYSIS/PERFORMANCE RATING

Job Title: Housekeeper
Company:
Job Trainer:

Dates:

Task Analysis

Clocking In Procedures:

- The worker comes into the establishment from the parking lot facing Bank and enters the door marked "_____."

- The security person at the door should be told that he/she is the housekeeper.

Note: Since most employees have arrived ahead of time, housekeepers are not usually asked. There is no sign in or out sheet.

- The worker proceeds straight for 10 feet and turns right into the entrance where the time clock is located. Time cards are located on the far wall facing the door. A numerical system is used to identify each individual's time card. The three-digit number located in the top left corner is the department code and the five-digit number located in the top right corner is the employee code.

Note: Housekeepers are in department # _____. Employees should not clock more than five minutes ahead of scheduled time.

After Clocking In:

- After clocking in, the worker should take his/her personal belongings to the locker. All packages and returned merchandise must be checked into the Customer Service Department. This is located in route to the Personnel Office.

- To arrive at the Personnel Office, worker leaves the room after clocking in and makes a right turn, then walks straight down main aisle until he/she meets the employee elevator on the left.

- The worker should take the elevator to the second level. After arriving he/she should make a left to right clockwise circle around the luggage display and he/she will be facing the Customer Service Department.

Transition To Work Project – Ohio RSC – March, 1987

FIGURE 15 (CONT.)

Client's Name: _____

TASK ANALYSIS/PERFORMANCE RATING

Page ___03___

Job Title: Housekeeper
Company:
Job Trainer: Dates: _____

Task Analysis

- Any packages or returned merchandise should be checked in at this department. The person at the Customer Service Department will give the employee a claim check for his/her packages.

- The personnel offices are located to the right of the Customer Service Department. The employee should inform the Personnel Supervisor, _____, that he/she has arrived. If _____ is not available a simple message left with the secretary will be fine.

- The housekeeper then places his/her belongings in the personal locker provided. The housekeeper provides the lock. The lockers are located through the door directly opposite the counter for the Personnel Office and behind the hallway leading to Customer Service.

- Leaving the Personnel Offices and walking past the Customer Service Department, the worker will be in the center aisle used upon arrival. He/she will walk counter clockwise right to left until he/she circles the luggage display and faces the employee supply room door. It will read "Employees Only."

Supplies

- Inside the supply room is a 6 foot white double door locker. It will have a lock on the handles. The key to the lock is given to the employee during orientation. If necessary, it can be left on the premises every night at the Personnel Office.

- Inside the locker are hangers for personal outerwear and room at the bottom for school bags or purses. There are also hangers to lay damp wash rags on to dry.

- At the bottom of the locker are two bags. The bag on the left side is where clean rags are found. The bag on the right side is where dirty dry rags are placed.

- Also at the bottom there is a yellow pitcher where the glass cleaner solution is kept. A spray bottle full of glass cleaner solution should be located next to the pitcher.

Transition To Work Project – Ohio RSC – March, 1987

FIGURE 15 (CONT.)

Client's Name: _____

TASK ANALYSIS/PERFORMANCE RATING

Page __04__

Job Title: Housekeeper
Company:
Job Trainer:

Dates: _____

Task Analysis

- On the top shelf is where the store keys are kept. These are the keys to supply rooms, tissue paper containers and feminine product containers. An empty shopping bag should also be in the bottom of the locker.

- Take the spray bottle and fill it to the neck with the glass cleaner solution from the yellow pitcher if it is not already full. Place it and some clean rags into the shopping bag. The keys should be placed somewhere on the employee. Replace the lock on locker handles.

- On the far wall behind the locker are shelves of supplies. Tissue paper and paper towels are located on the bottom shelves and inside the boxes in front of the shelves. Feminine product supplies are located under the bottom shelf in the left hand corner.

- Extra spray bottles are on the bottom left hand corner of the last shelf. Soap containers are located on the top shelf. The broom is on the right side of the shelves.

- The worker should fill the shopping bag with every item that they will need the entire day so that he/she will not need to come in and out of the supply room.

Cleaning Procedures:

- Walking out of the supply room past the employee elevator the worker makes a left at the telephone booths and another left immediately after, and will enter the second floor women's restroom. The employee should always clean this room first due to the fact that the other employees use this room before the store opens.

- The employee should use the glass cleaner solution to clean the basins and the mirrors.

- He/she should use the rags to wipe up any excess water, and do a quick dusting job on the counter.

Transition To Work Project - Ohio RSC - March, 1987

FIGURE 15 (CONT.)

Page __05__

Job Title: Housekeeper
Company:
Job Trainer:

Client's Name: _____

TASK ANALYSIS/PERFORMANCE RATING

Dates: _____

Task Analysis

- The employee should check each stall for cleanliness, but should not spend more time than necessary in each stall.

- The paper towel, soap, tissue paper, and feminine products machines should be filled.

- Filling the paper towel machine is done by opening the machine at the top center with the appropriate key. After opening it can be replaced with another roll if the old roll of paper is less than ½ inch thick.

- To remove the old roll of paper towel, the worker should insert paper towel roll on holder under the white roller, turn the crane and pull out the paper through the slot at the bottom.

- Filling the tissue paper containers is done by unlocking the container with the appropriate key and holding the wrapper of the tissue paper so that the arrows face downward. By lapping the last sheet of old tissue paper the container can now be filled.

- Filling the feminine products machine can be done by placing the appropriate key into the lock located on the side of the machine. Newer models have a two-key system where only one key is necessary to unlock two locks on one door. Upon opening the container, the personal products should be filled until the metal holder is at the top.

- Soap trays can be filled by squeezing the soap into the trays. The soap trays can be opened by simply pulling hand out toward yourself and lifting the lid directly upward.

- The employee should finish each bathroom by picking up any trash on the floor and placing it in the waste baskets.

Note: No sweeping, mopping or taking out the trash is done unless needed.

Transition To Work Project - Ohio RSC - March, 1987

Page 06

FIGURE 15 (CONT.)

Client's Name: _____

TASK ANALYSIS/PERFORMANCE RATING

Job Title: Housekeeper
Company:
Job Trainer:

Dates:

Task Analysis

- Walking out of the women's restroom, making a left and walking a few feet down the aisle is the men's restroom on the left side.

- Clean the men's restroom using the same procedures for the women's restroom.

- Walking out of the men's restroom to the left is the room where the mop and bucket, vacuum cleaner and sink can be found. On the door it is marked "Not an Exit."

Note: Employee is in charge of cleaning any major spills during his/her shift.

Telephone Booths and Water Fountains:

- After cleaning the restrooms, the worker should walk back down the aisle and clean off the telephone booths with glass cleaner.

- After cleaning the telephone booths the worker should clean the water fountains adjacent to the telephones.

Employee Lounge:

- Before the employee leaves the second floor he/she should walk straight down the main aisle from the elevator and walk on the aisle between the furniture on the left and Customer Service on the right. Before you arrive to the emergency exit door make a left and the second door on the right is the employee lounge.

- The Employee Lounge only requires light cleaning.

- Any paper should be picked up.

- Any spills should be wiped up.

- The room connecting to the eating area of the lounge on the right should also be cleaned.

- All magazines should be picked up and replaced on the table under the television.

Transition To Work Project - Ohio RSC - March, 1987

FIGURE 15 (CONT.)

TASK ANALYSIS/PERFORMANCE RATING

Client's Name: _____

Page __07__

Job Title: Housekeeper
Company:
Job Trainer:

Dates: _____

Task Analysis		

Mirrors - Second Floor:

- Returning to the main aisle the employee should walk clockwise circling the entire second floor starting with the Boys Department. The worker should clean all mirrors in the department or in the fitting rooms that need cleaning. After returning to the starting point the employee should return to the elevator.

Water Fountains - Main Floor:

- Taking the elevator to the first floor the employee should walk down the main aisle to the water fountains on the left. Clean the water fountains.

Men's Restroom - Main Floor:

- Next door to the water fountains is the Men's restroom.

- Clean the Men's restroom.

- Inside the men's room the employee should notice a door marked "Not an Exit." This is where a bucket and mop are located to clean spills on the first level.

- While the employee is in the restrooms the shopping bag or tissue paper trays can be left in the doorway.

Note: Always knock and call "Housekeeping" before entering the restrooms of those of the opposite sex.

Transition To Work Project - Ohio RSC - March, 1987

FIGURE 15 (CONT.)

Client's Name: _____

TASK ANALYSIS/PERFORMANCE RATING

Page **08**

Job Title: Housekeeper
Company:
Job Trainer:

Dates: _____

Women's Restroom — First Floor:

- Leaving the Men's Restroom the employee makes a right turn and another right turn to walk down the aisle to the First Floor Women's Restroom. This restroom is the most important part of a housekeeper's job. No special or different cleaning techniques are used, only the ones already explained in cleaning the other restrooms. However, unlike the other restrooms this one must be checked every twenty to thirty minutes for necessary cleaning and refilling. Because of the heavy people traffic on the first floor and particularly in this first floor Women's Restroom it is necessary for the housekeeper to watch it very carefully. This is also the only place where the Personnel Supervisor will definitely check.

Note: There is a long connecting basin counter that the customers are particularly concerned about due to the large amount of water that stays on it. The housekeeper should try to keep it dry at all times.

- The shopping bag full of supplies should be left in the first floor Women's Restroom under the changing table between the basin and the stalls on the far wall of the restroom. The tissue paper trays can be taken with the employee in order to keep him/her from coming back to the Women's Restroom before entering the Men's Restrooms. Also the glass cleaner and cleaning rag should be taken with the worker.

Washing Rags:

- Walking from the Women's Restroom directly across the aisle is the Beauty Salon. This is where a washing machine and dryer are located in order for the housekeeper to wash the cleaning rags. It is located inside to the left around the bend and to the right across from the sinks that hair is washed in, and through the door. The washing machine can be set on "Cotton" and washed for about ten minutes. Whenever washing, the housekeeper should check back after one-half an hour to place the cleaning rags in the dryer. It should only take twenty-five to thirty minutes to dry depending upon the amount of rags being cleaned.

FIGURE 15 (CONT.)

TASK ANALYSIS/PERFORMANCE RATING

Client's Name: _____

Page ___09___

Job Title: Housekeeper
Company:
Job Trainer:

Dates: _____

Task Analysis								

Escalators:

- Exiting the Beauty Salon, the worker should make a right turn leaving the aisle. Entering the main aisle the worker should make another right turn walking past the employee elevator to the escalator. The worker should stand in front of the escalator using the glass cleaner and spray the square metallic area just before the moving handrail.

- This is cleaned and then holding the moist part of the cloth downward on the metallic moving handrail the worker should enter the escalator.

- This is done in order to clean the metallic handrail while the worker is on the escalator.

- Arriving on the second floor the worker should enter the down escalator, after spraying it's square metallic area, and clean the rest of it the same way.

Mirrors - Main Floor:

- Leaving the escalator the worker should proceed to walk clockwise around the mall floor (the first floor) checking every mirror that he/she encounters and also checking every fitting room they pass. Remember: this is spot checking for major misses and the worker should not try to clean every mirror. (Also, the worker should stay aware of the time in order to stop checking mirrors and return to the first floor Women's Restroom.)

Shopping Bags:

- During the mirror checking the worker should check the shopping bag stations at each entrance (total of five - one mall entrance and four doorways) to see if they need refilling.

Transition To Work Project - Ohio RSC - March, 1987

FIGURE 15 (CONT.)

Client's Name: _____

TASK ANALYSIS/PERFORMANCE RATING

Page 10

Job Title: Housekeeper
Company:
Job Trainer:

Dates:

Task Analysis

Shopping Bags: (Continued)

- In order to have the shopping bag stations refilled the worker must call the Personnel Department at one of the cashier desks on the first floor. This is done by dialing _____ and informing the secretary of this information.

Paging:

- The Second most important part of the working job is to listen for a Page for the housekeeper. This Page is number _____. It is called by a bell system that rings, _____ bells, and then _____ bell with a brief pause in between each number. Any time a department needs the glass cleaner, some paper towels or maybe needs a major spill to be cleaned the housekeepers are paged. If the worker hears his/her page he/she should walk to the nearest cashier desk and ask to use the telephone.

- The worker dials number _____ to answer the page and find out who is paging them.

- If this number does not work, the employee should call _____ and one of these should connect them.

- A verbal page for the housekeeper can be done upon request by the workers.

Reporting Supply Shortages:

- During the course of the day the worker may run out of some supplies. He/she should always report this to the personnel department so that more supplies can be ordered.

Transition To Work Project – Ohio RSC – March, 1987

FIGURE 15 (CONT.)

TASK ANALYSIS/PERFORMANCE RATING

Page ___11___

Job Title: Housekeeper
Company:
Job Trainer:

Client's Name: _____

Dates: _____

Task Analysis

Daily Required Duties:

All Restrooms
Employee Lounge
Water Fountains
All Mirrors
Feminine Product Supplies
Shopping Bags
Phone Booths

Weekly Required Duties:

Filling Soap Trays
Dusting Ledges in the Restrooms
Dusting Ledges in the Fitting Rooms
Wash and Dry Cleaning Rags
Wipe off Doors to the Restrooms

Bi-Weekly Required Duties:

Supply All Departments with glass cleaning solutions and rags.

Monthly Required Duties:

Defrost two refrigerators (both located in Employee Lounge).

Spare Duties:

Vacuum, Mop up Spills and Pick up Paper

Note: Gloves and other materials will be supplied if a special job becomes necessary. This will be discussed ahead of time with Personnel Supervisor, _____.

Transition To Work Project — Ohio RSC — March, 1987

FIGURE 15 (CONT.)

Client's Name: _____

TASK ANALYSIS/PERFORMANCE RATING

Page __12__

Job Title: Housekeeper
Company:
Job Trainer:

Dates: _____

Task Analysis

Task Analysis

Skills Required:

1) Visual Discrimination
2) Auditory Discrimination
3) Figure Ground
4) Position in Space
5) Reversals
6) Midline
7) Visual Memory
8) Auditory Memory
9) Visual-Motor
10) Directionality
11) Co-ordinated Body Movements
12) Gross Motor Dexterity
13) Bi-manual Co-ordination
14) Motor Sequencing
15) Fine Finger Dexterity
16) Touch Sensitivity
17) Language
18) Organizational Skills
19) Judgement/Decision making skills
20) Short/Long Term Memory

Transition To Work Project - Ohio RSC - March, 1987

Chapter 6

JOB MATCH

THE JOB MATCH meeting is critical in determining if the client is placed in an appropriate job. The idea is simple; however, in practice, the job match itself may become difficult.

Before we discuss the meeting itself, let us discuss who should attend. Basically, anyone who knows the client well and whose input would be valuable for future planning should attend. Also, anyone who will be involved with the client while he is working should be a member of this team. Since our program works with high school students, the parents are always invited to any meeting dealing with decisions on the job. The others who attend include: the job developer, job trainer(s) (including the person who will be doing the training, the person who performed the job analysis, and, if the client worked previously, the person who trained him), coordinator of the program (I usually chair the meeting), teacher, state rehabilitation counselor, administrative representative of the school, group home representative, and, of course, the **client.** Many school programs are not used to having the student present at a meeting of this nature, and the rehabilitation counselors are not used to having parents attend. After a few meetings, it seems only natural to include everyone.

The reason for all these people to be involved is **communication and support.** Without the support and understanding of each person involved with the client, the job may be jeopardized. I have seen jobs sabotaged by any number of people who say that they "really want the job to work out" for the client. If the job can be decided with everyone in agreement, then things are headed in the right direction.

We need to look at the importance of having the client at the job match meeting. The first and most obvious reason is that **it is his life you are talking about.** He should hear what is being said about the job and him. You may be thinking that your client is too low functioning to get anything out of the meeting. He may not have the auditory skills, but you can draw pictures or even take him to see the job before a final decision is made. The client must be treated with the respect that you would want for yourself.

This is a good time to discuss your expectations with the client regarding behaviors and other problem areas. Transportation will be discussed, as well as uniforms. Including the client is imperative. He will be on the road to adulthood by attending and **participating** in this meeting.

The client has the right to say that he does not want to work in a certain job. His right as a human being must be respected. If he is not included in the job match meeting, you are not treating him with the adult-like behavior that you will expect from him on the job. He **must** be included in any decisions that affect his future!

We take notes at our job match meetings, and I have included several samples (see Figures 16 and 17). If there are any problems or concerns, these are noted. Once the notes are typed, they are signed by the administrators and parents. The parent keeps a copy, and copies are placed in the client's file. These can come in handy should there be a question later as to whether someone who attended the meeting was aware of an issue.

The procedure for the job match meeting is to first review the client analysis (see Chapter 4) in order to gain a complete understanding of the client's method of learning and of problem areas. Then, the job analysis is reviewed detail by detail. It is for this reason that the job analysis should have the learning channels included for the job tasks.

As each point is reviewed, there should be discussion as to whether the client is able to learn the job task. If there is a question, the item should be discussed and modifications to the problem explored. Sometimes this could be something as easy as a step stool so the client can reach higher, or it could mean asking the employer to restructure a portion of the job.

You may find that some of the problems are too monumental for the client to overcome in a reasonable amount of time, and you may have to decline the job because it is not a good match. This is difficult to do, as you have a willing employer ready to accept one of your clients. The job developer usually does not take this decision happily, as she is the person who has to tell the employer, then go find another job. I have found that employers tend to respect the decision and will be more anxious to hire from the program at a later date because you have examined the situation carefully.

At this point you may be wondering what some reasons may be to not match a job with a client. We have turned jobs down for the following reasons:

- The co-workers did not get along and tended to complain and bicker.
- There was not enough physical space for a large client. The client would have felt uncomfortable as would the co-workers.
- There were too many job duties included in the job.
- Too much judgment was required in the job. It was not routine, as the employer explained initially.
- The client could not catch a bus early enough to get there on time.

- There was too much contact with other people. The client needed a work station away from others.
- The client did not like the type of job. This is a valid point. Would you want to do a job that you hated, especially if you were pressured into it? Remember that your client cannot just quit and go find another job like you and I. The client must be asked throughout the meeting if he thinks he would like the job.

There can be many other reasons for turning down jobs. My advice is not to rationalize that a client will/may be able to learn a job when you are sure that he won't be able to do it. I have never seen this work. It only ends in disappointment for the client and a loss of the self-esteem you have tried so hard to build up. No matter how hard you try to explain the situation to the client, he will almost always think he did something wrong. I refuse to set up a client for failure. Remember, you are determining the outcome of someone's life. Would you want someone to set you up for a failure?

FIGURE 16

JOB MATCH MEETING

CLIENT: _____ DATE: _____

POSSIBLE TRAINING SITE: __Apartment Complex_____

DAYS/HOURS: Tuesday, Thursday – 9:00 – 5:00 p.m. (hours to be arranged with
apartment manager)_____ WAGE: $3.75/hr._____

PARTICIPANTS: _____, Mrs._____(Mother), _____
(Work Study Coordinator), _____ (BVR Counselor), _____
(Special Education Supervisor), _____ (teacher),
_____(Job Trainer) and _____(Transitional Coordinator).

DECISION AND REASON:

Place _____ in the job.

COMMENTS:
1. Client's perception of his job duties:
   a. Clean the laundry
   b. Sweep and mop
   c. Dust – handrails and mailboxes
   d. Garbage – take to dumpster
   e. Front doors – use water and soap

2. When discussing ___(Client)___ 's ability to work quickly, Mrs. __(Mom)__
   expressed concern because he can be "too meticulous."

3. __(BVR Counselor)__ was concerned that perhaps there were too many
   duties to accomplish in the amount of time alloted, i.e. 15 hours per
   week. __(WS Coordinator)__ will discuss this concern with the apartment
   manager to determine the importance of work speed initially in the job.

4. Transportation is a concern of everyone as there is no wait/walk light
   on _____ Avenue where __(Client)__ would have to cross the street.
   Mrs. __(Mom)__ was concerned about him walking from the high school to the
   job via _____ Road. Due to the flexibility with hours on this
   job, it was decided that for several reasons (transportation, classroom
   work), __(WS Coordinator)__ would request that he work from 9:00 a.m. –
   5:00 p.m. on Tuesday and Thursday. Mother will pick him up on a contin-
   ual basis as it is unsafe to cross _____ Avenue. After __(Client)__
   has settled into his job, he will be travel trained to go from home to
   his job.

5. Stamina was a concern of the group as this job requires physical
   activity throughout the day. __(Job Trainer)__ will probably do a
   majority of the job initially.

FIGURE 16 (CONT.)

Job Match Meeting

Page 2

6. The lack of supervision was the last concern.   (Client)   is a social person who likes to work with people. On this job he will work unsupervised, after the Job Trainer phases out. The comment was made that it may be easier for him to stay on task without social interactions. After his training period, he will be permitted to bring a radio, if the trainer feels this would help him.

The consensus was to place   (Client)   in this job as the group feels he is capable of performing all the required job tasks.

_____   _____
Parent/Guardian   **School Project Coordinator**

_____   _____
Date   **Kathy Morris**

FIGURE 17

JOB MATCH MEETING

CLIENT: _____   DATE: _____

POSSIBLE TRAINING SITE: _____

DAYS/HOURS: 2-3 days/week from 11:30 - 2:00 (?)
_____   WAGE: $2.01 + tips

PARTICIPANTS: (Client)   , Mrs._____(Mother), _____
(Teacher), _____(BVR Counselor), _____
(W/S Coordinator), _____(Job Trainer), _____
(Transitional Coordinator) and _____(School Project Coordinator).

DECISION AND REASON:

No match because of the requirements of the job and the lack of cooperation
of the manager.

COMMENTS:

1. Concern with her academic skills because she must do some writing;
    weak at attention to task, tends to hurry. However, on a trial basis,
    she could remember the things she was shown and has a very positive
    attitude.

2. Mother expressed concern over her ability to re-visit tables and to
    identify the different kinds of food.

3. __(The teacher)__ indicated that she remembers things very well that
    she's told and that once she has a job she'll retain it.

4. Mr. __(Employer)__ needs to understand that she cannot work without a
    trainer until after training. __(Transitional Coordinator)__ also said
    that 5 - 6 tables is unrealistic as a job load; __(Transitional
    Coordinator)__ observed that another busser was not able to clean the
    tables properly. Mrs. __(Mother)__ has doubts about whether
    Mr. __(Employer)__ will take into consideration __(Client)__ 's needs.

5. Concern expressed regarding the demand for meeting a "tip quota"
    required by __(Company)__ 's new policy.

6. __(Job Trainer)__ said she did very well on the judgement questions,
    i.e. what would you do if customer complained about a steak? - "Take
    it back."

7. Can us a calculator on the job. Able to do such with competence.

8. Concern over handling pressure. __(Teacher)__ and mother believe she
    could do so with assurance with the job.

9. She will not be able to do the job if she has to carry the tray over
    her head.

FIGURE 17 (CONT.)
JOB MATCH MEETING
PAGE 2
Client:

10. Concern with Mr. ___(Employer)___ 's attitude based upon past experience with him in the project; ___(BVR Counselor)___ suggested doing a job training agreement with the manager.

11. Compulsive handwashing has not occured since November, 1986. Mother ceased counseling for this reason.

_____   _____
Parent/Guardian   **School Project Coordinator**

_____   _____
Date   **Transitional Coordinator**

Chapter 7

TRAINING ON THE JOB

WELL, you made it to the first day of training your client. You probably are wondering what you are doing in this job. I did. You may be asking yourself, "What am I going to do? How am I going to teach this client the job?" Take a few deep breaths and relax. You'll do fine. You should have a job analysis that tells you how to do most of the job tasks, a client analysis that tells you how to approach new tasks with the client, and you have an employer that is interested in working with your client. He knows that your client will take some time to learn the job, after all, that's why you are there!

Many techniques will be used to help teach the client the job. The ones presented in this chapter are the ones I use most often. In-depth information about some of the techniques can probably be found in a library, however, you should be able to use the ones presented in this chapter without the necessity of further research. Many of these techniques are used in Work Adjustment programs, and if you have children, you may recognize some of the methods you use at home. (One job trainer reported success using some of these techniques with her teenagers.)

This chapter will be divided into several major categories, with specific techniques listed under each. References will be made to specific jobs; however, usually, techniques can be generalized to other jobs with slight modifications.

THE TRAINER—WHAT TO DO AND HOW TO ACT

Your job is not to be taken lightly. Many people are counting on you and are watching your every move: the employer, the client, the co-workers, your supervisor. There will be people who aren't watching you all the time but will be aware of your effectiveness: the parents, the administrators of your program, friends and acquaintances of the employer. My intent is not to scare you but to help make you aware of the importance of your job. You should never take this job lightly!

What Are Your Roles?

Your roles as a job trainer are teacher, advocate for your client, role model, confidant, intermediary, evaluator, supervisor, and friend. Because so many people are depending on you for your expertise, you must always **think before acting.** Your thoughts must include how a certain action will affect your client at the present and in the future. It is also necessary to think about how a certain action will affect the employer and the business.

When I interview prospective job trainers, I like to site several examples and have them tell me what they would do in given situations. My favorite is a story about a young man who had just begun a job as a dishwasher in a fairly busy restaurant. He was unaccustomed to the pace at which he should work during the rush periods, partly because he had not yet built up his speed and had not learned how to organize himself or his work area. He finally became frustrated at not being able to keep up with the work as well as having the cooks and waitresses constantly badger him for plates, silver, and glasses. He eventually threw an object across the room. What would **you** do? Take about five seconds and make a decision. You may not have even that amount of time to make a decision on a job.

I have heard a variety of answers:

1. I would find a place to let the client have some time out, then I would talk to him before letting him go back to work. (Time-out is when the client is permitted to sit alone in a room, usually for a specific time, in order to calm down and compose himself.)

2. I would try to calm him down and tell him he can't act that way on a job. Then, I would tell him to take his time and work at his own pace and forget the others.

3. I would tell the employer that there is too much work and he should hire someone to help the client.

4. I would tell him that things will get better, then pitch in and help, and talk about the problem later, after the work is caught up.

5. I would have started helping him before he became so frustrated, so he never would have progressed to that point.

Did you give one of these common answers? If so, hopefully it was one of the last two. Let's examine the ramifications for both your client, the place of business, and the community for each answer.

Answer number 1 is commonly given by applicants who have had coursework in psychology or education, especially classes that deal with behavior modification. In a classroom setting, this may be an appropriate way to handle the problem; however, in this job there are other variables to consider. For example, will that help get the dishes clean and to the customers? You might be thinking that time-out is what the client needs at the moment. He may very well benefit from that course of action. But think on, what will happen the next time? Might he say, I'm too frustrated and need to sit down for fifteen minutes. Some clients may do that because they learned the first time that if the job gets too hard that it is permissible to throw a plate. The

punishment for acting out is to sit down and rest. You may have a difficult time convincing the client otherwise.

Let's get back to my original premise that the dishes won't get washed if the client goes into time-out. If the dishes don't get washed in a timely manner, then the business will lose customers. The employer cannot afford to have all dishwashing stop for fifteen minutes while the client is in time-out or while you have a talk with him before he starts working. Thus, your client stands a chance of losing his job because the employer will say that the job is too difficult. He will be thinking that the client will never learn the job while sitting alone in a room.

Answer number 2 is also somewhat unrealistic, in that the client will have difficulty forgetting the others who are constantly asking him for supplies. The trainer must attempt to calm the client. All clients are individuals and react to things differently. Some may be able to hear, "You can't act that way on a job," if it is said in the right tone of voice. Chances are the trainer is flustered and would blurt out the sentence which may cause the client to react the opposite way. The client may say that he doesn't care about the job, and he's going to go home and never come back.

Answer number 3 is an almost sure way to get your client fired. The employer may say that if your client can't do the job, that he will find someone who can. The trainer's job is to make sure the client learns and completes the job. Yes, it may look overwhelming to you, too, but it's your job to stick with the client until he knows the job.

The other more obvious problem is that **it is not your role to tell the employer how to run his place of business.** You may think to yourself that the employer should buy more supplies or hire another person to share the job, but it is not your place to tell the employer what to do. The employer is the person responsible for the budget and for following the orders from his superiors. He has certain priorities that his superiors expect him to follow. Your wishes and his priorities may not be the same.

Answer number 4 is the answer that I hope to hear in an interview (answer 5 really isn't an option the way that I word the question). One of your roles is to make sure the work is completed correctly within the expected time. Therefore, you should pitch in and help. The way I usually accomplish this is to say to the client that it is really busy now and since his job is so new, I would be willing to help him through the rush period. I've never had a client refuse this assistance. On a dishwashing job I will put the client on the clean end of the machine and I will do the scraping and loading. I do this because on a new job, the client has not yet learned all of the tasks that make up his job, been taught how to organize the work area, or determine priorities. Also, the client isn't used to getting his hands dirty or working with less than pleasant looking plates. Usually, the stacking of clean dishes is the easiest part of a dishwasher's job and requires the least amount of skills.

By telling the client that you will help him because the job is new, he will not get the idea that you will always **do his job** for him. I usually assist the client only during the busiest times until he can manage the whole job alone.

By assisting your client, you are gaining credibility with the employer. He sees that you are not afraid to do the job and that you are really going to do what the job developer said you would. There is nothing worse than hearing that a job trainer **just sits there and watches** the client. The employer wonders why the trainer is there if she is never interacting or active with the client. The employer may not always be right there, but they always know what you and your client do.

Answer number 5 is not really an option. However, if someone prefaces their answer with this statement, I take note that the person was really watching the client and was watching for signs of stress. When I pursue that answer with an applicant, they usually say that they would have been helping the client when he first became stressed. By watching for signs of stress, the outburst could have been avoided.

It is extremely important to think of all the ramifications of your actions before you act in a given situation. You will learn to do this with time. The more experiences you have to build upon, the quicker you will be able to make good decisions. You will make mistakes, especially when you first start your job. That's expected. What's important is that you recognize and learn from them.

Be Prepared

Before you start working with your client on the job, be sure you have absorbed the client analysis. **Know how you will teach the client.** Practice in your mind how you will approach the tasks. Will it be through demonstration, verbal instructions, hands on, or a combination?

Think about your role and how you will relate to the client. Will you be supportive or stern? Will you be a friend or a boss? Will you joke with the client or will you be serious? There is no one way that is right or wrong. Remember that you are dealing with individuals, and individuals are all different. You must change to fit the role necessary for the client and the situation. For example, I once worked with a client who was rather **streetwise.** Many people think that I am mild-mannered and supportive at all times (a softee), as did this client. He proceeded to attempt to take advantage of my niceness by lying to me and generally acting inappropriately. Suddenly, my nice, supportive personality became serious and my tone of voice was authoritative. The client sat straight in his chair, looked me in the eye and stopped his inappropriate behavior. From that point on, it was necessary for me to always relate to him in that same demanding way. We had no communication difficulties as long as I related to him in a stern manner. On the other hand, there are many clients that need supportiveness and positive interactions. They may not be able to handle the tough authoritarian personality. The young, scared, naive person would probably crumble if you interacted the same way that you would with a streetwise or aggressive person who knows it all.

Be sure you have studied both the task and client analyses and have learned as much about the job as possible. Visual learners, like myself, will want to study the map of the work area. The more you know about your client and the job, the easier your job will be on the first day.

On the Job

There are many things to do the first morning on the job. You must make sure your client is comfortable in his new work place and knows the basic physical layout of the area. You will want to make sure that he knows where to enter and exit, to clock in, leave his belongings, where his work station is located and how to get to the restroom and break rooms. The first morning is sometimes confusing. But some places of business are organized and will begin the job with an orientation.

If your client has an orientation, you will want to be sure to attend this with him. Much of the information may be above his level of understanding, and you may need to review certain items with him later. He may have forms to fill out (i.e. income tax, insurance, emergency) or bring to the employer (e.g. birth certificate). If you have not already checked with his parents or guardians as to how they want the papers filled out, it is a good idea to send them home to be completed and returned the following day.

After orientation, when the client goes to his work station for the first time, you will suddenly feel pressured. This is it! The time is finally here! Now you have to produce!

Usually, the employer will assign someone to teach you and your client the job. If this person is the employer himself, he may or may not stay with you for a long period of time. If this person will be a co-worker, then your client will most likely be working with him for the entire work period. For information about working with the employers and co-workers, please see Chapter 8.

You will **establish your goals** for the day for your client and you. Your goals will change daily as your client progresses through the process of learning his job. For example, the goals for the first day of a dishwashing job may be for the client to learn where the clean dishes are kept and which dish racks are for the different dishes, glasses, utensils, etc.. Those are short-term goals, of course. The long-term goal for the client will always be to learn to become independent and complete all his assigned job tasks without assistance. By setting daily goals, you will be able to see improvement at a quicker pace than if you only look for the day the client is totally independent.

Before attempting to teach your client the job, it is wise to **observe someone performing the job task** the way it is expected to be completed. This is extremely important, as the job may have changed somewhat since the task analysis was completed. This is especially common in large corporations and in small new businesses. The large corporations must run as a unit for efficiency. They generally employ experts in this field, and often there are changes in the techniques to accomplish a task. In small businesses, it is quite the opposite. Especially in new companies, the employers are still trying to find the most efficient method of performing the jobs.

Therefore, the methods may change several times in a week or month, until the management is satisfied that the method is the most cost effective. I am not saying that your task analysis is worthless, I'm merely suggesting that you check to make sure there haven't been any changes since the time of the analysis.

While looking at the job and comparing it to the job analysis, **make sure that you understand all the specifications for the job.** I once had an employer criticize one of the trainers I was supervising because she was not requiring the same quality out of the client as the other trainer that was also working with the client. After questioning the trainer, I realized she did not have an understanding of the specific quality expected. Once she was shown, she had no further difficulty.

One important addition to that story is that **you should never generalize what you learn on one job to another job setting.** The reason is that although the job title may be the same, expectations are quite often different. We once had three clients in different laundry jobs. The expectations for each job were entirely different. One expected excellent quality, and quantity was secondary. One was exactly the opposite, neatness wasn't as important as working quickly. And the third was in between. The trainer mentioned above went from one setting to another and didn't realize the difference in the expectations. Had this situation not been resolved, the client may have lost the job. I have learned to **never assume anything.** It is always better to ask a question and be sure of the answer than to not ask it and jeopardize your client's job.

HOW DO I ACTUALLY WORK WITH THE CLIENT ON THE JOB?

In this section, we will look at two main areas: teaching techniques and job modifications. Although they will be presented together, there is a difference. **Teaching techniques** are the actual methods you utilize to teach a job task. For example, your client may have severe auditory problems but learns well through the visual channel. The technique used to teach the client would be demonstration alone, without talking to him.

Job modifications are changes you can make in the physical layout or environment or by giving the client aides (e.g. checklist, diagrams) in order to assist your client to perform all the expected job tasks. In the example above, you might provide a checklist of each step of the job for your client to refer. You may decide to draw diagrams of work areas or how to assemble specific items. Your client may be the only person in the company that is using a specific modification. Once an effective modification is in place, teaching the job task will be much easier.

Before specific techniques and modifications are discussed, we must look at some criteria and, of course, the ramifications of using a specific method. First, a job modification must be tailor-made to fit the client. You most likely will not use the same modifications to teach a visual learner as you would use to teach an auditory learner in the same job. Remember that you are working with individuals. Your modifications for the client will have to be compatible with his learning style.

A job modification must be affordable (i.e. cheap), easy to use, and adaptable into the environment easily. Some of the most successful modifications I have utilized were the cheapest to make. I have always been somewhat of a pack rat. It's amazing what you can make out of odds and ends. For example, in order to teach a low functioning mentally retarded woman to accurately count fish in a fast-food restaurant, I cut rug padding remnants into fish fillets. The client had figure-ground problems and could not understand that when the fish were stacked in rows, some were hidden from view. It was necessary to make the modification as realistic as possible to insure her understanding and the ability to transfer her knowledge to the actual job. The padding was the same color, I could make it the same shape, it could be manipulated into any configuration necessary (i.e. thrown into the pan), and it was cheap. The extra bonus was that my husband was glad to be rid of it!

The only limit to an effective modification is your creativity. Thus, if I would not have discovered the rug padding or something similar and instead made the fish out of paper, she may not have been as successful in learning to count. The fish would have lacked form and she would not have been able to determine if there were pieces of fish behind or under others.

If I am having a difficult time determining a modification, I may ask the employer if it is permissible to borrow several items of the product with which the client is working. Then I can take my time at the office or home and ask for ideas from friends, relatives, or co-workers. Two heads are often better than one.

The modification must fit comfortably into the environment. For example, you would not want to bring a large wooden box into a work area that is barely large enough for the client. The modification should be unobtrusive and non-interfering with co-workers performing their duties. Above all, the modification should be one that an adult would use. I have seen **happy faces** used on jobs with clients and do not consider that adult-like. My measure for the appropriateness of a modification is whether I would use it myself.

Modifications can be made for either the job task itself or for inappropriate behaviors as you will see later in this chapter. There are some modifications that are quite effective on clients with behavior problems. It is my opinion that **the reason most clients lose their jobs is because of behavior problems, not the inability to learn job tasks.**

You will find that **modifications will need to be concrete.** The modification must be easily seen or touched and be easily understood with the goal clear. For example, on a collating job in which the client must put five papers in an envelope, the modification may be to number the papers in the order in which they are collated. It is easily seen and understood and is adult-like. Do not present your client with a complex, multistep modification, as he will most likely have difficulty learning it. The purpose of making modifications is to **make the job easier** for the client. If the modification is complex, you will find yourself having to do twice the training, and both you and your client will become extremely frustrated.

The last (and perhaps most important) tip to give you is to try to teach yourself to **think modifications all the time.** By this, I mean that if you go out to eat, observe the busser, the waitress, and hostess. While observing them, think if there are any ways to make their job more efficient. I used to become frustrated when I went to a fast-food restaurant to get some iced tea. If I ordered a large tea, the front end worker was required to perform many unnecessary steps (in my opinion). After putting the ice in the large cup, she would set it down and get a small cup. She would fill the small cup with the tea and pour it into the large cup, then repeat this procedure. You may be wondering why such a process? This was because the spout from the container was about one inch too low and the large cup wouldn't fit under it. A simple and easy modification would have been to put the container on a phone book. Or, they could have moved the container to the side of the shelf so there would have been nothing under the spout. There are obviously more solutions to the problem than those two. The point is that modifications don't have to be expensive or flashy. They just have to be functional.

Before making any modifications that involve moving or adding equipment, you must always ask the employer's permission! In the example given above, the employer may not have wanted his phone book used for that purpose. Remember that it is **his** business, and if he doesn't want a certain modification used, you can't use it! If he doesn't want you to use one, then you will need to renegotiate for another modification.

I've given you all the basics; now I'll give you the specifics. **Remember that the following are only ideas and start-off points.** Have fun! This is where you begin your real work! Remember, it will be both fun and frustrating for you. During the frustrating times when your client is having difficulty learning the job tasks, calm down and try again. It will be worth it in the end!

MODIFICATIONS AND TEACHING TECHNIQUES

General Information

Now you will use the information from the client analysis to develop modifications. The following section is for those clients who can benefit from visual instruction or techniques. The information in this section may also be helpful for those clients who have visual difficulties in an area and modifications for the job task are necessary for the client to successfully perform his job duties.

The remainder of the chapter will consist of various ideas for modifications and teaching methods. They will be listed according to each learning channel and will follow the outline of Chapter 3 for easy reference. First will be general ideas, then ideas specific to traditional jobs: janitorial, dishwashing, bussing, laundry, clerical, and assembly/packaging.

In order to use this material most effectively, I would encourage you to **read the entire chapter.** Then, when you are working with a client and need to develop modifications, you will have some basic ideas. I have incorporated examples to help you understand how to implement the ideas. Remember, the following are ideas only. Use your creativity! Have fun! This is where you get to shine!

Visual Modifications and Teaching Techniques

General Methods

Demonstration

There are many ways to teach the person who learns best through the visual channel. The most popular method is **demonstration.** Most people think that demonstration is easy. However, with some clients, if you add **any** verbal instructions with the demonstration, they become confused. During the client analysis you should have determined if you can add verbal instructions and, if so, the amount. Can jobs with many steps be learned through a combination of the two, or is pure demonstration better?

When you demonstrate the task to the client, can you show many steps at once? With some clients you must go slowly, making sure the client masters the first step by practicing before introducing step two, and so on. This method of teaching is sometimes called forward chaining. Always be aware of how you are teaching a job task. And, more importantly, be aware of the client's level of understanding.

Written Instructions

Some clients learn from **written instructions** which they always have with them. I have seen clients that will use **only** the written instructions, with absolutely no verbal interaction whatsoever. You must always keep in mind the client's **language and reading level** when giving the client written instructions. I either have the client help me write the instructions or have him read them afterwards and demonstrate his understanding.

Depending on the client's need, you can place a line or box before each instruction and have the client check it off as he completes each task. Sometimes this helps the client see how much work he has accomplished for the day.

There are many ways in which to provide written instructions. But what about the visual learner who reads on an elementary grade level or not at all? The obvious is a **picture list.** One does not have to be an artist in order to draw pictures for a list. My clients have had many a chuckle out of my pictures, but they still understood what they meant. Some people will cut out pictures from magazines to use for lists. This is too time consuming for me, and the pictures are sometimes out of proportion and don't always fit on the paper like I want them. Therefore, I continue to use my stick figure people to show the job tasks. One hint for you: **always save your pictures** so you can use them later. I have a large file of janitorial pictures that I have handy to use when needed. When I have a client on a new job, I just arrange the pictures in the order of the task analysis for the client and he is set. I have become quite adept at **cutting and pasting** over the years.

Quite often I **laminate** the lists, that is, I place them in plastic so they won't get ruined if they get wet. Then they can be used over again, especially if the instructions have been made into a **checklist.** There are several ways you can laminate. One effective way is to use plastic report covers. They can be cut to size and sealed with tape around the edges. Clear contact paper can also be used. I have learned that some types of lamination will not take ink or markers; therefore, before investing a lot of money, or even a few dollars, you will want to make sure that you can both write on it with a marker and erase the marks easily. That way, the checklist can be reviewed at the end of each day, the check marks erased, and the list used again the next day. This is much cheaper and less wasteful than a fresh piece of paper every day.

Your client's needs and abilities will determine the type of checklist you will need. I once worked with a low functioning mentally retarded young man who could barely identify his own name. He also had severe auditory and language problems. Thus, the use of verbal instructions was out of the question. In order to help him remember the job tasks, I took **photographs** of him working at the specific tasks. I then made a workbook for him. The pictures were mounted two to a page, with a box under each picture. I placed the pictures in the plastic cover pages you can buy at a bookstore or even grocery and placed them in a binder. The first picture was the client clocking in and the last was him clocking out. After he clocked in in the morning, he would take the marker I provided him and place a check mark in the box under the picture of the time clock. He continued this procedure until he clocked out at the end of his shift when he turned in his book to the supervisor. He liked to see himself working and was able to follow the meaning of the book. He was proud of his book and showed it to all his co-workers. Also, by checking off completed tasks, there was no question if he had finished his work tasks. If someone left dirt in the area after he cleaned, his checklist indicated he had cleaned it earlier.

Checklists can be placed in binders (as mentioned above) if there are many pages. Sometimes I tape them to walls or work tables with masking tape (be sure to get the kind that painters use so the paint won't peel off the wall), with the employer's permission, or place them on a clipboard. I have also placed them on a large ring (shower curtain hooks work nicely and are inexpensive for a package) so the list for the day could be found readily if the job tasks change on a daily basis. Magnetic clips or suction cups with hooks can also be used to hang lists. You may want to place the list on a 3-by-5-inch index card so it can be kept in a pocket. One trainer had the client write his checklist on a pocket calendar (e.g. daily reminder) so he could refer to it throughout the day. This calendar looked like the same one that executives use and he was proud to have it!

Diagrams

Sometimes clients can easily follow **diagrams.** You draw each part of the job to be done in the proper sequence. In some cases, you may want to draw a floor plan or map. I once worked with a client who had severe short-term memory problems and could not remember how to get to her work station from the door, or to the restroom from the work station, or to the breakroom, etc.. I drew her a map of the building and drew her routes to go from one place to the next. In order to make it less confusing for her, I **color coded** the routes (e.g. work station — red, restroom — blue). By using the diagram, she was able to learn her way around the workplace. Before using a diagram as a map, you must be sure that the client is able to understand the meaning of the diagram. That is a fairly abstract concept and may be frustrating for some clients.

Diagrams that are used at a work station are smaller and not quite as abstract. For example, you may draw a picture of the way a box should look before a label is placed on it. Your diagram would include identifying marks on the box that the client can understand. A client may be able to use that type of visual aid and not the map. That should have been discovered during the client analysis. (For ideas on assessing the client's ability to follow a diagram, see Chapter 4.) Diagrams are becoming more prevalent in our everyday living, especially on directions on cake mixes and boxed foods that require preparation.

Color Coding

Color coding was briefly mentioned above. Color coding can be useful in helping a client pick out a specific object or line or group. Just think how color coding is used in your daily life. Road maps are color coded, interstates are one color and toll roads another. Traffic lights and safety signs (e.g. STOP signs and fire extinguishers are almost always red). Yellow is the universal color for caution.

You can do similar things with colors with your clients. I have used a different color for the days of the weeks on checklists in which the client could neither read or identify numbers. We decided on Monday's color (blue), Tuesday's (pink), etc.. I have seen colors used in a diagram of a salad bar. The dressings were labeled then circled with a specific color, as were the vegetables, fruits, and other items.

A client of mine once developed her own modification using color coding. She was responsible for many small items which she had to remove from one area, carry to another, then return after she had cleaned them. She was having difficulty remembering where each item went, so she bought a package of multicolored paperclips. In the morning, she would find color pairs and place them on the edge of her pocket. When she would pick up an item, she would replace it with a paperclip. After cleaning, she would look for the paperclips then replace the items. If, at the end of the day, she had an extra paperclip on her pocket without a mate, she would search for the clip and then she would remember the item. This modification worked for her, because she was able to remember what item went in the location once she saw the location. If she would not have had that ability, then this modification would not have been appropriate for her.

Models

Some clients need a completed model of the job in front of them. They can look at it to figure out the next step by observing the end product. For example, in an electronics assembly job, the completed printed circuit board with the components would be a help in determining if all the parts were placed appropriately. Likewise, a model of a chef salad may help the client to remember all the items. Obviously, models are more useful in assembly jobs than in dishwashing or janitorial jobs.

Manipulating the Environment

It may be necessary to change the environment to meet your client's needs by adding subtle visual clues for him. For example, when teaching a client to clean portions of a building, the trainer placed colored dots on an inconspicuous place on the doors of the rooms to be cleaned. These matched with the color coded daily schedule. The client, who could neither read nor tell time nor remember from day to day where to clean, could finally carry out the job on his own. The dots on the door didn't affect any of the daily duties of any employees and, in fact, were hardly noticed by the workers.

Placing a red X on a client's time card may be helpful if the client is unable to identify his name. Similarly, placing a red cloth on a client's work chair may assist him to remember the location of his work station. (I always use fabric, preferably knit, as it does not tear easily like paper and it can be washed.)

Enlisting the Help of the Employer

When working with a client on a job, it is imperative to **teach the employer how the client learns.** You should do this only after you have met with consistent success in teaching the client in that job setting. I once worked with a person in a job who was a visual learner and had extreme auditory problems. She had difficulty processing any information given strictly by verbal means. When communicating with her,

I would write instructions on my yellow pad (a necessity when working with a visual learner!). I would read them aloud and point to them as I read.

She had been on this particular job for several years, and the employer complained that, among other things, the client wanted to be promoted to a higher position. The employer had **told her over and over** that she had not yet mastered all the job requirements of the current job and would not be able to be promoted. The client, of course, did not understand, and continued to ask the employer the same question every week.

I explained to the employer that it was necessary to communicate through visual means when working with the client. This was a new concept for the employer. The employer was nervous about conveying the information to the client that a promotion would not occur soon, if ever. I was asked to explain this to the client.

I drew two circles on the paper and divided each into pie shapes. On the top one, I labeled the pies with her current job duties in spaces proportionate with the approximate percentage of time the duties assumed. On the other pie, I did the same with the duties of the other job. During the meeting, as we discussed the duties that she did well, I shaded in those pie pieces. We did the same thing with the other pie. Then we looked at the few unshaded pieces of the pie, those tasks that she was unable to accomplish on the current job. We did the same with the other pie, which showed about 75 percent of the pie unshaded.

The client's immediate reaction was, "I can't do that new job! I can't even do all of my job now! There is no way I could do well in the new one!" The employer's expression showed amazement and shock at how easy it was to communicate with the client. The discussion went on to let the client know that it was alright to stay in one job for a long time. Many people do that and it is normal. At the end of the meeting, both the client and the employer were satisfied. The employer now knows how to communicate effectively with the employee.

Specific Job Modifications

Visual Discrimination Modifications

Janitorial Work. If your client has a severe visual discrimination problem and does not perceive things in his environment as they were meant to be seen, he may have difficulty on a janitorial job. He probably would have difficulty seeing specks of dirt or smudges on mirrors or windows. If his problem is severe, it may be necessary to seek other employment for him, as modifications may not assist him to perform the quality of work expected. The following modifications may assist your client in a janitorial job:

1. **Clean everything.** Because he is unable to see if there is dirt or not, it will be necessary for the client to be taught to clean all surfaces daily. The client must do this, because if he was taught to clean certain items every other day, he may not

notice if the item is dirty on the day he is not to clean it. This obviously is time-consuming and will probably cause his work rate to be slowed significantly. Usually, janitorial jobs require the person to make quick judgments as to the necessity to clean an item. Thus, the janitor may dust a chair once or twice a week and more if it needs it.

2. **Verbalize while working.** If the client has problems reversing the order of things (e.g. items on a bookshelf), it may be necessary for him to verbalize the order as he takes them off the shelf to dust. For example, he may say, "large picture, small picture, tissue box, lighter." By verbalizing, he may be able to retain the order. Be aware that this modification uses not only the visual but the **auditory and kinesthetic** channels of learning. Auditory is hearing the verbalization while touching the object (kinesthetic).

3. **Provide exact measurement container.** If the client must mix chemicals, it is helpful to provide him with a measuring cup that is the exact measurement. Clients with other problems may be able to measure liquids to a line drawn on a cup, but the person with a visual discrimination problem will most likely have difficulty. The worst thing is to tell a client to pour in **a little** or **some** or **until it looks right.** You will be amazed at how many people use those measurements.

Dishwashing. A person with a visual discrimination problem will have difficulty determining if there is any dirt on a dish, utensil, or pot or pan. If the problem is too great, it may be wise to seek another type of employment for the client as he will not be able to obtain the quality necessary for the job. Quality is of the utmost importance in restaurant work due to the health factors involved. If the dishwasher does not clean the dishes well, the customers complain, they may get sick, and if the problem isn't corrected, the restaurant may eventually close. Modifications that may be helpful include:

1. **Use the sense of touch.** If the client is unable to perceive small amounts of food stuck to the plate, have him use his sense of touch and lightly run his hand across the plate. Obviously, this should be done **before** the plate is put through the washer. As in the janitorial job, this takes a tremendous amount of time and may slow him down too much.

2. **Compare sizes by using the sense of touch when sorting dishes and utensils.** Determining the difference between a soupspoon and a teaspoon can be difficult for a person with a visual discrimination problem. Therefore, when sorting silverware or plates, it may be necessary to compare the items by nesting them. If necessary, the client can touch them while nested in order to determine the difference. One trainer had the dishwasher arrange the plates in order by size. There were approximately ten different sizes and shapes, and the client was having difficulty placing them correctly. When he placed them in order, he made fewer errors and his work pace improved. When putting the dishes away, it was important to have him leave one of each size on the counter for reference for the next load of dishes.

3. **Adding soap.** Most dishwashers will buzz and flash a light when it is time to add more soap, and most soap is prepackaged with the right measurements. If it is necessary for your client to measure soap, you will want to make sure he has a container that holds the exact amount of soap he needs (see number 3 in the section above).

Bussing. If your client has a visual discrimination problem, he may have difficulty determining different sizes of utensils, dishes, or glassware. He may also have difficulty determining if there are crumbs on a table or how many napkins he is holding. Some of his problems are similar to those of a janitor and some are similar to those of a dishwasher. As in the janitorial or dishwashing work, if the problem is too severe, alternative employment should be sought for the client. The following modifications may help your client in a job bussing tables:

1. **Compare by kinesthetic means.** If the client has difficulty determining differences in sizes of spoons or plates, for example, he can stack them, then feel the rims for differences. This is similar to a dishwasher.

2. **Arrange sizes in order, use signs.** Placing items in order by size may assist the client in determining the correct size. Signs may be placed on the shelves to assist the client (e.g. dinner plates, salad plates, dessert plates), providing the client is able to read. If the client cannot read the words, picture signs may help. For example, a picture or drawing of a plate with the meal, a smaller plate with a salad, and a smaller one with a piece of pie.

Laundry. Visual discrimination is important to a laundry worker. If the client has a severe problem in this area, he may be unable to see small stains. In some settings, especially motels, this skill is a necessity. I have seen motels discard many linens or towels for one small smudge of makeup that would not come out in the wash. Nursing homes do not appear to be as fussy.

The laundry worker may also have difficulty operating the equipment if he has a severe visual discrimination problem. Machines generally have either a dial with numbers and lines or are computerized and may require pushing the correct buttons. Some machines have a card that is inserted, and the client must be able to determine the correct one for the load of wash. This should be included in the task analysis of the job, and the trainer should know before training begins if there is a problem in this area. The following modifications may be helpful for the client with a visual discrimination problem:

1. **Divide and conquer.** If the client has difficulty locating stains, divide and look at the article by sections. This may be time consuming and will most likely affect the client's productivity. (It is imperative to find out the quality and quantity standards before proceeding with the training.)

2. **Mark dial.** It is easier to make modifications if the machine is run by a dial. A red felt tip pen can be used (with the employer's permission) to place a mark next to

where the arrow should point when the machine is turned on. If the marker will not stick, then use a small piece of masking tape and place it on the machine, then put your red mark on it.

3. **Color code.** If it is necessary to place more than one mark on a machine, then you may want to color code. Clients generally know red, yellow, and green, as stop, be careful, and go. This coding system could be used if necessary.

4. **Charts.** If the machines are computerized and the client is required to put in numbers, a chart could be taped to the machine to help the client determine which buttons to push. If the client has problems identifying numbers, perhaps different-colored dots could be placed on them, with a coded list next to the buttons. Be sure to get permission before you mark or tape any walls or equipment.

5. **Envelopes.** If the machines are operated by the card system, perhaps each card could be placed in an envelope with a picture of the function. For example, a pillow for linens and towels for terry. Of course, this is only used if the employer approves.

Clerical. A person with a visual discrimination problem will have a difficult time performing some clerical tasks correctly. For example, filing will most likely be incorrect, as letters or numbers may be reversed or omitted. These problems will carry over to typing and the client will have difficulty proofreading finished copy. Any job task that involves reading will be very difficult for the client to accomplish well and in the time expected. For these problems, modifications will not be foolproof, especially when the client tires of using the painstaking methods. **I strongly urge you not to place a client with this problem in a position of having to fulfill the duties outlined above.**

Clients may achieve success in jobs that require using paper shredders, opening mail, and possibly inter-office mail delivery. Always be cautious before agreeing to place a client with a visual discrimination problem in a clerical job.

The following modifications **may** be helpful in working with a client with a visual discrimination problem:

1. **Windows.** When required to read, the client may use a window made from a **plain** paper. In the middle of the paper, a window is cut the size of either a line of print or a word. When reading, the client places the window over the text, allowing print to only show through the window. This modification is also used for clients who have figure-ground problems and cannot block out the print that is not currently being read. This modification is effective if the client must compare lists of names or proofread.

2. **Tracing.** When reading, the client can trace over the materials, thus introducing a motor movement component to the task. This can be effective if the client is a kinesthetic learner.

3. **Verbalizing.** When reading, the client can verbalize the entire word or each letter. This may be in conjunction with tracing mentioned above.

Assembly/Packaging. Jobs in these categories are so varied that it is difficult to give specific modifications. There are some general considerations that can be applied.

1. **Visual hint or guide.** Many times when either assembling or packaging, a letter, number, word can be identified to help the client determine if he is doing the task correctly. For example, on a collating task, one might use the page numbers, or if there is a window, the client should check to make sure the correct word is visible. If the client is working with metal items, sometimes control numbers or the manufacturer's name are stamped on the item.

If it is necessary for the client to count items and he has difficulty identifying how many items he has in his hand, you could draw boxes and have him place one item on each until they are all covered. Or, he could also be provided with a counter that sits on his worktable. When he places a completed item in the box, he clicks the arm on the counter. Counters may be purchased at office supply stores. By using these modifications, the client is assured that he has the correct amount of items. Be aware that the first modification mentioned above will slow his work pace, as he will be handling each item twice.

2. **Teach one method.** Sometimes the client may pick up items in several different ways when assembling or packaging. If the client has a visual discrimination problem, he may be unable to determine if the finished product is correct. You can teach the client to always pick up the item in the same way, and work with his motor movements to ensure quality. I will use a watch or ring that the client always wears as a point of reference. For example, I worked with a client who was collating and would sometimes pick up materials with his right hand and sometimes with his left. Sometimes his thumb was on the top and sometimes it was on the bottom. He was having problems with his work quality. I taught him to pick up the material with his hand so he could see his ring, or with his right hand with his thumb on the bottom. Once he learned consistency, his quality was fine.

3. **Organize the work station.** The client with a visual discrimination problem may have difficulty organizing. It is imperative that the client's work station is set up correctly by the supervisor or co-worker. If supplies are brought throughout the day, see that they are placed in their proper position on the worktable by someone other than the client, as he may reverse similar objects or place them upside down.

VISUAL SPATIAL PERCEPTUAL MODIFICATIONS

Janitorial Work. A person with a severe visual spatial perceptual problem in a janitorial job that involves cleaning offices, labs, or other things that are breakable or delicate is similar to a bull in a china shop. I don't advise it. Remember that the person with a visual spatial perceptual problem does not realize he has a problem in this area and cannot tell if he has made an error. Several modifications may help those with moderate spatial difficulties:

1. **Dust one item at a time.** When dusting, the client can be taught to pick up an item, dust it, dust the table where it was placed and replace it on the table. Be careful, because most likely the client will be unaware of items near him and he may accidentally knock something over with his elbow or the corner of his rag. You will want to make sure he holds **all** of the rag in the palm of his hand so there are no loose ends to brush against other objects.

2. **Organize the job.** The client with spatial problems, if left to his own methods, will probably clean something on the right side of the room, then hop over to the left, then maybe to the right or middle. His method of **attacking a room** is unorganized. For dusting, he should be taught to always start at the door and move around the outside of the room, then clean the items in the middle. For cleaning the floor, he should always start at the point farthest from the door and proceed to the door. This saves the client from mopping himself into a corner.

3. **Kathy Morris's Bump'em Method.** When working with a client who cannot comprehend number 2, it is necessary to add motor involvement. I tell my clients it is my **bump'em method** of cleaning. You start at the door and clean the first thing that you **bump** into. I usually demonstrate this to the client in exaggerated movements, without actually touching the furniture, and the client chuckles but seems to understand the concept.

4. **Use the lines on the floor.** When teaching a client to mop a floor, use the lines that are on the floor for guidance. For example, a tile floor has lines where the tiles meet. Hopefully, your client will be able to perceive and use those lines. I once worked with a client who was unable to determine the long side of a 36-inch dust mop. She regularly used the small side of the mop (approximately 6″ wide) and was unaware of the difference in the amount of surface she was covering. Also, she was unable to perceive the lines on the floor. When she was mopping a room, instead of walking behind the mop, she would push the mop toward the wall and pull it back towards her. By using this method she left a row of dirt around the edges of the room. In order to teach her to mop, I tore several pieces of yellow paper from my pad I always carry and spread them all over the floor. (If you are prepared to teach this skill, you can use the holes from paper punches. Be advised that sometimes they tend to fly around because they are so light. I have also seen rice used for this purpose. Be sure that whatever you use does not scratch the surface of the floor.) Although she tried hard and we practiced for hours, she was **never** able to mop a floor with the quality expected on a job. I had to recommend that she not be placed in a job that required cleaning floors.

5. **Provide exact measurement container.** As for the client with a visual discrimination problem, it is necessary to provide a container for the exact measure-

ment, if the client is required to mix chemicals. For more information on this modification, please see number 3 in the "Janitorial Work" section above.

Dishwashing. The client with a spatial problem will most likely have difficulty placing the dirty dishes in the dish racks efficiently. He will probably also have difficulty arranging his work area in an orderly manner. Several modifications which may assist you in working with your client in a dishwashing capacity include:

1. **Place big items in the back.** When teaching the client to fill a dish rack, the large items (e.g. plates, platters) should always go in the back. If the client learns to fill the rack from the back to the front, then his chances of leaving empty spaces are less than if he goes from front to back. Obviously, when working, this may not be possible at all times, as there will be salad and dessert plates and bowls. If it is possible without breaking dishes, I try to have the client find all the large items first.

2. **Verbalize.** If the client is placing items at random, you might have him verbalize the general size and where it should be placed. For example, big—back, little—front. Sometimes adding the verbal component assists the client in making the decision.

3. **Organize work area.** It will be necessary to help your client to organize his work area. You will want him to place each item in a specific area in order to help him identify sizes.

4. **Provide an exact measurement container.** The client should be furnished with an exact measuring device as was mentioned for the client with visual discrimination problems as well as the janitorial client.

Bussing. As in janitorial work, a client who is bussing tables may have some accidents. He may place a glass on the edge of a table or bus tray and not realize it until it falls to the floor. He may stack the plates to the side of a round tray and place the glasses in the middle, causing it to be off balance and tip over when lifted with one hand. He may bump into tables, stands, or customers unintentionally. When setting a table, he may place items off center. Some employers are very fussy about the placement of the condiments on the table. If your client has severe problems in this area, you may want to think twice about the placement. The following are some modifications that may assist the client with mild visual spatial perceptual problems:

1. **Diagrams.** If the client is having problems placing items on bus trays, for example, you could draw a diagram the size of the tray indicating where the different items are to be placed. You could draw a large circle in the middle for the plates or heavier items.

2. **Use the sense of touch to check placement of objects.** If the client has a tendency to place items so close to the edge of a table or tray that it falls, you could teach him to check the placement by feeling the object. You may want to make a work rule that all items are to be placed one thumb width from the side.

3. **Measuring stick.** If the client has difficulty placing the condiments in the middle of the table, perhaps you could devise a measuring stick or method of measuring. This could be a ruler or a piece of cardboard cut to the width the condiments are placed in from the side of the table. You could also write or draw the names or labels on the end of the measurer to help him determine the correct order.

4. **Belly button or stomach.** Everyone knows what a belly button is, even clients who are mentally retarded. Most of your clients will know what a stomach or tummy is. I use this as a frame of reference if I want the client to place something directly in front of him. For example, if he is having difficulty setting a table, I have him stand behind the chair and set the place mat on the table in front of his belly button, then the plate. This may sound juvenile, but if the client has a language problem in addition to his spatial problem, it is a way of communicating with him. Of course, you change your language depending on the understanding level of the client.

Laundry. A client with a visual spatial problem will most likely have difficulty folding sheets evenly. He will be unable to tell if the edges are even and the corners match. Some employers expect each corner and edge to be even, while others are not as particular. A client may also have difficulties if required to fold an item in thirds, as he will be unable to determine one-third. Setting dials may also present problems for the client. Sometimes, employers will not allow the trainer to make modifications that would allow the client to perform the job tasks easier. If that is the case, there is not much you can do, except use the knowledge and skills you have to teach the client, using the approved method. Before attempting to teach any other method, **always ask the employer if it is permissible.** The following modifications may assist the client to improve his quality of work:

1. **Stretch arms.** If the client has difficulty determining the long and short side of a sheet, have him hold one side. If there is little or no extra sheet, it is the short side; if there is a lot of extra, it is the long side. You cannot count on using the hems of sheets to determine the long or short sides, because not all sheets are made the same way.

2. **Use identifying spots in the room.** I once worked with a client who had the problem described in number 1 above. His arms were so short that there was extra sheet by both hands. The laundry was equipped with a **third arm** or **helping hand** which is a pole that has a clamp at the top that is activated by a foot pedal. The sheet can be inserted into the clamp, then stretched out and folded more easily. When this client stretched out sheets, he was to be standing next to the first dryer, if he had the correct side. If he folded the sheet wrong, he would not have been as near the dryer and he knew he had to use the other side. The room itself provided the guide he needed to fold correctly.

3. **Match corners.** In order to match corners evenly, I suggest having the client grasp two corners in his hand. Then teach him to run his forefinger between the two sections of sheets until he comes to the other two corners. Then have him grasp them, then fold the sheet in half. Continue in this manner until the sheet is folded completely.

4. **Color-coded guide or line.** When the client is required to fold in thirds and is having difficulty determining the correct width to fold, you could place a line on a paper or table that shows where one-third is. The client then places the item to be folded on top of the paper and folds until he sees the line appear.

5. **Cardboard cut to size.** If number 2 is impractical for the particular situation, you could cut a piece of cardboard which he must place **on top of the fabric** even with the side. Then he folds the opposite side until it hits the cardboard. Of course, he must then remove the cardboard before completing the task, which is time consuming.

6. **Mark the dial.** It is easier to make modifications if the machine is run by a dial. A red felt tip pen can be used (with the employer's permission) to place a mark next to where the arrow should point when the machine is turned on. If the marker will not stick, then use a small piece of masking tape and place it on the machine, then put your red mark on it.

7. **Color code.** If it is necessary to place more than one mark on a machine, then you may want to color code. Clients generally know red, yellow, and green as stop, be careful, and go. This coding system could be used if necessary.

8. **Charts.** If the machines are computerized and the client is required to put in numbers, a chart could be taped to the machine to help the client determine which buttons to push. If the client has problems identifying numbers, perhaps different-colored dots could be placed on them, with a coded list next to the buttons. Be sure to get permission before you mark or tape any walls or equipment.

Clerical. The client with a visual spatial perceptual problem will have a difficult time centering typing on a page. I once had a secretary (she was not a client) who had some spatial problems. She could center the items by counting, but if the text was crooked on the page she was unable to tell this by herself. A client would also have difficulty identifying copied material that is off center. The following modifications may assist the clerical worker with a visual spatial perceptual problem:

1. **Measure.** When I would ask my secretary to type the paper over because it was off center, the only way she could tell that it was crooked was to use a ruler and measure the typing from the bottom of the page. She was constantly amazed that I could see that it was crooked, and I was amazed that she couldn't. We gained an understanding about this problem; however, your client may not be as lucky. It may be necessary to teach your client to make a quick measurement check after typing each paper.

2. **Windows.** As in the client with a visual discrimination problem, the client with a spatial problem can also use windows to his benefit. For example, if your client must fill out forms by writing in a small space, he could use a window made of light cardboard cut to the dimensions of the space. Likewise, if he has difficulty reading because of spatial problems, he could use a window to assist in reading.

Assembly/Packaging. Once again, it is difficult to give specific ideas because of the wide variety of jobs in this category. Some general ideas for modifications would include:

1. **Jigs.** Sometimes a jig could be made to assist the client. A jig is an object that is made to hold or guide work. For example, when stapling headers (the cardboard tops) onto plastic bags, the employer usually wants the staple to be located in a precise location. A jig to assist a client in this situation would be that the stapler is affixed to the table and a piece of wood is nailed to the table so that when the header is slipped into the stapler, it must stop at the exact location where the staple is to be.

A jig for material that has been collated could be a box with two sides cut away, so the client pushes the envelope into it until it touches the sides.

The only limit of the type of jig used is the creativity of the person making it. Rehabilitation engineers make jigs and modifications for a living, and can be called upon for assistance.

2. **Organize the work area.** As in the person with a visual discrimination problem, it will probably be necessary for you to organize his work area. I have seen clients with spatial and organizational problems make many unnecessary movements to accomplish a task. It is not uncommon to see a person reaching over the finished product in order to assemble an item.

3. **Hints or guides.** When assembling a box, for example, a client can identify which end to fold first by looking at a written guide on the box. The guide can be numbers or writing. For example, the name of the product may be written larger on the top than on the bottom, or the writing on the box is upside down when the bottom flap is folded first.

Visual Figure-Ground Modifications

Janitorial Work. A client with a severe visual figure-ground problem will have great difficulties on a janitorial job. He will be unable to pick out dirt from its background, especially in a rug with a pattern. Likewise, he will have difficulty when dusting. A trainer once worked with a client whose problem in this area was so severe that he held the broom a few inches off the ground when sweeping. Sometimes the term figure-ground is referred to as depth perception. Modifications that may help a client include:

1. **Touch and hand-over-hand.** For the client who was unable to sweep the floor, it was necessary to use his sense of touch to help him become aware of the area to be swept. It was necessary to exaggerate the movements of touching the broom to the floor. In his case, he was using a 36-inch push broom and was instructed to let it hit the floor then sweep. He was taught this motion by the hand-over-hand method, where the trainer placed her hands over his and practiced placing the broom on the floor a few times before sweeping.

2. **Verbalize.** In the example cited above, it was necessary to attach a short verbal instruction to assist him in performing the task correctly. For example, he was taught to say, "up...down...push...step...up...down,..." etc.. The first three commands were for his hands with the broom, and the last was for his feet. He eventually learned to sweep the floor with the expected quality; however, the training process was long.

3. **Clean everything.** Because the client has difficulty sorting a thing out from its background, it is necessary to clean everything. For example, if the client is unable to determine if there is a speck of dirt on a rug or table, then the entire rug or table should be cleaned to insure that the client cleans everything expected. You cannot rely on the client with a figure-ground problem to work with the quality expected if he is to use his judgment as to what he cleans. Remember that using this method will slow his work pace while improving his quality. Be sure to check with the employer as to his priorities.

Dishwashing. The client with a figure-ground problem will have difficulty performing all the required tasks on a dishwashing job. He will most likely have difficulties placing the dishes on the dish rack, sorting silverware from the flat rack (the flat dishwashing rack on which **all** silverware is placed); perhaps he will have difficulty fitting stacks of dishes onto shelves or tabletops. The trainer must realize that with a figure-ground problem, **the client may injure himself** by accidentally jabbing himself with a knife point, or dropping a plate or glass because he thought it was on the shelf correctly. The following modifications may help the client in the dishwashing job:

1. **Touch.** In order to place the dishes in the dish rack, you may want to teach the client to touch the back of the rack. Then as he brings his hands forward, he can feel the last row of prongs. He can then place the plate between the back and the prong that he is touching. When placing the second plate next to the first, he can use the first as a guide. This procedure will need to be followed until the dish rack is full. Remember, the client should work from the back to the front, placing the larger items in the back and the smaller in the front.

2. **Change the job method.** Many times changes in the work method can be made which help the client. For example, the client with the figure-ground problem facing a whole flat dish rack of silverware is overwhelmed at best. The most logical way to assist your client is to have him sort all the silver **before** it is to be washed, then he can place it in there in sections or wash each utensil individually (e.g. forks, then knives, then spoons, etc.). If the employer is agreeable to this method, it should help your client. If the employer insists otherwise, then it would be helpful to teach the client to start at the side of the dish rack and work inwards. He can move most of it to the side, leaving a small portion in the middle or side. **Be aware of safety hazards when handling sharp knives and forks.**

3. **Identifying a specific location for each item.** Sometimes, the dishwasher is required to place the clean dishes on a shelf or cart. If the shelf or cart does not have

sides on it, the client may not be aware that the dishes on the other side will fall off when he places one more stack of dishes on the shelf. Thus, accidents can occur. If the client has an established place for all items, then the opportunity for this occurring will not be as great. If the items will always be different, then make up a concrete number of items allowed on the shelf that he is not to go over. He may place five stacks of plates on the shelf, for example.

Bussing. The client with a figure-ground problem who is bussing may have difficulties, also. He may have difficulty determining when the bus pan is full, or where he can fit in just one more plate in the bus pan. Wiping off tables may be difficult for him as it is for the janitor listed above. Filling glasses or cups may present a problem, and maneuvering through a crowded room with a bus tray may be difficult for him. The following modifications may be helpful in working with the client on the job:

1. **Organization.** It will be important to help the client organize the job. During the training period, you will help him determine how many tables of dishes will fit into one bus pan. He will need to be shown where to place the items in the bus pan to allow for the best use of space. By teaching him these things, you are also teaching him to be safe.

2. **Hand-over-hand.** If the client is having difficulty learning the organization of the job, it may be necessary for you to place your hands on top of his and guide them in the correct motion.

3. **Clean the whole table.** The client needs to be taught to clean the whole table in order to make sure all the food and crumbs are removed. In food service, the entire surface should be cleaned each time anyway.

4. **Determine a path for the client.** If the client has trouble walking through the dining room with his bus pan, you may want to make him a route that he can follow. Once he gets used to his route, then he will be fine, until a table is placed in his way. When determining a route, consider that this may happen and try to make the route pass tables that will not be moved.

Laundry. The client with a visual figure-ground problem who works in a laundry will probably have difficulties folding. It will be difficult for the person to determine if he has folded evenly, because he will be looking at white with a white background. He may also have difficulty making neat stacks of folded items, especially if they are the same color. Some modifications that may help the client include:

1. **Match corners.** Perhaps the easiest way of making sure the corners match is to feel them. I have had laundry workers tell me it takes a lot more time to fold sheets if they are held at the corners. They insist that the sheets should be folded in half by holding them in the middle and dangling the corners. If you are in a position where the employer insists that you use their method, then you have no choice. I would explain to the employer that you are not sure the client's quality will be what he expects, but you will try it that way.

2. **Contrasting colors.** If the client is folding on a table, try placing a contrasting color on the table (with the employer's consent, of course). Be careful of the material that you use. If you choose to use construction paper, for example, the color may bleed onto the item you are folding and ruin it. You certainly would not want to paint the table, unless the employer suggested it. Perhaps the best thing to use is a piece of fabric that won't bleed.

Clerical. The clerical worker with a visual figure-ground problem will most likely have difficulty reading and proofreading. This would affect filing correctly, using a computer or typewriter, operating a copy machine, and operating a multiple line phone, for example. The following modifications may help the client with a visual figure-ground problem on a clerical job:

1. **Window.** If reading is necessary, perhaps a window could be used. A window can be made by cutting out the equivalent of a line of writing from a piece of cardboard or **plain** paper. The window is placed over the material to be read, blocking out all writing except the line to be read.

2. **Pull files up.** If the client is required to file and is having difficulty finding the correct file, he could be taught to pull the file about halfway out of the file drawer and then look at the label. By doing this, he will not be required to try to sort out one number from a drawer full of numbers when replacing the files.

3. **Type without looking at hands.** For the person with a figure-ground problem, attempting to type while looking at his hands would be terribly difficult. Therefore, he must learn to type without watching his hands, only by the sense of touch.

4. **Repetition.** Your client may be taught to operate a copy machine by repetition. He will probably succeed in learning the mechanics of which button to push for the correct number of copies. He may or may not learn how to refill the toner or fix the machine when a jam occurs.

5. **Find a co-worker willing to help.** If the client cannot seem to master a portion of the job, attempt to enlist the help of a co-worker who could help for that specific problem. For example, when the paper jams, the client could request assistance from this person.

Assembly/Packaging. The job duties would determine what, if any, problems the client would have on an assembly or packaging job. There are some general considerations that may help the client in this setting.

1. **Only necessary items at work station.** If the client's work station is cluttered with unnecessary items, the clutter may make it difficult for him to find the items he really needs. For example, if his job is to punch out a rectangular piece from a roll of paper, he should have a place to discard his scraps from the punch-out. If he leaves the scraps on the table, he could easily become confused and lose the product with which he is to be working.

2. **Keep work area neat.** Everything must have its place in the work area. In the example used above, he should keep the items he needs in special areas on his work table. They should be distinctly separated so they will be easily recognized.

3. **Contrast colors.** If the client is assembling brown objects on a brown table, he may have difficulty. However, if you were to place a white paper or cardboard on top of the table, he will be able to see the items easier.

Visual Closure

Janitorial Work. A client with a closure problem will most likely have difficulty determining if he has cleaned an entire surface. He may also have difficulty replacing all the objects, for example, he may leave off the object on the end. It will be necessary to use his sense of touch and some modifications where he can concentrate on remembering how many objects there are in all. The following modifications may help the client with this problem.

1. **Verbalize.** In order to help the client remember all the objects, it may be helpful to have him count the objects as he removes them from the table. He could also name the objects, if his memory is good enough to remember all the items. When he replaces the items, if he should have five and there are only four, then he would know to look for the other object.

2. **Place fingers over the sides of tabletops.** In order to insure that the client dusts the entire surface of the tabletop, he can be taught to place his fingers on the edges of the tabletop instead of only on the top. Of course, this applies only when the client is dusting near the top, bottom, or sides. When he is dusting in the middle, he should be taught to go from side to side and place his fingers over each edge when he reaches them. This technique not only insures that the entire top surface has been cleaned, but the sides are also cleaned in the process and you don't have to teach the client an extra step. This modification applies to anyone who must wipe off surfaces, whether in a janitorial or food service job or any other which requires this task to be completed.

3. **Bump'em method.** If the client has difficulty determining if he has cleaned an entire area, he can gently move his body or hands to help him see if he has cleaned all surfaces. Of course, he will need to be careful not to destroy any breakables or knock things onto the floor. This method was explained during the discussion for clients with visual spatial perceptual problems.

Dishwashing. The client with a severe closure problem may only partially fill the dish rack. He may make many stacks of dishes at the clean end of the machine, because he is unaware that there is already a stack of the same size plates. As mentioned for the janitorial client above, it is necessary to use modifications that utilize his sense of touch and help him memorize a system. Some assistance with his organization will be helpful.

1. **Teach by counting.** It may be necessary to determine how many plates can be placed side by side in a dish rack. Usually, two large plates fit on the same row. It will also be necessary to show him several other combinations of how plates and bowls fit. By showing him different combinations and teaching him that at least a certain number of plates, dishes, etc., can fit into a dish rack, he will be more aware of what he is doing.

2. **Arrange plates by size.** When stacking plates at the clean end of the machine, teach the client to arrange them by sizes. By doing this, he should not create a mass of small stacks but, instead, several piles of plates of like sizes.

3. **Use hands to clean the sides of a table.** As in modification number 2 for the janitorial client, the sense of touch can be used effectively. By feeling for the edge of a table, his touch can assist in making the decision as to whether he has placed the item on or near the table edge. This modification should help his awareness.

Bussing. The client with a closure problem will most likely have difficulty determining if all the items are off the table and if he has included all items when setting the table. As in the other occupations, modifications will center around his sense of touch and his organization.

1. **Divide and conquer.** If the client is aware of only a portion of the table, he can be taught to section the table in fourths, for example. Sometimes this can be accomplished by using the folds in the table linen. If there is no tablecloth, then perhaps the space can be divided according to the chairs. The area in front of a chair is the area to be cleaned.

2. **Count.** If the client neglects to place a utensil, for example, then he can be taught how many are to be placed at each setting. When the place is set, he can count the utensils to make sure he has not forgotten any.

3. **Verbalize.** As in the modification above, the client can be taught the name of the item and this can be combined with counting. For example, "little fork, big fork, napkin, knife, round spoon, long spoon." If that is too involved, it can be shortened to "two forks, one knife, and two spoons."

Laundry. The client with a closure problem will probably not have as difficult time performing job tasks in a laundry as he would in a janitorial or food service job. The client would be working with rather large objects as a whole, not single items that placed together make the whole. If the client is having problems, the trainer should refer to modifications listed previously in this chapter.

Clerical. The client with a visual closure problem would most likely have problems in a clerical job. Filing, typing and any other tasks involving reading or identifying information as a whole would be difficult. My experience with clients with this problem on clerical jobs is not extensive. However, the clients with whom I have worked tired of the modifications and after a period of time used them only sporadically. When this happened, the work quality deteriorated accordingly. Thus, my advice would be to either find a job with different duties, or incorporate a contract to follow the modifications with your follow-up services.

1. **Use a window.** As in the suggested modifications presented earlier in this chapter, I suggest that you try using a window. By blocking out the visual information on the page that you do not want the client to see, he may better be able to see the whole words rather than just the beginning, for example.

2. **Point and verbalize.** In order to assist the client to read the entire word, it may be helpful to have him point to each letter and say it aloud or softly to himself.

3. **Comparing.** When filing, for example, it is helpful to point to both the word on the paper to be filed and the word on the file. You may also want to add the verbal component as in the previous modification and have the client say the letters aloud. By using this technique, hopefully the papers for "Stroud" will not be filed with "Strong."

Assembly/Packaging. As in other occupations, it will be necessary to use techniques that involve the sense of touch and organization. Numbering steps or parts may be helpful. Using an uncluttered work area may also be helpful for the person with a closure problem. For additional ideas, look at the modifications listed above and see if any are applicable to your client's job.

Visual Memory and Visual Sequential Memory

The modifications for this area are similar for all jobs. If a client has difficulty remembering the job duties, supplies, work schedule, layout of the facility, the modifications will be the same. They vary only in what you place on the checklists and where you might post them. For that reason, **the modifications will not be listed by occupation.**

1. **Checklist.** Checklists are perhaps the most popular modification used for clients who have difficulty remembering all aspects of their jobs. Perhaps the reason they are so popular is that most people use checklists at some point in their life. Grocery lists are prime examples of checklists and are an accepted method of helping one remember what they are to buy at the store. Because checklists are so widely used, it is only natural to use them with the client. Different types of checklists were discussed earlier in this chapter along with some hints of materials to use.

2. **Diagrams.** Diagrams are a form of written instruction that shows the client the different steps to accomplishing a task. This was also discussed earlier in this chapter.

3. **Step-by-step instructions.** Sometimes clients become confused when a multistep job is presented all at once. Most clients learn the job at a quicker rate and remember the steps in sequence better when they are presented step-by-step. By using this method, the client is able to practice each step before learning a new one.

4. **Repetition.** Most clients remember multistep jobs after they have performed the job for a period of time. Checklists may be needed at first but may not be necessary after the client has repeated the job for several weeks or months.

5. **Verbalize.** Some clients find it easier to remember the steps of a job if they repeat them to themselves. This technique helps them to concentrate and focus attention on the job. You can use key words the client needs to remember when performing the job. These words can be numbers of the tasks or descriptive words (e.g. in, over, under, top) that you and your client decide describe the job tasks.

6. **Close eyes when teaching.** In extreme cases, it may be necessary to withdraw all visual stimulation when teaching a new task. I once worked with a man who needed to spell some words in order to be successful on a job. Due to several visual perceptual problems and his visual sequential memory problem, it was necessary to teach him to spell with his eyes closed. In addition, it was necessary to have him write the words with his finger on the table. He was successful in learning to spell several words using this method. This is an extreme case, one that you would rarely see.

Eye-Hand Coordination

The modifications for a client with eye-hand coordination problems are similar in each job. They can be adapted to be used with any job in which the client is working. The comments about the specific jobs will be made first, then the modifications will be listed.

Janitorial. If your client has an eye-hand coordination problem, he is in the wrong job. He will have difficulty dusting, sweeping, vacuuming, mopping, washing windows and mirrors, and mixing chemicals. He may also be what some people call **accident prone** and break things or run into things with the vacuum, broom, and mop. Modifications may be helpful if the client cleans the same **exact** items every day in the same location within the same room. If that **consistency** can be maintained, then there is hope. If he cleans a different area each day with different items to be dusted, then he may have difficulty. Your job as a trainer will be to **teach the client where things are in the room** and how to maneuver around them. Your client will probably be able to learn the job with repetition and training time.

Dishwashing. A dishwasher with an eye-hand coordination problem is in a similar situation to a janitor. He may misjudge where the plates belong in the rack. Likewise, he may reach into the soaking liquid where the silverware is and cut himself on a knife. Since the dishwasher is in the same location and the job has consistency, it is usually possible to teach the client the job tasks. It takes time and patience. The same considerations should be used as were listed for the janitor job. You would need to show him how to use the sprayer, for example. (You may want to wear old clothes or a rain slicker that day!)

Busser. The table busser will use the same considerations listed above. It will be important to teach him to have deliberate movements and to organize the silver, for example, when he removes it from the table so it doesn't fall off the plate.

Laundry Worker. The laundry worker quite often folds by touch. If your client is able to use the sense of touch only, then he should not have great difficulty learning his job.

Clerical. I once worked with a client who was unable to type faster than about fifteen words per minute. She explained to me that she could "see the words, but it just won't come out my fingers right." This is a classic eye-hand problem. In her case, it was necessary to recommend that she pursue another occupation, because the problem she had would prevent her from ever typing at a speed that employers require for clerical workers. I feel that a client with a problem in this area will not perform well on clerical tasks of typing and filing. The client would do better running a copy machine or delivering inter-office mail.

Assembly/Packaging. The trainer would need to evaluate the specific job to determine the appropriateness for the client. Some jobs can be taught to the client with an eye-hand problem; some are more difficult.

Modifications for Visual-Motor Problems

1. **Organize the job.** It will be necessary for you to organize the job for your client. By doing this, you can control what he learns first. You will probably want to proceed slowly, because you will have to teach him in a deliberate manner.

2. **Hand-over-hand.** In order to teach the specific task, it may be necessary to place your hand on top of his and teach him how to move it. For example, when teaching him to dust a table, you will need to guide his hand to show him the motions he should use. It may be necessary to do this with each item with which he is going to work.

3. **Verbalizing.** The client may be able to learn the job by using key phrases as were mentioned in the previous section on visual memory.

4. **Repetition.** Repeat the steps of the job with the client until he remembers them. It will be necessary to correct any errors immediately after they are made so he does not learn incorrect techniques through practice.

Auditory Modifications
and Teaching Techniques

If your client has a problem processing information he hears, the best thing you can do to assist him to learn new job tasks is **not to talk to him.** When you do talk to him, which will happen, use short phrases, making sure that he understands what you are saying.

When teaching him new job tasks, it will be necessary to use the visual teaching techniques discussed in the previous section and the motor techniques discussed in the next section of this chapter. If the client has difficulties in all three learning channels, then you will probably need to use a combination of all three methods of teaching. Therefore, it will be necessary for you to become familiar with the modifications and teaching methods listed throughout this chapter and use those that apply to your client.

There is one modification that must be mentioned in this section, as it is useful for clients with **auditory figure-ground problems.** When a client has difficulty blocking out background noise, wearing **earplugs** can be of great help. I have had clients who were so distractible that the slightest noise caused a lapse in concentration. Once provided earplugs, they were able to relax and focus their attention on the important matters at hand. Earplugs will allow the wearer to hear voices or conversations while they muffle other noises like air vents, cars outside a window, a T.V. in the next room.

There are several kinds of earplugs available. Some have a little plastic cord that connects them, so during breaks, the wearer just lets them hang around his neck. There is also a kind made out of foam that conforms to the inside of the ear. Earplugs can be purchased in industrial supply houses as well as discount stores and stores that sell guns and other noisy items that can damage ears.

I usually have several kinds that I present to a client. Remember that you are working with an individual with his own tastes. Preferences in earplugs vary with the individual, just as they do in clothes or shoes. Some clients will be interested in the cosmetic effect, while others look for comfort. Some are washable and reusable, and some are disposable.

Motor Modifications and Teaching Techniques

The techniques found in this section will be needed if the client is having difficulty gaining the speed required on the job, if the client is having difficulty coordinating his hand movements, and/or having difficulty performing motor tasks on the job. As in the other learning channels, a client with a severe motor problem should be working in a job that does not require the use of his hands to perform the major job task.

The following modifications can be used with a variety of motor problems, i.e. fine finger dexterity, gross motor, bi-manual, midline, motor sequencing. These modifications can also assist your client to learn what the word **fast** means in relation to the job. Usually, the client has to be taught this concept which is abstract. He may grunt and groan, but without adequate speed, he stands a good chance of failing in the job.

By observing your client performing his job duties, you may discover that he is unable to work at an acceptable pace in a consistent manner. He may have the **ability** to do the task and work at the rate expected without prompting but is unable to actually work at his ability level. You may discover that the client is able to keep up with a job if the **job duties dictate the speed** at which to work, but he is **unable to initiate** the required work pace on his own.

I worked with a client once who had this problem. He worked in a factory and was required to assemble an object. He had the potential to perform the job well, but he sat alone and faced what seemed like a never-ending pile of materials to assemble. I tried all modifications I could think of to help him learn to pace himself, all without success. The factory had a packaging machine that he was able to work on at times. His job was to take the finished product off the machine after it was packaged. The job (machine) dictated the speed to him and he was able to keep up. He was transferred to this work station and became successful on the job.

In the interest of space and your reading time, the modifications will be listed with any comments regarding specific jobs listed in that section.

1. **Hand-over-hand.** This technique has been discussed in previous sections. If the client is having difficulty learning the job task initially, it may be necessary to guide his hands to **show** them how to work. In order to do this, you must place your hands on top of the client's and move them in the direction you want them to go.

WARNING: **Never** stand behind a client without first telling him your intentions to do so. Some clients do not like to have anyone stand behind them, especially if the person is going to touch him!

Hand-over-hand is helpful when teaching a client to apply pressure, for example, showing a client how to use the right amount of pressure to sweep a floor, dust, or wipe a table clean. This technique is also useful for teaching the motion necessary to complete a job task. For example, the motions required to clean a mirror are side-to-side, and the motions to mop a floor are the **figure eight,** i.e. to move the mop sideways in the motion of the figure eight. For a dishwasher, it may be necessary to use the hand-over-hand technique to teach the use of pressure when cleaning pots and pans. Laundry workers quite often need to be shown the tremendous amount of pressure necessary in order to stuff all the sheets into the washer, as well as the actual tasks of folding the laundry. Clerical workers need to be shown how to fit files into full file drawers.

2. **Step-by-step.** Sometimes clients learn best by the repetition of the hand movements. It is quite often necessary to have the client repeat a step until it is learned, then add the next one, repeat the two, then add the next and so on. The manner in which the information is presented, whether through the visual or auditory channel, depends on the learning style of the client.

3. **Pacing with an individual.** There are several ways of assisting a client to improve his speed. The first we will discuss is using another individual, usually the trainer and sometimes a co-worker. The trainer will work next to or across the table from the client and have the client attempt to keep up with her. Depending on the intellectual and functioning level of the client, you can race with the client. I do caution you not to get too **gimicky,** because the client may only improve if there is a game. You want him to improve even without the game.

If it is possible to arrange, you may want to ask the employer if your client's work station could be placed next to a fast worker. Quite often, employers do this anyway, but if you think it could help keep your client moving quickly, it couldn't hurt to ask. If it is impossible to have the client sit next to the person, then try to position your client so he can see the co-worker. You will want to make sure that the client is not sitting next to someone who moves so quickly as to discourage him so that he gives up.

4. **Verbal pacing.** Verbal pacing can be extremely helpful in working with a client. In addition to teaching the client how fast he must work, you are also focusing his concentration on his job. When using this technique, you will want to choose short words or phrases and give one to each movement. For example, when attempting to build speed with a laundry worker, we attached numbers to the folds. I said the numbers aloud and his job was to keep up with me. Of course, when you do this you will not start off at the final speed expected. You should start at the speed at which he is able to work, then increase your pace slowly. This can be extremely frustrating for the client, especially if you continue to count for a long period of time. I usually will count for a while, then stop and see if the client can maintain the speed without the extra stimulation. If the client has some behavioral problems and verbalizes his dislike for you and your methods, you may want to tell him that when he is able to reach the speed necessary and maintain it, that you will not have to use the methods anymore. Sometimes this helps tremendously.

5. **Pacing with a timer.** Timers are extremely helpful when working with a client who needs to increase his speed. Two ways you can use the timer are presented in this section. First, show the client what you expect him to accomplish in a short amount of time, e.g. ten minutes. Set the timer and check him at the end of the time. Your instructions may be, "I want you to finish this pile before the timer goes off." This is effective on janitorial jobs, dishwashing (although somewhat harder because each bus pan has a different amount of dishes with a different amount of food stuck to them), bussing (the problems are similar to dishwashing), laundry, clerical (for filing, for example), and assembly/packaging work.

The second method you can use with a timer, which is not as effective because it is not as concrete, is to set the timer and see how much he can accomplish in the set period. Your instructions may be, "See how much you can get done in ten minutes."

There are several kinds of timers available on the market. I prefer to use the kitchen timer with the dial as opposed to a digital timer. The client can see the dial moving at a glance and can tell if there is a lot or a little time left. Also, it is easy to put a mark on the timer where the client should set it before he starts a task. Thus, he can use the timer without your assistance. Digital timers are also being manufactured and can be helpful, if the client has good number skills. There are digital timers that count down as well as count up.

6. **Watch co-workers.** If you are having difficulty figuring out a method that could help your client work more quickly, you could watch the co-workers and find the one that works with the most fluidity and observe that person. This might give

you some clues as to the most efficient method to use to help your client. (Co-workers are discussed in depth in Chapter 8.)

7. **Organizing the work area.** Sometimes a client's speed will increase when the work area is organized to allow him the maximum efficiency. Always be aware of the handedness of your client. Most jobs are arranged for right-handed people. If your client is left-handed, you will need the work area reversed.

If your client has a midline problem, his work area will need to be arranged accordingly. He will need everything placed in front of him if he is to work on tasks bimanually, and he will need verbal reminders from you to use both hands. Most likely, he will be unable to use both hands simultaneously, but will be able to use one then the other.

If your client has a touch sensitivity problem, he should be aware of where the materials are for the job. He should not be working with objects that could be dangerous to him.

8. **Counters and goals.** Counters and goals can be used to help the client become aware of how many of the product he has assembled. I must caution you in the use of the counter, because it has the potential of **slowing the client's work pace.** For example, a client is to count the number of products he has assembled. He is provided a tally counter. (I am familiar with two kinds: hand-held and one that sits on a table and can be affixed to the table with screws.) As he places the completed product into the box for completed items, he hits the counter handle and it tallies one. You can use the tally counter to set goals, e.g. he must complete 100 before break, 200 before lunch, etc..

For some clients this is an excellent method of helping increase the speed. For others, they become too involved in the novelty of the counter and use exaggerated movements to hit the counter lever. Some clients tend to look at the number on the counter after each click, and sometimes a client may forget to hit the lever, thus giving an inaccurate count.

Before deciding that this is the modification you want to use permanently, be sure you have observed the client closely with the counter, that he is accurate, and that he is not spending extra time playing with it.

Language Modifications and Techniques

If your client has a language problem, you should already be aware of the amount and type of verbal communication you should use. You should have discovered this from the client assessment.

As I have mentioned throughout the book, it is necessary to communicate with the client on his own language level. For example, you will not want to discuss the physical properties of an object or the comparison of computer languages with a mentally retarded client.

When working with a client who has a language problem, it will be necessary to use other learning channels when teaching him jobs. You will want to use visual cues and modifications involving motor activities. Please see those sections in this chapter for ideas.

Planning and Organization Modifications

Modifications for the client with difficulty planning and organizing time, space, motor movements, and his personal day can be the influencing factor in whether or not your client retains the job. The success of the modifications depend on your creativity and ability to pinpoint the problem. There are several aspects to planning and organization that will be discussed.

Time Concepts

A client without a sense of time will have great difficulty comprehending what speed is. He also may have difficulty telling when it is break or lunchtime or time to go home. The client may also sit down to lunch during the morning break on an eight-hour job. (Issues regarding time in relation to getting to work on time will be discussed in the section about the personal day.)

If the client is having difficulty telling when to go on break, the obvious thing is to have him follow a co-worker to break. This works fine as long as there are co-workers around. But what about the client who works independently on a cleaning job, for example? Before the question is answered, let us think through the problem and determine the type of modification to use.

1. He can't tell time.

2. Why? Time is an abstract concept. You cannot touch it or manipulate it. It cannot be seen or heard. To a person with mental retardation or brain damage, if it is not real it is not understood.

3. Can he be taught? Consider the special education high school student or graduate. Teachers have most likely spent at least twelve years attempting to teach this concept. If they were not successful, the chances of your ability to do so in a short period of time are slim to none.

4. Does he know numbers? The answer to this question may be yes. If it is, he has a positive skill.

5. Does he know numbers in relation to other numbers? Does he know that 25 comes before 30, or 33 is after 30? If he does, consider both of you lucky, the client because he has another skill, and you, because it will be easier to make modifications. If he has this skill, you could probably use a digital watch and tell him to watch for a certain time. If he can identify numbers but they have no meaning, you are wasting time asking him to compare numbers. If he misses the exact number, he has another twelve hours to go before it comes back! He won't be able to say, "It's 11:33

and I was supposed to clock in at 11:30." What he will say is, "It's 11:33." If he doesn't have this skill, read on.

6. What is the real problem? Something is going to have to tell him the time. You cannot rely on him or a co-worker to determine the time of day. Perhaps the easiest and most socially acceptable modification in a situation like this is a digital watch with an alarm. In this age of electronics, they are now manufacturing a watch with at least five alarms that can be set during one day. Thus, you could set them at break, lunch, end of lunch, afternoon break, and going-home time. They also make watches with countdown alarms that warn you that the alarm is about to go off. It may also be necessary to incorporate other methods with this. For example, a chart with the time and a picture of what he is to do. He can compare the time and drink a soda pop, eat lunch, or go home. You may also need to have a kitchen timer that he can set for the ten-minute breaks so he knows when to go back to work.

Speed

Teaching a client the concept of speed is difficult. Usually, when a client is in a new job setting, it is so overwhelming that the client is spending all his effort trying to fit into the setting. However, you must be always aware of his work pace, as most clients are paid by the hour. If your client never gains enough speed, he may be fired so the employer can hire someone who will pay for himself. Therefore, it is up to you to help him increase his speed.

Modifications to assist a client in improving his speed are found in the section on motor modifications. Speed is directly related to how fast a client can manipulate his hands and how his work area and job task methods are organized. Organizing the method and area will be discussed in this section.

Organizing the job task method. The job task method should be organized in such a manner that when the client works on the job, there is a flow to his work. For example, if he is to assemble an item, then package it with an instruction sheet into a plastic bag with a header, he should start with the assembly work. You should always remember that **the more times an object is handled, the more time that takes and the slower the client works.** Usually, the employer has already worked out the most efficient method and may insist that you teach your client that specific method. However, there are times that the employer is working with a new product and he is not yet sure how he wants it to be done. I worked with one employer who designed the product but had no idea how to assemble it in an efficient manner.

As mentioned earlier in this manual, it is wise to look around the work area and find the person who appears to be working the quickest and with the smoothest movements. Examine how the co-worker has organized the job task. Does he make a pile of the product and then assemble them, or does he assemble and package all in one string of motion? Sometimes this will depend on the amount of materials needed for each part of the operation. It may be a more practical use of space to assemble for an hour and then package for an hour.

While watching the co-worker, notice the position of the hands. How is the product held? Are the fingertips used only, or the whole hand?

I learned about labeling from my client's co-workers. When working with **labels** that were printed on computers, tear approximately one-fourth to one-half of the backing off the back. This is usually a fairly easy procedure. You grab the top corner of the backing and pull it away from you so that it tears the backing only.

When it is time to affix the stickers, it is easy to grab four at a time, one with each finger, except the thumb. Then they can be placed on the products one at a time quickly and efficiently, beginning with either the index or pinky finger and using each in turn. I have seen people place stickers on their forearms with half of the sticker off the arm. When applying the stickers, they took one or two off their arm from the bottom to the top.

While organizing the work method, watch the client closely for awkward movements. Most clients won't realize that if the object is turned slightly, or if the supplies are shifted slightly, the materials would be much easier to reach. You need to teach your client to do this.

Organizing one's materials is critical to working efficiently. If a client is continually going to the storage room to get supplies, he is not working efficiently. **Checklists** for materials help the client to organize himself for the workday.

If there is only **one** thing you can do for your client to help him succeed on his job, organizing him is the obvious choice. If he doesn't work in an efficient manner, he will lose his job.

Organizing the work station. The organization of the work station is also critical to the client working efficiently. It is imperative that the client not reach over finished work to get the supplies to do the job. In a **janitorial** job, it is important that the client work in an organized manner, otherwise valuable time will be wasted. The client should be taught to work in either a clockwise or counterclockwise direction from the door when dusting. Thus, he begins and ends at the door. Should he decide to skip around the room, he will most likely have some difficulties remembering if he has completed all the job tasks.

A **dishwasher's** efficiency depends upon his ability to organize the area as well as the sequence of the job tasks. For example, each job has its own peculiarities as far as what items are needed. Mid-morning in a coffee shop will require that the dishwasher always make cups, saucers, and spoons a priority. Lunch or dinner in the same place may require the silverware to be washed often. Once the priority item(s) have been determined, then it is the trainer's responsibility to insure that a method is being used to insure the priority items are being cleaned regularly. Sometimes this must be made concrete for the client. When there is a specific amount of silverware in the soaking pan, then the silver should be washed. Sometimes it needs to be more concrete than that, and the client should be instructed that after he sends three dish racks, for example, through the dishwasher, he must do silver.

Sometimes this type of modification must be made when the client forgets about the clean end of the machine and continues washing, forgetting about the dish racks coming out the other end of the machine. The trainer must decide how many dish racks can sit at the clean end of the machine without having any stuck in the dishwasher. Then the client can be trained to send only that amount through without stopping to unload the dish racks. This is extremely important to teach the client, because if the dish racks become backed up in some machines, the client runs the risk of **breaking the machine.**

The dishwasher should have everything within easy reach without having to take more than a couple of steps. That is, the empty dish racks, the glass and cup racks, the silverware soak, etc., should all be within an arm's reach. If the kitchen is not organized this way, then you should attempt to organize the area for the client.

For the **busser,** the table is always a mess and no two are ever left looking the same. He must be organized in the method of taking things off the table. Some restaurants have rigid guidelines that they want followed. The glasses come off the table first, as they are usually fragile and easily knocked over. The plates are placed in a certain place in the pan, as is the silverware. Some restaurants want the plates scraped at the table, some in the kitchen. Follow the requirements of the employer and that will help in organizing the client.

Laundries are usually fairly well organized. When your client starts a job in a laundry, he will usually be assigned to folding. He just picks the next article out of the bin and folds. As he becomes more at ease in the job, he will assume more duties, and they will be taught with the organizational methods used by the co-workers.

Clerical workers must be organized in their approach to jobs. When filing, for example, the client should not be reaching over the stack of items to be filed in order to reach the drawer. If the client is working on a mail route within a place of business, then his route should be a logical one. He should also use the same route on a consistent basis. I once worked with a client who had a physical impairment, cerebral palsy, and had a pronounced limp and held her hand to her chest due to hemiplegia. She held the stack of mail in her affected arm and, as she walked on her mail route, it tended to slip. She would hoist it up with her other arm, but as she did so, the mail would become mixed up and consequently would end up in the wrong mailbox. The modification for this problem was to provide her with an accordion-folded file box (without a lid). She labeled each section with the names of the staff, in the order of her mail route, and when she sorted the mail, she sorted it into the file box. When she started on her mail route, she picked up the box and was on her way. She mentioned at a later time that she liked the file box very much, as she thought that she looked more **important** when she carried it.

Social Perception or Judgment-Making Modifications

Attempting to come up with specific modifications for this area is difficult at best. The reason is that no two social situations or individuals are the same; thus the number of situations that your client may encounter are infinite. So much communication in our culture depends on subtle non-verbal messages. We learn to interpret these messages as children by parents explaining the incident. After this happens several times, the child tends to generalize to other situations. The client with whom you will be working most likely thinks in concrete terms and is unable to understand the abstract subtleties of a given situation.

Likewise, our clients quite often do not understand the cause-and-effect relationship. They do not understand that their actions may cause negative reactions in others. For example, a client who insists on sleeping to the last minute and arrives late may not understand that his behavior is likely to cause him to lose his job. Another example of this problem is the client who insists on performing a job task **his** way is likely to be reprimanded. He may argue that his method was fine since the finished product looks the way it should. The problem is that it may have taken him an extra five steps to complete the job.

For this reason, it is up to you to interpret the environment in which the client is working. It will be necessary for you to teach him appropriate responses to situations that arise while you are working with him as well as give him guidelines to use while you are not there. For example, one of my clients worked in a rather high pressure situation. She was capable of doing the job and she worked steadily at it. The supervisor became nervous during the stress periods and was concerned about giving quick service to the customers. He would raise his voice at the staff during this time, yelling for a specific person to work quicker. After a few days on the job with the client, it was apparent to me that he was holding back on yelling at my client, for whatever reason. I realized that sooner or later it would be her turn to receive his stress, so I attempted to prepare her for it. I started pointing out that he got like this almost everyday, when there were many customers. I also pointed out that he wanted to make the customers happy which made him nervous and that caused him to yell. I then pointed out that her co-workers were working hard and as fast as they could, but he was still nervous.

The day finally came that he yelled at her. She took it hard, but I pointed out that there was no way that she could make the machinery go faster, and he wasn't really mad at her but at the machines. After consoling her a few more times, she could better understand him and his way of handling his stress.

Work Rules

One modification I have used since working with my first client is **work rules**. Anyone who has ever worked with me chuckles when work rules are mentioned. Work rules are common rules that you and I know about work. A good worker is on time to work, works instead of talking, stays at his work station, etc.. When I have a client that needs to work on a goal, instead of saying, "your goals should be...," I prefer to say, "a work rule is...." The term **goal** is used often in schools in the classroom. Of course, it is also used in jobs, but I prefer to relate the goal with work and thus use the term **work rules**.

Some examples of work rules include:

- Use both hands while working.
- Always work as fast as you can.
- Do not sit with _____ because you had problems with her.
- Keep your mouth closed while chewing.
- You may only wipe the table one time (this helps prevent wiping the same spot six times).
- Do what your supervisor tells you.
- Use your checklist.
- Choose your work clothes the night before.
- Look at the supervisor when talking.
- Wear your hairnet (earplugs, etc.).
- Go to bed at 10:00 P.M.

When making work rules, you simply figure out the areas in which your client is having difficulty then make a work rule for the problem. **I consider that any problem the client has that affects his ability to maintain his job is subject to a work rule.** This could include anything from washing clothes and body to breaks and lunch to performing the actual job duties and communicating with supervisors and co-workers. Remember that **most clients lose jobs for reasons other than their ability to perform the actual job.**

For example, a client had difficulty dealing with personnel during lunch. She insisted on sitting with professional staff and monopolizing the conversation. She was finally given a work rule of not being allowed to sit with those people. If that behavior would have continued, she may have lost her job.

Likewise, clients who perseverate while cleaning can be given several work rules. A common rule is that you only clean things one time. Another may be that he starts cleaning with a specific room or place in a room, in order to help him become consistent in his work.

I never give a work rule unless it is necessary, and I have had quite a few clients who never had to be given work rules. If the list of rules is long, I may only give a few at the beginning and add more as some of those are accomplished. You will not want to overload the client with a long list, as he will feel overloaded and defeated. When expanding the list, it is wise not to remove the rules already learned. That way the client is constantly reminded that he needs to maintain what he has learned, and it can help boost his self-esteem because he has been successful. If the client is extremely sensitive to negative criticism, I may include some rules that the client has already achieved or has never had as a problem. This lets the client know he is doing some things right.

Work rules should be written, either in words or pictures, in language and vocabulary levels understood by the client. Whenever possible and time permits, I have the client write them. He then owns the rules and should understand them.

Frustration Tolerance

Working with a client who has a low tolerance for frustration is also frustrating for the trainer. There is a fine line as to how far the client can be pushed for the speed required for the job, for example. When the trainer reminds the client to work quickly, the client may answer with, "I'm doing the best I can. If you want it done faster, you do it!" This obviously is not the response trainer is seeking, but it's the one that was given. What do you do as the trainer?

There are many responses you could give and many ways of delivering the response. You could yell back, but that probably would not be productive. (You may feel like yelling, however, you need to exert self-control.) You could not respond and walk away, ignoring the behavior. You could respond with a positive response such as, "I realize that there is a lot of pressure and this job is not easy. You have been doing a good job and working hard. It is important for you to know that you must keep working as quickly as you can." I tend and like to give responses such as the last, if the client's personality lends itself to that type of response.

Some clients would take that response as a signal that it is alright to talk that way. For the client who would learn negative behaviors from that response, it may be necessary to discuss the behavior with them, away from the work station. If the behavior continues and seems to be an ongoing problem, I would give him a work rule about not displaying this attitude.

Another way that you can help your clients deal with their frustrations is to **pitch in and assist them during the rush periods.** That way, the frustration will not build up. As the client learns more and more of his job, you will help less until he is working independently. By assisting the client during those periods, he is more able to concentrate on the job duties he is performing rather than his mounting frustration.

Obviously, if his inability to handle his frustration interferes too much, it might be necessary to remove him from the job, if he isn't fired first. Sometimes, clients who exhibit behavior problems learn from experiences of losing jobs as a result of those behaviors. There is a saying in the field of rehabilitation that, **"Our clients should be given the same opportunities to succeed or fail on a job as anyone else. They also have the same opportunity to learn from their successes and failures."** I truly believe this and have seen clients grow from losing a job. The investment in the next job is much bigger and the client will work harder to make it succeed. This does not mean that every client should fail at a job. Not every client must go through that experience to grow.

The best advice I can give you is to know your client, his frustration point, and how he responds to a variety of interactions. By knowing your client in this manner, you will be more successful on the job.

Diet

Diet is extremely important in the functioning of an individual. In the past few years, there has been quite a bit written about nutrition. If you find your client has slump periods during the day, it may be caused by his diet. I have worked with many clients whose breakfast consists of a soda pop or who don't eat breakfast at all. Some clients say they would eat breakfast, but they get up too late. Although there is not too much you can do about this problem, you may discuss the problem with a family member, or you could make a work rule that he must eat breakfast.

Lunches are also important. The client who eats no breakfast and has only a soda pop and a bag of chips for lunch is not going to be in the best shape to perform his job duties in the afternoon. You can monitor lunches, although you really have no control over what the client brings for lunch. It is possible to encourage him to bring a well-balanced lunch by withholding work privileges.

If your client is heavy and he is performing a physical job, you may suggest that he go on a diet. In our program, one of our Down's syndrome clients is going to a nationally known diet program in order to lose weight. The trainer reports an increase in stamina and ability to perform his job tasks with greater ease.

Although you do not have much control in the area of diet and nutrition, you can make suggestions based on work performance.

Attention-Seeking Behaviors

Attention-seeking behaviors can cause a client to lose a job. Some clients are so used to being the center of attention at home, school, or church that they have a hard time dealing with not receiving the attention they are used to and want. Probably the most effective way to deal with this type of problem is to use a **behavioral program.** This is an area in which many books have been written. Courses are given in behavior modification at colleges and universities in the education department and sometimes in the psychology department. I do not pretend to be an expert on behavioral programs, however, I do know the basics and have used these techniques for years.

For the purpose of this manual, a behavioral program is a program that is designed to change one or more negative behaviors that are interfering with the client's ability to adequately peform his job duties or maintain his job. I will discuss the simple programs that I have devised that have worked with my clients. The following suggestions can be used with any behavioral problem. I usually try the easiest method first (work rules), then work into the more complex. The less complicated the program, the better the client will understand it and the chances of success are greater.

In order to determine the most effective method to use with your client, it will be necessary to assess the severity of the problem, the expected response to different methods, the people affected by the problem, and who needs to be involved in the implementation. I try not to involve the employer, if possible. He is usually a busy person who does not need or want to become involved in extra work with your client. Another reason to not involve the employer, especially if it is necessary to use a behavioral program at the beginning of the employment, is that he may be frightened or unsure of what working with this client for a long time may be like. I definitely would involve the employer if the client has been working for a period of time and the employer is concerned and would like to learn to manage the client on his own. This is really dependent upon your judgment of the situation.

The first type of behavioral program would be the **work rules** discussed earlier in this chapter. This would be viewed as an incomplete behavioral plan by some, however, I believe that if the simple things work, there is no need to introduce complex methods. For the person who interrupts, a work rule is that he may not talk while others are talking. Likewise, for the client who asks numerous questions, he would be allowed to ask a question only one time during the day, for example.

For some clients who interrupt quite often, ask unnecessary questions, or ask for help when they really do not need it, **ignoring** may be helpful. Before starting a program in which you will ignore your client, be sure you have explained to him what you intend to do. I usually tell the client that he does not need to ask a question over and over, and I will answer it only one time. After that, I will not answer him and will probably walk away from him when he does that.

For ongoing serious behaviors, I will write a **contract** between the client, myself, and employer, if necessary. Usually this is necessary for the client who is an excellent manipulator and will push you. A sample behavioral contract may look like this:

I, _____, realize that the following behaviors are keeping me from doing a good job. I also realize that if I don't stop these behaviors, I may lose my job. The behaviors I must change are:

- talking while working. I may only talk about work when it is necessary. For example, I may ask for supplies.
- interrupting. I may only talk to people on break when they are not talking.
- taking extra breaks. I may use the restroom and get drinks only during break time.

_____

Client Signature   Job Trainer Signature

_____

Date

Anything can be included in the contract with your client. It must be written to meet your needs at the time. You could add a reward for performing well, for example, a soda pop at break or lunch. If you do offer rewards, I would caution you on several things. First, only offer a reward such as I mentioned above as a last resort. Eventually, the client will need to exhibit those behaviors without the reward. Sometimes it is hard to end the reward system. The second thing to remember is that the reward should be age-appropriate (i.e. not happy faces or stickers) or something an adult or person his age would want. For a teenager, a tape may be appropriate, for example. Never get toys or things that will encourage immature behavior.

Compulsivity

Work rules tend to help the compulsive person work quicker. Rules such as you may only touch the item one time, or you may only wipe an area one time, are helpful. If you introduce work rules like those mentioned, be prepared to stand over your client and supervise him, reminding him to only touch once. You may want to arrange with the client how he wants you to remind him. Sometimes it can be done verbally, other times a touch to the elbow. Whatever works for you and your client is acceptable.

Pacing and timers also can help people who are compulsive about their work. Please see the section in this chapter on motor modifications for descriptions on implementation.

Distractibility

The environment is important to the person who is distractible. I once worked with a client who was highly distracted by visual stimuli. His work station faced the busiest walkway in the work area, where supervisors and suppliers were constantly walking in front of him. Once his work area was changed to an area in a corner facing a wall, his work improved greatly.

For the client who is distracted by auditory stimuli, earplugs are a great help. There are different kinds described in the auditory section of this chapter.

Sometimes clients are distracted by inner thoughts. For these clients, a radio with a set of earphones is sometimes helpful. If you find the client is into the music more than his work, then this modification must be discontinued.

Perseveration

Work rules help the client who perseverates. As in the compulsive person, you must stand over the client to insure that he is following the rule. He may need prompting by either touch or verbal methods, and, at times, it may be necessary to remove the work or place your hands on top of his to stop them. Working with a client to eliminate this behavior is time consuming. Don't expect to be successful in a few days.

Unwillingness to Accept Supervision

Behavioral contracts are sometimes effective when working with clients who will not accept supervision, that is, if they haven't yet been fired. Unfortunately, clients who are unwilling to accept supervision tend to lose jobs. Sometimes they learn from their past and are more willing to try to change. It is a difficult task to change a life-long behavior.

Inappropriate Interactions/Advances to Co-Workers

Depending on the severity of the problem, I have found that work rules are usually sufficient to assist the client in improving these behaviors. It worked with the young man who wanted to see what was under the blouse. Work rules also worked with clients who hugged supervisors and co-workers. For the more severe behaviors, a contract may be more effective in extinguishing the behavior.

Boredom

When a client becomes bored on the job, it is wise to try to pique his interest in the paycheck. What does he buy with the money? Is he saving for something? If so, a plan or chart could be devised in order for the client to see that by doing his work he will be able to buy what he wants. I often explain to my clients that everyone is bored at one time or another on their job and that he is no different.

Praising the Client

Perhaps one of the most effective ways to change a person's behavior is to praise him. This is true for clients, employers, co-workers, professionals, and anyone else with whom you work. When working on a job with your client, praise him for the small steps he learns. Sometimes it is a great feat for him to learn what may seem very basic to you.

Praise can come in many forms. Most people respond to verbal praise such as, "You did it! I'm so excited that you can do that step!" Many times, you will see a grin on the client's face because he feels like he has accomplished something worthwhile.

A smile or nod of the head can also be a form of praise. Buying the client a soft drink for a job well done is sometimes an excellent method of acknowledging the client's job.

The client who feels good about himself and the job he is doing will continue to improve his work performance. The value of praise cannot be stressed enough. Use it and you should see results that may surprise you.

Summary

Modifications and teaching techniques can be fun. In order to be effective, they must be functional and use the client's learning style. If that is not the case, then no matter how hard you push your client, he will not learn the job or change the behavior.

PAPERWORK

Every job has its fun and not-so-fun parts. I consider the training fun and the paperwork a necessary part but not as fun. Unfortunately, paperwork is a part of the job. The paperwork you turn in verifies that you have been working with your client. Of course, the client and employer know that you have worked, and the client is learning the job, but you must document the client's progress and any problems that have occurred throughout the training.

In our program, I strive to keep paperwork at a minimum. Sometimes, the trainers would argue that point because it is possible to become bogged down. Unfortunately, it is difficult to keep everyone informed without notes and reports. In this section, I will describe the paperwork required of the job trainers in the Transition to Work Project in Cincinnati, Ohio. The paperwork required of you may be similar or differ somewhat to that which is required in your program.

If you are an administrator who is just starting a program, you may want to think long and hard before introducing paperwork to the trainer. If the trainer becomes too laden with paperwork, his work with the client may suffer. For this reason, before I introduce any new paperwork to the trainers, I evaluate the purpose of it, the amount of time it will take, whether or not the benefits are worth the cost of producing it, and if the particular format I am considering is the quickest and easiest for the trainer while still giving me the information I need. Also, I sometimes ask the trainers if they have any ideas as to new forms and formats for paperwork. They have helped develop some of our paperwork. They are a good resource; remember that they were hired for their creativity, among other things.

Daily Log

The trainers in our program are required to keep a daily log. The daily log is a record of the events of the day, the client's progress, and any problems from the minute the client leaves his home until he returns at the end of his shift. Logs should be written describing events and behaviors as the trainer sees them. For example, instead of saying "Mr. _____ was extremely rude to _____ today." The trainer should describe the behavior, "Mr. _____ interrupted (the client) and his supervisor while the supervisor was explaining a procedure. When Mr. _____ interrupted, he did not apologize for his behavior or excuse himself."

Logs are important for several reasons. First, they document the client's progress for the day, including any problems. Many times, we have had to delve through the notes to find the date and particulars of an incident.

Another reason for a daily log is to verify that the trainer was actually working with the client on a specific day during certain hours. During controversies, this is important information to have. Not only is the trainer able to tell if and when she worked on a certain day, she can tell what happened while she was working.

The client's progress can be followed and patterns in behavior noted. Sometimes the trainer may discover at a later date that the client is having a behavioral problem and vaguely remembers a similar incident happening before. She can go back in her notes and compare incidents and chart the behaviors. She can use the information when forming a behavior plan.

The daily log is just that. A journal of the daily happenings at the job site. Usually, at the beginning of the job, the entries are rather lengthy, as there are more problems encountered. As the client becomes accustomed to his job and training is completed, the logs become much shorter, with only the date, time, and a few short statements.

At the beginning of the job, it is necessary for the trainer to write in her log at home after she has finished working with the client. We pay our trainers for this time, as the log is a requirement of the job and valuable information. As the training progresses and the trainer fades on the job site (see Chapter 9), the log can be written at the job site.

Very few trainers have complained about keeping a log (after a few weeks), because they can refer to it to see the progress, if any, the client has made. Sometimes, it seems as if the client is progressing so slowly, it is nice to look back and see how far he has come.

Task Analysis Sheet

The Task Analysis sheet was filled out during the Job Analysis (see Chapter 5 and Figures 13–15). However, you will use it faithfully while your client is working. It is the breakdown of every job duty and portion of a job to be completed. As the client progresses in his job, you will need to document his progress on learning the job.

There are many ways to document the client's progress. Included in this chapter is the method by which we document our clients in jobs. We use a numbering system according to the cover sheet (see Figure 12). Thus, we can see when a new job task was presented to the client. We can also see when the client begins to become independent and the trainer can step back and allow the client to perform the job without assistance.

This system has helped us in working with the employer at times. Sometimes, the employer cannot understand why the trainer is still with the client, and he suggests that the client knows the job well enough for the trainer to leave. Usually, this has happened when the trainer was working with a problem and cannot leave the client for fear of the client losing the job. The trainer showed the rating sheet to the employer who was then satisfied that the trainer needed to be there. The concrete data seems to help employers understand the need for the trainer to continue working with the client.

The time lines for filling out the data are listed on the cover sheet, however, the trainers are encouraged to fill more of it out if they like. Sometimes, the trainer may fill it out daily for the first few weeks to document how quickly the client is learning.

As the job changes, which happens fairly frequently, the trainer writes an addendum to be added to the original job analysis. An N/A is placed in the squares next to the portions of the job that are no longer being performed. The addendum is treated as the original was.

Supervisor Evaluations

Once a month, a supervisor's evaluation sheet is given to the employer to fill out (see Figure 18). In our program, the trainer is responsible for the evaluations while the client is in training, then the responsibility falls to the job developer after final phaseout.

It is always helpful to have a written and signed evaluation from the employer, as he will tend to think carefully about what he puts in writing. Be careful of the employer who after one month thinks you should no longer be working with the client, especially if you feel strongly that you should still be involved. You need to have a meeting with him to clarify what you are doing and what goals you are working toward. This may be a good time to show the employer your task analysis rating form, to back up your statements.

It is also just as important to watch out for the employer who becomes dependent on you and thinks you should stay for an extended period of time. This also would require a meeting, and the job analysis rating sheet can be of assistance. If the employer keeps on finding small insignificant things for you to work on with the client, he may need to be told in a tactful manner that the client has learned the job skills and you are worried that the client will become dependent upon you if you do not begin phasing out. Actually, it is the employer who is dependent upon you. Phasing out and the problems associated with it will be discussed in Chapter 9. You may also wish to refer to Chapter 8 regarding working with employers.

Summary

Working with clients on jobs is complex. In this chapter, I tried to give you ideas for teaching techniques and modifications for six traditional jobs in which your clients may be employed. The techniques were discussed in relation to the learning modalities presented in Chapter 3, in order to give you a sense of how it all fits together. Paperwork was also discussed as it pertains to the training. I hope you weren't discouraged or too overwhelmed when reading this chapter. This will be a handy reference when you begin training.

Good luck and have fun!

FIGURE 18

Supervisor's Evaluation of Employees

Trainee/Employee's Name:_____

Company:_____ Position:_____

Date:_____ Supervisor's Name:_____

Please circle the answer that best represents your opinion about the trainee/
employee's present situation.

	Comments
1. The employee is working up to your standards to maintain the position. Less than As Required More than Required Required	
2. The employee arrives and leaves <u>on time</u>. Yes No	
3. The employee maintains good attendance. Yes No	
4. The employee takes meals and breaks appropriately. Yes No	
5. The employee maintains good appearance. Yes No	
6. The employee completes job tasks within the appropriate amount of time. Seldom Usually Always	
7. Communication with the employee is: A problem Not a problem	

Transition To Work Project - Ohio RSC - March, 1987

FIGURE 18 (CONT.)

	Comments
8. The employee works consistently. Yes No	
9. Does the employee have appropriate social interactions on the job? Yes No	
10. Is the employee accepted by others? Yes No	
11. Do you feel the employee still needs a Job Trainer to improve his/her performance? Yes No	

Additional Comments:

_____
_____
_____
_____
_____
_____
_____
_____
_____
_____

Signature_____

Chapter 8

WORKING WITH EMPLOYERS

EMPLOYERS ARE people, too. They have emotions, ideas, and opinions just like anyone else. As in the general population, there are **good ones** and **bad ones.** Some are wonderful to work with because they are caring and understanding; some seem aloof and preoccupied. At times, the trainer will think that the employer doesn't care about the client. How many times I have thought or heard others say, "All that he can think about is how much money the company is earning!" When one thinks about that statement, the reality of the situation becomes apparent. That is his job, he was hired to make sure the company runs smoothly and stays solvent.

Unfortunately, sometimes our clients have an adverse effect on the economy of a business for a short time. That is when you hear, "John's a good worker, but he's too slow. If he doesn't pick up speed soon, I'll have to let him go."

A statement such as this quite often puts a great fear into trainers, as they say to themselves, "But John's doing the best that he can, in fact he's doing better than I thought he would at this time."

In order to decide how to handle situations such as this, let's take a look at some of the factors involved in working with employers.

WHO ARE EMPLOYERS?

For the purpose of this manual, an employer is a person who has supervisory responsibility over your client. Thus, an employer could be an owner of a business, a direct supervisor in a competitive job, and, in some cases, a staff person from a rehabilitation program or school. In any case, the information found in this chapter is applicable to the relationship you establish with your client's direct supervisor. For the most part, the employers mentioned in this chapter are people who have hired clients of mine as employees.

One of the most important things I always feel the need to keep in perspective is my relationship to the employer. **As a trainer, I am a guest in his place of business.** It is not my place to tell him how to run his business, although there have been many times when I wanted to do so! As a new trainer, it is sometimes difficult to understand the importance of this position. I have had new trainers say to me, "What the manager needs to do is get more help!" or "The business would run more smoothly if the manager would just…." I don't know one trainer who hasn't thought they could improve something about a business at least once.

Try to put yourself in the place of the employer. You have forty employees and are responsible for the quality of food and service at a steak house. You deal with employee absenteeism, laziness, and apathy at times, as well as stopped-up plumbing and broken equipment. The dishes have been washed a certain way since the opening of the restaurant, and the manager is satisfied because the work is done quickly and efficiently. It may slip his mind that your client needs a new scrubbing pad. It may not be the top priority for him as it is for your client.

Likewise, the employees may all seem overworked. You wonder how they ever got their jobs completed within the alloted time without your help. You would like to tell the employer that his expectations are unrealistic, that no one can get the job done in the time allotted, handicapped or not! (Remember that the job was done by someone before, without the assistance of a job trainer.) No matter how strongly you feel about the situation, if you tell the employer exactly how you feel, **you may be jeopardizing your client's job!**

The way I sometimes approach the subject is to ask the specific production standards for the job. I may probe the employer to ask how the production figures for my client's job were obtained. If equipment is broken, I ask if that was taken into consideration when the standards were determined. It is helpful to let the employer decide for himself if changes in the standard are necessary. Sometimes a few questions will start him thinking, and eventually changes may occur on the job. Sometimes, a person will be more willing to make changes if the ideas are his own.

If an employer is extremely busy, I quite often leave a note for him. Generally, this is an acceptable method of communication, especially when the employer appears to be overloaded with work problems. Some employers prefer a note that is always in front of them as a reminder.

Remember that you are a guest in the employer's company, and you and your client can be asked to leave if the employer so chooses. I have always felt the major responsibility for the relationship lies with the trainer. As a trainer, you **never want a client to lose a job because of your relationship with the employer!**

EMPLOYERS' KNOWLEDGE OF DISABILITIES

Many employers have had little or no experience working with people with a disabling condition. Many times the trainer will work with an employer who had a cousin who "lost a leg in the war" or "had a customer who was blind." They may discuss this person with you at length, since this is the employer's frame of reference. More times than not, their prior experiences will not have any similarities to the client with whom you are working.

Therefore, you must tactfully educate (or train, if you will) not only your client but the employer. This is accomplished in a variety of ways, each of which will be discussed individually.

HOW DO YOU TEACH EMPLOYERS ABOUT THE CLIENT'S DISABILITY?

Written Information

A common method of educating employers about disabilities is to give them some form of written information. For example, brochures have been written by agencies or associations, such as the Association for Retarded Citizens, specifically for employers who hire a person with the particular disability. This form of communication is a good start.

Consider, however, the manager of the steak house. He is responsible for perhaps forty employees and the quality of food and service for the full time it is open. He may not have the time to read and fully comprehend several brochures.

Some employers may resent this form of communication as being too impersonal. For this reason, it is recommended that this form of educating the employer not be used alone but combined with other methods listed below.

General Explanation of the Disability

Most likely, the employer is wanting firsthand knowledge from the **expert.** That's you! This is a sensitive topic to discuss with anyone. **Client confidentiality** must be kept at all times. For this reason, one must speak only in general terms.

To further explain, let us look at several examples. Many employers have asked me questions such as, "What's wrong with him? He seems okay. Why does he need help?" This is **not** a time to expound on your knowledge of the client's background, I.Q. scores, or behavioral problems. In fact, **you are expected to keep the exact nature of the client's disability strictly confidential.** You must **never** give I.Q. scores or psychological diagnoses to an employer. If you give information such as this, you are leaving yourself open for a lawsuit.

Before getting into a situation of being questioned by an employer, it is preferable to discuss with the client and/or guardian exactly how he wishes the disability to be presented. It is wise to have a release of information signed by the client and/or guardian. Better yet, **prepare the client to explain his own disability.** Depending on the disability, clients may be able to explain their strengths and limitations well. For example, a mentally retarded person can be taught to tell an employer that he learns slowly. Likewise, a learning disabled client can learn to ask the employer to demonstrate how to do something rather than explain it verbally.

Several ideas of what to say to an employer follow. It is better to speak in general terms about a disability and offer information the employer already has or would know after working with the client a short time. For example, when questioned about a mentally retarded client, I quite often will explain that my client takes a longer time to learn than many people that the place of business generally hires. Sometimes I add that once the client learns the job, he will retain what he has learned and be a consistent worker. This is information the employer would realize himself after working with the client for a few weeks.

Notice the words used to describe the client. It is always important to **use words the employer understands.** It is tempting to use psychological or educational jargon to help explain a client's disability. However, the employer will not understand you. For example, few employers would understand you if you were to say the client has visual discrimination problems. You would instead say that the client does not see things the way they were meant to be seen. Explain by using examples that pertain to the job. For example, the client **may** have difficulty seeing the difference between a soupspoon and a teaspoon.

Your response to the employer will vary with the disability. When working with a learning disabled client, one might say that he doesn't learn in the same way that many people do. Therefore, he must be taught by showing him or demonstration. Likewise, when working with a person who suffered a closed head trauma, one might explain that the client has difficulty remembering things. Explain that you will show the client and the employer how to work around this problem.

Sometimes the employer will insist that the trainer give him the name of the disability. Before doing this, again, I would try to give him information he already has. For a mentally retarded client, one might say that he was in special education classes in school because he is a slow learner. (This information is usually found on the job application.) Amazingly, this satisfies many people. If the employer continues pressing, I would discuss this with the client, and/or guardian, and the job developer (if that is someone other than the trainer). A strategy can be planned to put the employer's mind at ease. One must always remember that an I.Q. score should **never** be given to anyone!

Of course, one should always **be positive about the client.** Granted, sometimes that is difficult when working with a problem client, but, remember, you are selling your program and your client to the employer each minute you are in contact with him. If a client has behavioral problems, they were most likely discussed with the employer before the person was hired. **The trainer must be truthful at all times**

with the employer or all credibility is lost. Remember that the truthfulness must take into consideration **confidentiality.** An example of this approach might be to tell the employer that the client responds best to a structured environment. He works best with only one supervisor and in a small work area with few people. He becomes somewhat confused if more than one person gives him instruction. If he works in a large area with many distractions, he may become interested in watching others. This is a positive way of saying that this person becomes frustrated and acts out by yelling and throwing things when more than one person tells him what to do. Hopefully, the employer will place the client in the environment described. If not, then the employer should be forewarned of possible resulting behaviors.

In summary, there are several things to consider when talking to an employer about a disability:

1. Obtain a **release of information** as to what information the client and/or guardian want divulged to the employer. Include broad, general statements which will be used first, as well as the most specific information the client will permit, if the trainer is pressured by the employer. (Your agency should have Release of Information forms available for your use.)

2. **Never** give I.Q. scores or psychological diagnoses! You could get sued!

3. **Be positive** about the client. Even though he has perhaps displayed negative behaviors before, the employer may be frightened if that is mentioned. Of course, if the trainer expects to encounter that behavior on the job, it was most likely addressed before the employer hired the client.

4. Whenever possible, have the client explain his disability. After all, it is his life you are talking about!

5. Remember to use words that the employer can understand. It does not help the employer when psychological or educational jargon is used. It only confuses him and makes him more concerned about working with you and your client.

Modeling

Quite a bit of information has been written about modeling. For the purposes of this manual, modeling will be discussed briefly as an effective way to deal with employers. When one models behavior, he is behaving the way that he wishes the other person would. For example, we teach children to say **please** and **thank you** by demonstrating that behavior in front of the child. The same principle applies when working with the employer.

Some employers are nervous and uncomfortable when working with persons with disabilities for the first time, especially if there is some physical involvement. I once placed a client who had Down's syndrome in a large manufacturing company to do assembly work. The supervisors were nervous about this, as they had never worked with a person with this disability. They had, however, worked with mentally retarded persons before. Because of the visibility of the disability, the long title of the disability, and the fact that the supervisor had "never seen one," it made it necessary to model the desired behavior. In order to assist the employer and put him at ease, I gathered some written information for him and brought the client to the company for a tour. I interacted with this client no differently than I would any other client. The employer saw rather quickly that there was no difference between this client and other clients I had placed in his employ.

It is usually not too difficult to tell if an employer is inexperienced working with persons who are disabled. Perhaps the most noticeable trait is that **the employer will address the trainer rather than the client.** I have had employers ask me questions such as, "What would John like for lunch?" or "Would you tell him to clean the restroom next?" Quite often this happens with the client standing next to you. It is almost as if the client is invisible.

It is my opinion that employers don't realize they do this. Sometimes it seems as if they are more nervous than the client. In situations such as those listed above, I usually look at the client and wait for the response or redirect the question. Once this behavior has been demonstrated for a period of time and the employer learns that the client can respond to his questions or commands, the employer becomes more comfortable. Eventually, he will begin to address the client. This is your goal, to teach the employer to communicate with your client. It is an important step toward independence, both for the client and the employer. The client must learn to respond to the employer, and the employer must feel comfortable communicating with the client in order for the job to be successful. This step is imperative, as you will not be with the client every minute of every workday for the client's career.

Employers are no different than the general population as far as naivete is concerned. As a job trainer, it is likely you will be asked many questions about your clients. **It is important not to laugh or answer in disbelief when a question is asked.** One of the first employers with whom I worked used to ask some questions that I thought were rather unusual. One that I may never forget occurred while I was training a young man who was mentally retarded. He had a cleaning job and was usually alone in the building during his shift. One morning the employer asked what would happen if a woman were to walk by while he was working. This seemed a rather odd statement to me at the time, after all, what did he think I was! (Actually, he was referring to cocktail waitresses, which I was not.) However, I remember being pleased that he felt comfortable enough to ask me the question. After making a quick mental recovery, I answered that he would probably take a quick look then continue working because he was on a time schedule. I then added that his reaction would probably be no different than the other man that worked for him. The employer seemed to give a sigh of relief and went on working. I never knew what he expected to happen, and supposed he had either watched a movie or read an article in the paper about a maniac and generalized that to my client. After that incident I always encouraged him, and every other employer with whom I have worked, to ask questions about behaviors he either did or didn't expect. It's better that questions are answered than left to the imagination.

It is important to **respect the employer's position.** When he hires a client of yours, he knows the person has problems, otherwise the person wouldn't need a trainer. When the employer hires someone off the street, he usually assumes (sometimes incorrectly) that the person doesn't have problems. Your job is to help the employer feel comfortable with his decision to try your program. This means that sometimes **the trainer must train the employer to work with the client as well as train the client to work with the employer.** Of course, this is done rather discretely.

Honesty

As in working with anyone, it is imperative that the trainer is honest with the employer at all times. As a job placement counselor, I worked with several employers who regularly mentioned that they would only work with one or two programs in the area (luckily one was mine!), because the others would promise wonderful things from their clients that were not true. These employers stated that they prefer the placement counselor and/or job trainer, because they were up front about the client's abilities and limitations rather than presenting the clients falsely. By being honest with the employer, you have gained **trust** which sometimes will make an employer more willing to work with you and your client. You are also avoiding unpleasant surprises. Thus, by being honest, you may have opened doors for job restructuring and modifications (see Chapter 7). You also will keep the doors open for future employment opportunities for clients from your program.

If, at some point in the training, the trainer is sure that the client will **not** be able to perform some aspect of the job, even through the use of modifications, the employer must be informed. Perhaps, the job could be restructured in some way to allow the client to adequately perform the task in question.

At times you will work with employers who do not always tell you everything about the job or who seem to forget what you tell them. For example, I have worked with clients who were unable to work evening or night shifts. This information had been thoroughly discussed before the placement was made, then two weeks into the job, the employer informed me that all employees must work evening shifts and that it is a job requirement. In this particular case, it is probably necessary to contact the job developer to inform her of the problem. Perhaps a compromise can be reached where the employer will keep the client on the day shift for the first few months until the original problem can be resolved. If there is no resolution and the employer is insistent on the night shift, it may be necessary to locate alternative employment for the client.

Often, employers will disguise their discomfort by dealing with the client in this way instead of talking over his feelings and/or misgivings about hiring the client.

Depending on the employer, it is sometimes possible to help him through this period of adjustment to the client by being supportive and reassuring that you will stay with the client until he is comfortable enough with the client and satisfied with his work performance.

However one deals with the problem, it is necessary to remember that **the trainer always represents the client, the program, future clients, as well as himself.**

HOW DO I DEAL WITH DIFFERENT EMPLOYERS?

Naive and Overconfident Employers

Sometimes you will be assigned to work with an employer who is extremely overconfident in appearance but in reality is **naive.** This person will insist that he can do all the training himself and that the client really doesn't need all the assistance that you or the job developer insists that he does. This type of employer may not allow the trainer to work with the client on the job. Beware! This person usually does not know what he is talking about! **Unfortunately, it is not uncommon for this type of situation to end in failure.**

Your program may decide to place the client on the job and take the risk, which is a common method of dealing with the situation. (We no longer will do this in our program in Cincinnati.) The client starts the job and a week or so later, if that long, the job developer receives a call informing her that the job "just isn't working." One of several outcomes usually occurs. Either the employer insists that the client will never learn the job and terminates the relationship immediately, or he will finally allow a trainer to come into the situation.

It may be an understatement to say that the trainer is facing an uphill battle at this point. Not only does the trainer have to go into the situation with some modifications that will demonstrate immediate improvement, but quite often the employer will place a time limit on the client. I have had employers give me one week to "have him improve or I'll have to let him go."

During that time period you must also convince the employer that the client can handle the job (if you are convinced he can). I try to do this very **subtly.** If the client masters a difficult task that the employer was aware he could not do, then I will ask the employer to observe the client performing the task independently. Also, I like to report on the client's progress daily. Depending on the resistance of the employer, this may be extremely difficult to accomplish. He may be unavailable by either being genuinely busy or avoiding the trainer at the end of the day, making it impossible to talk with him. When this happens, I usually **write him a short note** telling of the progress. Sometimes, if speaking to him in person, I will summarize all that the client has learned in order to help him see the progress.

Sometimes these tactics work; other times, the employer has already made up his mind and for some reason he allowed you to try (e.g. he may be afraid of a discrimination suit, or he may want to prove to himself and the trainer that it wouldn't work). No matter what you do or say, or how much progress the client makes, he will not acknowledge it.

I have also heard of an unusual rare situation where the trainer was not allowed to touch anything at the work place. This situation involved a higher functioning client who was working with heavy machinery. In a situation like this, one must do what the employer asks. After all, he is the boss. Obviously, the trainer was unable to use the hands-on approach in that situation. She did the best she could with the materials available.

These are extremely difficult situations and I wish anyone luck who finds herself having to deal with it. Just remember, others have been through this situation, too. Hopefully, this will not happen to the new trainer until after she has had some experience.

Of course, the person who suffers the most is the client, who usually does not understand the dynamics of the situation and feels he has done something wrong. He will need quite a bit of support and assistance working through the situation. He will need to be reassured that he **did not fail** and that the problem was not because he is a bad person. Remember to use his open learning channel when explaining the situation to him (see Chapter 3). Hopefully, he will find satisfactory employment quickly and feel success in his next job.

Well-Meaning Employers

Opposite of the employer discussed above is the well-meaning person who is giving the client a chance for some reason that fills an internal need. While there is nothing wrong with this reason for hiring a client, some employers who mean well actually can unknowingly **sabotage** a job for the client.

Consider a young woman who has Down's syndrome and knew the employer prior to her hire. The nature of the job required the trainer to structure the job for the client. Because the client knew her co-workers prior to employment, she was interested in continuing the social relationships during work. She enjoyed talking rather than working and consequently was not completing all of her job tasks. The trainer provided her a list of work rules which included taking a break only at specified times. The client, who was sweet but manipulative, told the employer that she was thirsty but her **trainer** wouldn't allow her to have a pop. The employer verbalized that when doing hard work (i.e. cleaning for four hours), one depletes body fluid and it is necessary to get a drink.

It was clear that the employer did not understand the position in which he placed the trainer. The situation was handled by having a meeting with the employer, client, job developer, and trainer. At this meeting the work rules were presented and the reasons for them were explained. Cooperation was enlisted from the employer and parent in working with the client.

In summary, working with employers is almost always interesting. The trainer rarely knows what challenges await her when assigned to a new job site. The trainer does know that she must assess the employer quickly in order to determine how to work effectively with him for the good of the client and the program. Working with employers is a responsibility that should not be taken lightly!

Co-Workers

For the purposes of this book a co-worker is any person who works at your client's place of employment and is not his supervisor or works in a job level that is considered a higher position than your client's. It is important to remember the distinction between co-worker and supervisor, as many times a co-worker may **think** he is your client's supervisor. A co-worker is usually performing a job function that is the same as or similar to your client's.

Your client's co-workers are extremely important to your client. Quite often, they can make or break a job. Usually, the co-workers have been working for an amount of time before your client is hired, and have knowledge of both the job and the politics of the work place. The co-workers may exert quite a bit of control over the supervisor and manipulate information about your client that is given to the supervisor.

There are several things to remember when working with co-workers. First, these are the people who will be working with your client for possibly a very long time. Therefore, you will want to make sure that a positive relationship is developed with the co-worker. I quite often strike up conversations with the co-workers, as they are usually wondering why I am with the client. (Hopefully, they will already know the situation.) I usually explain that I am there because my client needs some initial assistance to learn new tasks and it is my responsibility to assure that he learns his job tasks correctly.

If the co-worker appears to be interested in the client and me, I may ask the co-worker to show me a certain aspect of the job. Helpful co-workers love to show their expertise and seem to enjoy the involvement with you and your client.

If it is the first day or very early into the training and we do not yet know any co-workers, I will look for the person who appears to be working the fastest and in the smoothest manner with the fewest movements. Because that person has found the most efficient method of completing the job, I will task-analyze the method used and teach it to my client. I have learned many timesaving tricks by chatting with and watching the client's co-workers.

I have a favorite story that helps illustrate positive interactions with co-workers. The first day on a dishwashing job with a client, I was asking a co-worker about the methods she utilized to bus the banquet tables. After she gave me some tips, she began asking me about my client, myself, and a professional I was training. She was interested in the job of trainer and asked questions about my background. When I told her I have a master's degree, she was amazed and said she was doing that job so she could go to school, and once she did, she certainly didn't want to bus tables. When the trainee worked with her shortly after our conversation, she asked if the trainee "has a master's in dishwashing and bussing, too."

At times, you may find the co-worker is somewhat threatened by you and your client. After all, here is a person who is obviously a **slow** learner who is going to do the same job as the co-worker has done for the past five years. Some people have difficulty dealing with this, although they will not verbalize it. They may become involved in some passive-aggressive acts by setting your client up to fail at a portion of his job. Or the co-worker may say some negative things about your client to other co-workers and/or supervisors. This is a difficult attitude with which to deal. It takes your best diplomacy. Although you want to tell the person exactly how you feel, you must be positive and congenial.

If the co-worker is extremely difficult to work with, it is best to discuss the problem tactfully with the employer. For example, one trainer worked with a client whose productivity was lower than expected. After the trainer observed the situation, it was evident that a co-worker was requesting the best work from the material handlers. They readily fulfilled her request which left the undesirable and more difficult work for the client. The trainer requested a meeting with the supervisory staff to discuss the client and presented possible reasons for the lower productivity. Among those reasons listed was the fact that the choice jobs **appeared** to be going to the co-worker. The supervisors were surprised and mentioned several times during the meeting that they would correct that problem immediately. Supervisors can be extremely helpful in dealing with co-worker problems.

WHAT ARE SOME METHODS TO CONSIDER USING WHEN DEALING WITH EMPLOYERS?

Effective Communication

Communication is perhaps the single most important aspect of job training. Communication is crucial between the trainer and employer, the trainer and client, the trainer and co-workers, the client and employer, the client and co-workers, not to mention all the people involved in the client's placement in the particular job.

Without open communication, the client will have great difficulty maintaining his job. There are several basic factors in communication that I consider to be of the utmost importance. First is the willingness to communicate. Unless you as the job trainer are willing to ask questions and be ready to learn from the answers, you will not be able to train the client properly. You must also be ready to take correction as you learn the job tasks. You must show the employer that you want to learn the job correctly so that you can teach your client to perform work of the highest caliber, both quality and quantity. If you are not willing to communicate with the employer, you are in the wrong job.

Communication is, of course, a two-way street. The employer must be willing to communicate with you and your client. Many times, the person who was responsible for hiring your client is not the same person who will be supervising the client on a daily basis. Thus, there may be a communication delay between the employers as to expectations, for example.

Several times I have been in the position when the personnel manager was excited about hiring the client and working with the program, but he failed to lay the proper groundwork with the direct supervisor. In cases like this, the direct supervisor may not know who you are, why you are with the client, or any of the information the job developer so carefully gave the personnel manager. At these times, you must become the salesperson and convince the supervisor that your client will be an excellent employee with your assistance. It will be up to you to deal with the supervisor's questions and fears.

A major component of communication is the choice of **language** that people utilize. As I mentioned earlier, an employer can become frustrated attempting to talk with you if you are using professional jargon. On the other hand, it is necessary for you to learn some of the jargon that your client will have to know in order to keep his job. While working in southern California, many of my clients were working in the electronics industry. I found that I had more credibility with employers once I could use their language. So I learned terms like strip and crimp wires and stuff PC boards.

Enthusiasm

Communication as mentioned above is a form of showing the employer that you are enthusiastic about your job at his place of business. Enthusiasm is extremely important and there are many ways of showing it. Showing an eagerness to learn the job and some about the business is one way to show this.

I try to learn about the business, as I am always interested in knowing how my client fits into the overall scheme. Once I know this, I can tell him how important his job is. For example, I can almost always become enthusiastic about a client on a janitorial job. I explain the importance of people working and living in a clean environment. I sometimes tell clients that there are two professions that people cannot live without: janitors/housekeepers and garbagemen. When the client finishes cleaning a room, we may pause to look at the difference and imagine how happy the person will be to come to work in a clean office. (Part of my respect for janitors is the complexity of their job. I think that cleaning is one of the hardest jobs our clients do.)

Nothing saddens me more than to see a job trainer looking bored on the job. This does not look good for either the trainer, the program, or the client. Obviously, there will be times when the trainer will be bored, especially when preparing to phase out, but a good trainer will never let anyone know that she is bored. It is difficult to expect your client to be cheery and enthusiastic about his work when it is clear that you are not.

Follow Through

It is extremely important that if you say you will do something, that you do it. A major reason that some employers will not use certain programs is that there is little or no follow through. If you say you will be at the job site at 8:00, be there! If you come in at 8:05, the employer will wonder about your dependability. If the trainer cannot get to the job on time, how will she ever teach the client?

Using the excuse "I just didn't have time" can be translated by the employer that you don't care about him or his job. If you think that you may not be able to follow through on something, don't offer to do it.

Sometimes I find time management difficult if I am starting a new client and am not quite phased out with another. I have used several tactics which worked, depending on the situation and the personalities. I may ask the employer with whom I have been working for some time if it is alright to drop in sometime **early next week.** Then I offer to call first. Sometimes I may explain that I am working with a client who is having great difficulty in another job and will need to be with him for a few days. If you have maintained good communication and dependability, this should not present a problem. Since this client is doing fine, I would like to call the employer daily to follow his progress while he works independently.

Sense of Humor

Displaying a sense of humor is extremely important to me. I think that if a person is able to smile or chuckle, he is more apt to be relaxed. The more relaxed a person is, the more accepting he may be. Therefore, I assume the responsibility of helping my client's co-workers and employers to be relaxed around my client and me, and thus with each other.

This does not mean that one does not act in a professional manner. One can smile and display a sense of humor and still be professional. I do not accomplish this by telling jokes but rather by adding some wit to the situation. For example, a client apparently displayed some negative behavior immediately before the supervisor and I entered the room. The trainer had already worked through the problem with the client. Upon entering the room, the client hurriedly walked over to the supervisor and announced she had had a bad attitude that day, apologized, and wanted to know if she was fired. The supervisor assured her that she would not be fired if she could improve her behavior. After the supervisor and I left the room, I commented to her that she would never have to worry about her new employee keeping any secrets. She chuckled and agreed, and the client has maintained the job for over one year.

One employer with whom I worked rarely smiled. He was always serious. Thus, when we first met to discuss the client's progress, he was rather rigid and had difficulty seeing the progress the client had made. His affect caused me to be somewhat nervous, so I worked hard at being relaxed and at the same time serious about the subject. After several meetings, he became more relaxed also, and eventually he even smiled!

Summary

Your client's employers and co-workers can either help or hinder your efforts to train your client. Sometimes they can sabotage your work without realizing it, and when you speak to them, they are unwilling to face that fact. For the most part, I think that you will find employers to be open to you and your client. After all, it was the employer's decision to hire your client.

If you only remember one thing from this chapter, remember that **you are a guest in the employer's place of business.** He can ask you and/or your client to leave at any time. He is the boss. His decisions are law for his business. If you feel the need to complain or vent your feelings, wait until you get back to your office.

You can always learn a lot from employers and co-workers if you are willing. You will meet some interesting and fun people during your tenure as a job trainer.

Chapter 9

PHASING OUT
OF THE WORK PLACE

THE PHASEOUT period is of extreme importance to your client maintaining his job. If you phase out too quickly, the client may not have the confidence or full understanding of the job and his performance may suffer. If you stay on the job too long, he may become so dependent on you that his confidence suffers when you leave.

The phaseout process is systematic. It should be carried out in a specific manner, with **communication at all times** with the employer and people involved with the client. The phaseout period can be lengthy, taking several months. I have seen people try to rush the process and have to go in later and retrain the client, which takes much more time than approaching it systematically.

The phaseout period begins when the client is able to perform all the duties of the job independently, **without any prompting, while you are standing next to him.** In the Transition to Work Project in Cincinnati, we use the rating system on the task analysis sheet for documentation as to when the client has reached this point. He should have maintained this point for **at least** a week, preferably more, before you start the phaseout process. You are setting the client up for possible failure if you start phasing out after he has finally completed a step independently one time. Make sure he can do the task on a repetitive basis before you start the process.

Step 1: Stand back. The first step in the phaseout process is to step back and watch the client perform his job duties from a distance. You should inform him of your intentions so he will not wonder what you are doing and why you are not right with him. He may be frightened at first, but, most likely, he will be happy to do the job without you watching every move he makes. You will still be in the same room with the client, just not right next to him. By doing this, you can step in and intervene if necessary. For example, he may forget a step or use a different method. If this happens, you can correct the error at that time before he uses the incorrect method all the time. Once you are convinced that he is performing the job independently to the expectations of the employer, you can go on to the next step.

Step 2: Leave the Room. The next step in the process is to leave the room for short time periods. For example, I will say to the client, "I'll be back in five minutes. You should be finished with this stack of dishes by the time I get back." I usually start out with five minutes, then gradually lengthen the time period as he meets the short goals. As the time increases, I usually do not give him a goal, but, instead, I just inform him that "I will be back soon." If he maintains the quality and quantity of work expected, you can go on to the next step.

It is extremely important to inform the employer of your intentions. If you are not with your client, he may become concerned and wonder where you are. He may even contact your supervisor and complain. **Communication** is so important to the success of your program and keeping your client in his job.

During this phase, you should be discussing your client's progress with him and find out how he feels about your not being with him on a regular basis. It is important that he is ready for the next step. Usually, the client will be pleased that you are finally going to allow him to work on his own without you there all the time.

Step 3: Meet with employer, job developer, and client, if possible. At this point, a formal meeting is called with the employer and job developer for the purpose of discussing the client's progress. If possible, the client should be involved; however, sometimes it is impossible because the client is working and is needed at his work station. As the progress is discussed, it should be apparent that the client is able to perform at least a portion of his job independently. You will want to ask the employer if he is comfortable with you shortening the amount of time that you spend on the job. If he is, you can develop a plan of how you will phase out. For example, it is common to start this step by coming in fifteen minutes late if the client knows the clocking in and setup procedures. You may also leave fifteen minutes early if the client knows the procedures for the end of the day.

The employer should be given a phone number where he can reach you in case of emergency. He may also want the job developer's in case you are not available when he calls. This will put the employer's mind at ease, knowing he can reach someone if necessary.

It is crucial that the employer is in agreement with you. If he is not, your client may lose the job. On the other hand, many employers are more nervous about this process than the client, and he may not be sure about your leaving the premises. If that happens, remind him that the client has been working without you in the same room for some time. You may need to show him the task analysis sheet where you have documented your client's progress. And, of course, reassure him that if there are problems, you can come in full time again until the client is stabilized.

I have found that most employers wonder why you have stayed around as long as you have, and are in agreement with your leaving. (For more information about working with employers, see Chapter 8.)

Step 4: Phaseout according to outline in Step 3. The next step is to carry out the agreement you have with the employer. **Communication** is so important in this step. When you come in late, always ask the employer how your client did without you. Most of the time, the answer should be that he did fine. Then you will want to ask your client how things went. If there was a problem, I like to have the client tell me without confronting him, if possible. If there was a problem, we discuss it and possible ways of dealing with the problem should it happen again.

You will want to gradually shorten the amount of time that you spend on the job, as you find that the client is progressing without you. Before you change your time, you must discuss this with the employer. As the two of you agree, the phaseout period can proceed. You may decide to have at least one formal meeting to discuss the phaseout, like you did before the phaseout, to formally communicate the progress.

When you are down to a relatively short period of time, you may want to vary the times of day that you come in so the client is not dependent upon you. Some clients may not be performing at their best at other times of the day but perform well while you are there. If you come at different times unannounced, the client must perform well at all times.

Step 5: Meet with employer and job developer. The last step of the phaseout is to meet with the employer for a final phaseout meeting. At this meeting, you will want to discuss no longer coming in to work with your client. The client should be independent in all aspects of his job and performing up to the expectations of the employer. At this time, you will want to make sure the client and employer have your phone number and can reach you in case of emergency or if the client needs to be retrained on some aspect of his job. They should have always had the numbers, but sometimes they misplace them. Of course, you will need to fill out whatever paperwork your program requires. The phaseout report for the Transition to Work Project can be found at the end of this chapter (see Figure 19).

Step 6: Develop a Follow-Up Plan. The last step in this process is to develop a follow-up plan with the employer. This will be discussed in the next chapter.

Helpful Techniques

Now that you know the steps involved in the phaseout period, you may wish to know some techniques of how to assist your client if he starts having problems on the job. The first thing to do is to determine exactly what the problem is and the cause. For example, a client with a behavior problem or one who is stubborn may perform well while you are at the job site, then take the opportunity to do the job the way he wants once you leave. This may not necessarily be the way that the employer wants the job to be completed. If your client is a dependent person or has a low self-esteem, he may become frightened when you leave. These are two entirely different cases, and both may happen to you. You will want to work differently with each one.

Let's look at the client who is stubborn. He may need a **stern approach and be told in a straightforward manner** that he had better do the job as he was told, or he may not be working there anymore. I will never forget the first time that I confronted a client on his behavior. I always considered myself as a supportive type of person, and thought that positive reinforcement was the approach to take. After several months on the job, I realized that my client was taking advantage of my kindness. I got together my courage and told him that I thought that he was making excuses for not working well. He had proven that he could do the job, but he was lazy and was blaming others for his laziness. I went on to tell him that he had better straighten up or he would not be working anymore. I was not going to help him with his job anymore, because it was his job, not mine.

Once I started talking, I kept on going on and on. I know that my voice quivered because of my nervousness. And I was sure that the client would quit then and there because I was not positive. Much to my amazement, he agreed with me and said that he would do better. He did just that, and I phased out not long after.

I was happy that I did confront him, because I learned that **not everyone responds to the positive, supportive approach.** I was also lucky, because he was my first client I placed and trained in a job. I learned this early and could put it to use when necessary.

Obviously, that technique is not for every client, especially the second example above. The approach to that client must depend on the outcome of further investigation of the problem. Is he making errors on his job so that you will come back to work with him? Or does he not know the job well enough? If he is seeking attention from you, then you will need to turn the attention around to **reinforce the positive behavior** of doing well on the job. For example, if you are certain he can perform the job well without further training, you may say that you will be in touch with the supervisor. If the client is doing well, then you will come to visit him at the job site and you can talk together at his break. If, however, he is not doing a good job, then you will not be able to see him at the job as often. This usually works quite well if the reinforcer is your attention. It will not work if the client does not care to see you or want your attention.

Another technique that you could use is a **picture of yourself.** You could leave that with the client to let them know that you are always thinking about him and that you care about his work. This technique can also be used with a client who is not doing well because of behavioral reasons, to let him know that you always know what he is doing. Even though you are not there, you will know if he is working well.

We have been using **spies** in our program if we have a client who we think is possibly not following his work schedule and is working in a restaurant or place where the public can see him. For example, one of our clients was cleaning a fast-food restaurant during operating hours. The trainer suspected that he was performing differently when she was not there. I sent another trainer in to the restaurant to **spy** on the client without the client knowing who she was. (The client had been told that this may occur.) The second trainer watched him for several days and observed him working with the trainer and after the trainer left. There was indeed a change in behavior. The second trainer estimated that he worked approximately 10 percent of the time and talked the rest. After she had gathered enough data to show that this happened consistently, the client was confronted with the data. We then began to see some improvement in his behavior.

Every situation is different; therefore, there is no sure way to handle all situations. My advice is to think through the problem well. Look at all the data you have about the client and the situation. I highly recommend **talking** to your client about the problem before you start on a behavioral program. When the trainer talked to the client mentioned above, he denied that he talked during work time. For this reason, it was necessary to send in a spy. It is wonderful to send a second trainer to observe the client and have the trainer come back with good news! That is what we all want to happen.

Some clients will not make it in the job. You will need to evaluate the reason. Maybe it wasn't a good job match. Perhaps the client's behavior was inappropriate and/or he sabotaged his job for some reason. In our program, if a client has worked on several jobs and the same behaviors occur in those jobs, then they go onto what we call the **ROT** program. (This title is only used by the job trainers. The clients never hear this name. We may say they are in **interrupted status.**) This program was named by one of the school administrators who also manages our program. The ROT program is just that. The client sits at home for a certain amount of time, for example, six months, without our services. (Usually, when a client goes on interruption, he has certain goals to meet, such as counseling or a traditional Work Adjustment program.) At the end of that time, we will meet to discuss what, if any, changes have taken place. If the goals have been met, then the client will be reinstated into the program.

Summary

The phaseout period is extremely important to your client (see Figure 19). This is the time that he becomes independent on his job and no longer requires your services on a full-time basis. Most of your clients will make it and a few won't. If the client has difficulties, take a close look at the problem before acting on it.

FIGURE 19
PHASE OUT MEETING

_____ Initial
_____ Final
_____ Other

Client: _____   Date: _____

Job Site: _____

Work Schedule: _____   Wage: _____

Participants:

 Supervisor(s) _____

 Job Developer _____   Job Trainer _____

 Others _____

Comments (If initial phase out, portions of shift. Time line decided upon for future meetings.):

Decision: Job Trainer _____ will phase out for portions of the shift (listed above)

 _____ will no longer be training, client in follow-along status.

_____ Employer received phone numbers of job developer and trainer to contact in case of emergency or changes.

The contact person(s) at the work site are:

 Name(s): _____

 Title(s): _____

 _____
 Signature of Job Trainer

Transition To Work Project - Ohio RSC - March, 1987

Chapter 10

FOLLOW-UP

THE AMOUNT OF follow-up and the length of the follow-up will depend on the program for which you work. For supported employment programs, the length of the follow-up (or follow-along as it is sometimes called) can be an ongoing process spanning many years. Other programs may limit follow-up to several months. Because of the wide difference in the amount of time you may devote to follow-up, you will need to fit the material in this chapter to your needs.

In Chapter 9, a follow-up plan was mentioned. This plan should be written at the final phaseout meeting, and everyone should be in agreement about all aspects of the plan. A plan should include several key items and any information that is particular to your program.

FREQUENCY

The follow-up plan should include the frequency of the follow-up contacts. For example, you may want to contact the employer weekly for the first month, then decrease it to every other week, then monthly. The decision as to how often you contact the employer should directly relate to how the client is progressing. You will want to be careful not to bother the employer too much, especially if he thinks that your calls are unnecessary. He will view this as interfering with his precious work time and will not be pleased with you.

On the other hand, if you find that your client is having difficulties, you will want to work with him to rectify the problems so he can keep his job. You may need to develop a behavior plan (see Chapter 7) in order to make sure the client is maintaining his job. If you do this, you will want to involve the employer, if only to inform him you are doing this. Sometimes, the employer will want to monitor it, which is beneficial, as he is with the client all the time.

CONTACT PERSON

While writing the follow-up plan, you will want to determine who the contact person will be. Sometimes, the employer will prefer that you contact the immediate supervisor, sometimes the personnel person, and sometimes the head of the company. Make sure you have this firmly established.

PREFERRED METHOD OF CONTACT

While writing the plan, make sure the method of contact is established. Some employers prefer to talk on the phone, others will suggest you **stop in** to see him. I like to visit the work site occasionally, as I know the expectations that were placed on the client originally, and can see quickly if he is keeping up. Also, I have found that **talking in person** to the employer is more effective than on the phone. While talking in person, it is possible to read the expression on the employer's face, which may give away a problem that you would not know to ask about otherwise. Also, it shows more interest on your part, to actually make the effort to come to the business.

If the client is working in a restaurant, I will try to patronize the business whenever possible. This may not be included in the plan, but it does help with ongoing communication. The employer sees an interest and may be interested in hiring more clients from your program. This has happened with our program.

CONTACTING THE CLIENT AND FAMILY

You will want to establish with the client when you will contact him, as you did the employer. If the family has been involved with you, you will want to do the same with them. It is important that the client and family have your phone number so they can reach you, if necessary. The family may see a change in the client's behavior and want you to check on the job and see if there is a problem that can be resolved. The client may have a question and want to contact you.

CARRY OUT PLAN

After the plan is written and agreed upon by everyone, the next step is to implement it. Be sure to look for changes in supervision or job duties, as those are the major reasons clients lose jobs after phaseout. If you see that there is a new supervisor, you will want to go in and have a talk. You may want to explain a little about your client's history in the company and your role with the client and the company. You will most likely want to contact him more often for a few weeks until you are sure he is satisfied with your client. Sometimes new supervisors have different expectations from the original supervisor.

The same principle applies to new job duties. Quite often, it is the **policy** in businesses to promote workers within a certain time period. If your client is working for a company who practices this, you will need to discuss your client and how this may not be in his best interest. If they insist and promote him or add duties, you will need to become involved for further training. He may not be able to stay in this company for an extended period of time, as he will eventually be promoted to a job that is beyond his capabilities. You will probably see this philosophy most in the food service industry.

Sometimes a client will be given additional duties or promoted because he is doing so well on the original job. In this situation, it is **not mandatory** to promote the client but is considered a reward for a job well done. This is a difficult situation, as you do not want your client to fail and you want your client to progress. I would discuss the promotion with the employer and ask him if you could do a job analysis (see Chapter 5) on the new position and determine if he can learn all the jobs. You may need to remind him of the amount of time it took for the client to learn the original job. Most likely he will learn the second job quicker, since he is used to the environment and has seen others performing the duties. This is an area in which you will need to use your judgment, weighing information about the client and the job. You may want to ask the employer if he can try the new job for awhile, and if he is unable to do it, could he return to the original. Sometimes employers are agreeable with this.

NEVER ASSUME

Never assume that things are fine with your client. Problems may be occurring about which you are unaware. Follow-up is extremely important for your client. The hour or two you spend a month doing follow-up may prevent you from retraining on a new job.

WHAT HAPPENS
IF THE CLIENT FAILS?

Perhaps the most devastating thing that can happen to a job trainer is for the client to fail on the job. The trainer has invested time, energy, and a portion of her life to help this client become successful on the job. I have learned that the trainer cannot be responsible for the client's behavior and should not take the blame for failure. Of course, this makes sense when you are not in the emotional throws of a situation. The natural feelings surface when an incident actually happens.

Let's take a look at reasons that client's lose jobs. The most common reason is that the client demonstrates inappropriate behaviors on the job. He may become lazy, talk back to the supervisor, come back late from breaks and lunch, refuse to do work or do the task his own way. The client **chooses** to carry out these behaviors. There is nothing that anyone can do to **make** the client act appropriate all the time. This must come from within. The only way you can prevent a client from displaying non-work behaviors at the work site is to be with him all day, every day for the rest of his working life. And you still can't guarantee that his behavior will be acceptable. Our program is not set up for a commitment as extensive as that.

Another major reason that a client may lose his job is an inability to complete all the job tasks in the manner that the employer requires. Once on the job, you may discover that the client does not have the dexterity to accomplish the task. Or he may have a midline problem that you had not previously identified. Again, it is not the trainer's fault that the client does not have the skills or abilities to do the job. If a client of mine loses a job for this reason, I explain to him that it wasn't the right job for him at this time, but I learned more about him and will be able to make a better choice for the next job.

The third reason that a client may not be successful on a job is that the job may be different from the original job analysis. Perhaps the duties have changed to include some tasks that are too difficult for the client. I worked with a client who was a diabetic amputee (leg). The employer agreed to a certain work station that was accessible to her. Two weeks into the job, her work station was changed to the second level, which required her to walk up a flight of stairs. She also was required to carry her supplies to her work station. The employer could not change back to the previous work station because of complaints from co-workers who were in the union. Obviously, she could not stay in that situation.

Clients also lose jobs due to changes in supervision. The supportive supervisor who hired your client is transferred and is replaced by a person who is not as understanding of the situation.

Before you start to get down on yourself, look at the actual reason the client lost his job. Was it something you could have or should have controlled? Most of the time the answer to that question will be no. Look at the situation as a learning experience. What did you learn about the client? What about the employer? If the client had behavioral problems, will placing him in another job immediately help him? What has changed for him? Does he need to sit at home for a while and think about not working and not having a paycheck? Or does he need professional assistance for his problems? What did I learn about the way I handled the problem? If faced with a similar problem, how will I handle it? By answering these questions you will get a true picture of what actually happened and some ideas for working with the client in the future.

Summary

You now have the necessary information to become a job trainer. This is a complex job, but if you follow the guidelines in this book, you should do fine. The responsibilities are great when you consider that you are helping a client to begin a career. But you will also feel very proud of yourself when the client is working successfully on the job because you trained him well.

Have fun with this job! It is easy to look at the responsibilities and become bogged down with the thought of what you are doing. If you allow this to happen to yourself, you will not do as good a job. Relax and enjoy your client and the place of business. If you don't particularly like the kind of work your client is doing, remember that **you** will not be doing it for a long time. You will be working with another client in another job.

The most important thing to remember is that your job is to help the client become independent. You will do this using a variety of methods, but at all times you must evaluate your performance to determine if your actions are helping the client to become more **dependent** or **independent.** If you can honestly answer that you are helping him to become independent, then you are doing your job.

Good luck to you and your client! Remember, relax and enjoy!

APPENDICES

Appendix 1

TRAVEL TRAINING

TRAVEL TRAINING deserves a section of its own. It is not exactly training on the job, but unless the client can get to his job, he is unable to work. I did not want to include this information with the section on job training, as you will not always be able to teach the client according to his learning style. If your client learns best through his motor channel, it is not practical for him to trace the number of the bus to make sure it is the correct one. You may or may not need this information with every client, as your client may walk to work (see the "Pedestrian Skills" section) or the parent drives him.

What is travel training? It is teaching the client to ride public transportation. Some clients will know how to ride the bus and may have been doing so for years. If this is the case, it may only be necessary to accompany the client once or twice, to be sure he knows the landmarks and where to pull the cord. Your client may have never been on a bus, and if that is the case, you will need to teach him to ride the bus, in addition to learning the job skills. There is a certain order in which you teach a person to ride a bus. That is what this section is all about.

PEDESTRIAN SKILLS

You will want to make sure that your client has pedestrian skills before you attempt to teach him to ride a bus. For example, can he safely cross a street? Does he understand the WAIT/WALK light? Does he know what to do if there is only a traffic signal? Does he know what to do if there is no signal, but a stop sign? How about if there is heavy traffic on a turn lane? Does he always look both ways before crossing the street? He must be able to do this with 100 percent accuracy. If not, he could easily get hit some day and you may be liable. If your client is unable to learn pedestrian skills, I would locate an alternate form of transportation.

MONEY SKILLS

Can your client identify the correct change for bus fare? If not, he will need to be provided with the exact fare each day. Can he identify the correct amount of money to make a phone call in case he misses his bus? Does he carry money for emergency phone calls?

SURVIVAL SKILLS

Can your client use a pay phone? Can he use both a dial (if there are any still in use) and a push button? I once had a client who was unable to call me because she had not yet learned to use a dial pay phone.

Can the client read the address off the pay phone, even if it is just spelling the word? I had a client call me from a pay phone after he had taken the wrong bus. When I asked him if there was a sign to spell to me, he proceeded to spell the sign he could best see, "S-H-E-L-L," the name of the gas station. I had not trained him in the necessary emergency skills.

If you live in an area where the client will work in another telephone area code, will your client know how to place a long distance call to his home or work place? When I worked with clients in the southern California area, this was a reality. They carried cards that instructed them in the procedures of making the call to home. They were taught to place collect calls, with the parents' approval. The clients practiced the procedure several times.

Can your client identify a street sign? Can he spell the letters of the street names to you?

Does your client know what to do if approached by a stranger?

BUS TRAINING

Before we start the specifics, it is important for you to realize that **you will need to accompany your client on the bus,** until you feel confident that the client can ride safely and get to his destination without assistance. That will be discussed later in this chapter.

Step 1: Correct Bus

The first thing that you need to do is determine the appropriate bus. Most likely, you will need to read the schedule for the client. He will need to learn to identify what the sign on the bus should say. You need to be aware that in some cities, there may be as many as five different routes with the same number. When that happens, the client must correctly identify the sign. This is becoming more difficult, at least in Cincinnati, as the new buses have computerized signs that flash and move. They are no longer stationary, which helps the person who reads slowly.

Step 2: Ask the Driver

Once the right bus is identified and you board the bus, the client should **ask the driver** if it is the number _____ bus going to _____. If it is the right bus, then he stays on; if not, he gets off.

Step 3: Money and Transfer

The next thing to do is to **insert the money into the slot and ask for a transfer,** if necessary. The money part is usually easy to teach. It may take a while for the client to remember to ask for a transfer.

Step 4: Sit Down

I always teach clients to **sit as near to the front as possible.** That way, should the client encounter any difficulties, he is near the driver.

Step 5: Watch for Landmarks and Pull Cord

The next step is to **watch for landmarks.** This can be a store, a house, a sign, or something that will always be there. When the landmark is spotted, then the client **pulls the cord** or pushes the strip. Different busses have different methods of letting the driver know that you want to get off. Be sure that you ride with the client long enough to identify all possible ways to let the driver know he wants off.

Step 6: Identify Bus Stop Location

Once you are at the destination, you may want to identify where the bus stop is for the end of the day. This may comfort the client so he isn't worried all day. Then you proceed to the work place and train him in the job.

Step 7: Going Home

At the end of the day, you proceed with the same steps as you did on the way to work.

Step 8: Phaseout on the Bus

After you have ridden with the client for a few days and he is able to identify the bus stops by himself, then you can **sit a few seats behind him.** When you do this, tell him that **he** must decide when to pull the cord and get off, but you will be there in case he forgets. Usually, the client becomes quite anxious at this point and will turn and look at you about the time he should pull the cord. At this point, I usually shrug my shoulders or look away but not tell him what to do.

If he pulls the cord too late and doesn't get off at his regular stop, that is alright, as this may happen after you have stopped the training. You are there to help him think through the dilemma. Ask him what to do. Where is your job? **If at all possible, have him solve his problem without your assistance.** If he has no idea, then give him hints, and if he is still totally confused, then show him the way. If he is unable to figure out the problem on his own, then I would have him get off the bus at the same place and train him how to find his way. This experience may be all it takes to pull the cord at the correct place the next time and ever after.

Step 9: Follow the Bus

After the client is getting off the bus at the correct place consistently, then you can move on to the next step. **Follow the bus in your car.** This step of the process almost always produces some fun stories. But before we get into my favorite, let me tell you what you have to do. You will tell your client that he will ride alone because he knows how to ride the bus, but you will follow the bus in your car, in case there are any problems. You will have to decide where to wait in your car, but you will need to be able to see the client and the bus number. If you have a choice of one or the other, make sure you see the bus number, especially if several different busses stop at his stop.

Once your client is on the bus, you will follow the bus. Thus, you will stop at almost every bus stop. When the bus stops, you will want to make sure that your client is still on the bus, if he should be, or gets off if he should. I have often thought that the bus driver would wonder why the bus was being followed and call the police on me, but it has never happened.

Now comes the fun! If your client fails to get off the bus at his regular stop or the next, if you trained him at that one, then you will need to get him off the bus. The only way to do that is to get in front of the bus and when it stops, you stop and get the client off.

I promised you a story. When I was still fairly new at this job, I worked with a client who fell asleep to the sound of motors. When he rode in my car, he fell asleep as soon as the motor was turned on, and he did this on the bus, too. After extensive training on the bus, I thought he was able to stay awake, as he had done so consistently. Also, we always had the same bus driver. Well, you guessed it. On his first day solo, he fell asleep and had a new bus driver. The bus wandered through a residential community where it was impossible to pass the bus. When the bus stopped at a stop, it was not there long enough for me to get out of the car and get the client. So I followed the bus for four-and-a-half miles, until it came to a four-lane road. When it stopped to pick up more passengers, I pulled my car in front of the bus so that it could not pull away without hitting the car, left the car running, got on the bus and woke up my client, with a rather loud voice. He came immediately, sensing that he had made a mistake. The bus driver was rather awestricken and watched the whole thing with his mouth open. Since that incident, I have not become quite as panicked, although I still pull my car in front of the bus, because the bus never stands still long enough.

I will guarantee that if you travel train enough, you will have experiences you never expected. And you will never forget them.

Step 10: Meet the Client at the Job

After you follow your client on the bus and are sure that he can do this alone, then tell him that you will see him at the job site. Although I tell the client that, I usually hide and watch the client get on the bus then wait at the other end to make sure that he gets off at the correct place.

Once you are absolutely sure that he can handle the whole procedure, then your travel training is finished.

Documentation

Travel training is not to be taken lightly. You are taking on a huge responsibility any time you take a client into the community where there are so many possibilities for accidents. Be sure that you document what you do with the client and any problems he has. If he does have problems, document modifications or things you did to try to teach the client. If something happens to a client and you were aware of a problem and did not notify the parents or people on your team, the liability rests on your shoulders alone. If you see a problem, be sure to discuss it with the appropriate people.

Do not let this warning keep you from doing your job. Travel training is always an experience. Have fun and relax!

Appendix 2

DRAWINGS FOR CHECKLISTS

THIS APPENDIX is short but valuable to anyone who has difficulty drawing pictures that make sense. The idea was Keith Kleespies's, my husband's close friend since high school. He not only drew all the pictures in this book, but he was also kind enough to read the book to see if it made sense. After looking at my drawings for the checklist I made for the cleaning job, he suggested that maybe the reader would like to have some pictures that she could photocopy, then cut and paste into checklists. (I guess that tells you how bad my pictures really were!)

After some discussion and permission from the publisher, Keith drew the pictures for Figure 20 for you to use. I have a few suggestions for you when using the pictures:

1. Don't cut up the book. Make copies with a photocopier.
2. If you need the pictures larger or smaller, use a copy machine that enlarges or shrinks the original.
3. Always save the extras, as you never know when you will use them.
4. Try to get the entire checklist on one sheet of paper. It was impossible to do that with the checklist in this book and keep the spacing right and the pictures the same size. You may need to improvise.
5. Some checklists work better with the boxes to the side of the paper, instead of underneath. You may need to change that.

The empty boxes are for you to fill in with pictures of your own. Remember that **they don't have to be beautiful, just functional!**

Again, I would like to thank Keith for his wonderful idea, and for doing the drawings. I know that they will come in handy for many trainers. I wish I would have had these pictures years ago!

FIGURE 20

FIGURE 20 (CONT.)

BIBLIOGRAPHY

Wallace, G., and Larsen, Stephen C.: *Educational Assessment of Learning Problems: Testing for Teaching.* Newton, MA: Allyn and Bacon, 1978, pp. 187-188.

INDEX